CONTEMPORARY FRANCE

An Introduction to French Politics and Society

David Howarth
Georgios Varouxakis

A member of the Hodder Headline Group
LONDON
Distributed in the United States of America by
Oxford University Press Inc., New York

First published in Great Britain in 2003 by
Arnold, a member of the Hodder Headline Group,
338 Euston Road, London NW1 3BH

http://www.arnoldpublishers.com

Distributed in the United States of America by
Oxford University Press Inc.,
198 Madison Avenue, New York, NY10016

British Library Cataloguing in Publication Data
A catalogue record for this book is available from the British Library

Library of Congress Cataloging-in-Publication Data
A catalog record for this book is available from the Library of Congress

ISBN 0 340 74186 4 (hb)
ISBN 0 340 74187 2 (pb)

1 2 3 4 5 6 7 8 9 10

Typeset in 10/12 Palatino by Charon Tec Pvt. Ltd, Chennai, India
Printed and bound in Great Britain by MPG Books Ltd, Bodmin, Cornwall

What do you think about this book? Or any other Arnold title?
Please send your comments to feedback.arnold@hodder.co.uk

For

Gilly, David's lovely wife, and Georgios' recently born nephew Markos

CONTENTS

The regions of (metropolitan) France

PREFACE

France is a country of extremes. There certainly is something in the widespread belief that the French, in their collective behaviour, can in turn inspire or exasperate their foreign observers, but rarely bore them. As two of the sharpest observers of modern French society and culture, Alexis de Tocqueville and Charles de Gaulle, have put it in texts that serve as epigraphs for Chapters 1 and 5 of this book, in their collective comportment the French seem to be capable of the best and the worst, but somehow not of average or 'normal' behaviour. This view was not original with de Gaulle or even with Tocqueville, but is rather much older. Since Roman times, already in the writings of Tacitus or Julius Caesar, a stereotypical view of the Gaulois (or 'Galli') has survived, which has striking resemblances with French self-descriptions and self-perceptions in this early twenty-first century.

Few recent instances have been as characteristic in this respect as what happened, and what was commented upon, during the four successive electoral contests that took place in France between 21 April and 16 June 2002. During this period of collective action the French people certainly lived up to the reputation for extremism, hyperbole and a capacity to astound the rest of Europe and the world, as well as themselves. The first round of the presidential elections, characterised by record levels of voter apathy and abstention, resulted in Jean-Marie Le Pen, the Extreme Right leader, getting through to the second round, at the expense of the candidate who was expected to do so, the incumbent Socialist prime minister, Lionel Jospin. Following the shock ('political earthquake', Jospin called it), the 2 weeks between the first round and the second (5 May) saw an extraordinary mobilisation of all the mainstream parties against Le Pen (*barrage à Le Pen* was their watchword) and the xenophobia and racism that he is seen as standing for: a real *sursaut antiraciste* that resulted in a 'bloc républicain' with all parties except the Extreme Right supporting incumbent President Chirac's re-election as a way to stop Le Pen and save 'the republic' and France's 'honour'.

All sorts of things happened and all sorts of hopes were raised as a result of the particularly high voter participation in the second round. A revival of citizenship, citizens' participation in politics and public concerns were immediately hailed by many, and a golden age of citizenship was predicted. Self-congratulation was the order of the day; it was now believed that nothing would be the same again. France had shown herself capable of the worst (Le Pen's relative success and passage to the second round) and of the best (the extraordinary republican and patriotic rally behind the other candidate, Chirac, who had never compromised with the Extreme Right). And yet, the self-congratulation was premature, and the revival of citizenship was short-lived. When the legislative elections came, in June 2002, both rounds were characterised by the striking extent of abstention (almost 40 per cent of those eligible to vote). A whole circle had been drawn, with France scaring, inspiring and then again letting down itself and its observers abroad.

All this is not isolated. It is part of a broader picture, related to the age-old discourse of 'crisis' and the *malaise* of French society and politics. What seems to be peculiar to France is that the country is, or rather that it sees itself as being, permanently in crisis. Since the French Revolution started through a series of events and processes in 1789, France has always been ill at ease with itself, the French people fighting their 'Franco-French wars', and looking for the right direction. With the possible exception of some years in the 1960s, when, under de Gaulle's leadership, most of the French felt a degree of self-confidence that had not been felt for a very long time, France has not been seen as settled. And the exception in question, if it can be said to have been an exception, did not last for more than a few years, with the revolts of May 1968 plunging France into a new cycle of confrontation and 'crisis'. Thus, when people discuss continuity and change in France, they should bear in mind that what in the short term looks new, peculiar to its time and a recent 'crisis', may be more than that; it may be part of a longer process, inherent in French culture itself, representing continuity more than change.

This having been said, some things do change in France, sometimes very rapidly in fact. The impressive economic development that took place during the so-called *trente glorieuses*, the 30 years after the Second World War, did represent an important departure. Similarly, in the past 20 years or so, some impressive intellectual processes have been taking place, and some major French analysts have referred to some very important aspects of these processes as 'the end of the French exception'. The degree and kind of confrontation that characterised France for around two centuries are no more, according to those who speak of the end of French exceptionalism. There has been reached an unprecedented degree of consensus regarding the basic institutions of French society and political life and some fundamental principles. France is no longer an exception among the most advanced western democracies; it has become a 'normal' country, where the fundamental institutions, rules and values of liberal democracy and the rule of law, as well as some at least of the fundamentals of a market economy, have been at last accepted. In the words of the historian François Furet, the French Revolution is at long last over. In the chapters that follow we will evaluate the degree to which this view is valid.

This book does not purport to be exhaustive and there are numerous aspects of French society that could legitimately claim one's attention more than they did here. We do think, however, that we have focused on the most important aspects of French life and the French polity, and that, as far as these are concerned, we have brought to bear the most sophisticated and up-to-date scholarship and commentary. The final outcome will be judged by the supreme tribunal, of course: our readers.

We would like to thank the numerous academics who, over the past decade, have contributed immeasurably to our understanding of contemporary French politics and society: our colleagues at Oxford University, Aston University and Queen Mary, University of London and in particular Anne Stevens, John Gaffney, Michael Sutton and Raymond Kuhn; our former colleague Catherine Fieschi who helped set this project on track and contributed so much to its design; our former teachers and employers, including Vincent Wright and Jack Hayward; and the numerous UK-based academic experts on France with whom we have collaborated on projects on France over the years and who have contributed so much to our understanding of this fascinating country, in particular Jeremy Jennings, Alistair Cole, Sue Milner, Helen Drake, Robert Elgie, Cécile Laborde, Sudhir Hazareesingh, Martyn Cornick, Nick Hewlett, Douglas Johnson and Bernard Cottret. David had the wonderful opportunity of studying the French state from the inside as a student at the *École Nationale d'Administration* and profited from the considered reflection on French politics and society by his fellow students, many of whom remain good friends. Our (most recent) editor at Edward Arnold, Eva Martinez, must be thanked and praised for her impressive sang-froid, demonstrated without fail upon receipt of our umpteenth request for an extension to complete this text. Our dear friend Libby Jukes was always willing to listen to our ideas about French politics and history – or at least she demonstrated no obvious audible or visible signs of *ennui*. David's wife, Gilly, a great fan of all things French, helped to convince him that many French films – even the recent ones – are definitely worth watching.

Martin Haiden demonstrated impressive patience with Georgios at the computer and both he and our dear friend Uwe Schütte have taught us a great deal about German sensitivities.

LIST OF ABBREVIATIONS

AIDS	Acquired Immune Deficiency Syndrome
ANRS	*Agence Nationale de Recherches sur le Sida*
BEP	*Brevet d'Études Professionnelle*
CAE	*Conseil d'Analyse Economique*, Council for Economic Analysis
CAP	Common Agricultural Policy
CAP	*Certificat d'Aptitude Professionnelle*
CEEC	Central and East European countries
CEFISEM	*Centre d'Études pour la Formation et l'Information sur la Scolarisation des Enfants de Migrants*, Centre for the Study of the Training of Information on the Education of the Children of Immigrants
CEPR	Centre for Economic Policy Research
CERES	*Centre de Recherche et d'Études Socialistes*, Centre for Socialist Research and Studies
CESDP	Common European Security and Defence Policy
CFDT	*Confédération Française Démocratique du Travail*
CFSP	Common Foreign and Security Policy
CGC	*Confédération Générale des Cadres*
CGPME	*Confédération Générale des Petites et Moyennes Entreprises*
CGT	*Confédération Générale du Travail*
CID-UNATI	*Confédération Intersyndicale de Défense – Union Nationale des Artisans et Travailleurs Indépendants*
CLIN	*Classes d'Initiation*
CMU	*Couverture Maladie Universelle*, sickness benefit
CNAL	*Comité National d'Action Laïque*
CNEC	*Comité National de l'Enseignement Catholique*
CNJA	*Centre National des Jeunes Agriculteurs*
CNPF	*Conseil National du Patronat Français*, the former name of the leading French major business association
CPGE	*Classes Préparatoires aux Grandes Écoles*
CPNT	*Chasse, Pêche, Nature et Traditions*, Hunting, Fishing, Nature and Traditions
CSG	*Contribution Sociale Generalisée*, supplementary income tax
DEA	*Diplôme d'Études Approfondies* (Master's degree)

DEUG	*Diplome d'Études Universitaires Générales*
DL	*Démocratie Libérale*, Liberal Democracy
DOM-TOM	*Département Outre Mer – Territoires Outre Mer*, Overseas Department – Overseas Territories
EC	European Community
ECB	European Central Bank
ECOFIN	Council of Ministers of Economics and Finance
ECSC	European Coal and Steel Community
EEC	European Economic Community
EHESS	*École des Hautes Études en Sciences Sociales*
EIB	European Investment Bank
EMS	European Monetary System
EMU	Economic and Monetary Union
ENA	*École Nationale d'Administration*
EP	European Parliament
ERM	Exchange Rate Mechanism (of the EMS)
ERRF	European Rapid Reaction Force
ESCB	European System of Central Banks
ESDI	European Security and Defence Identity
EU	European Union
FEN	*Fédération de l'Education Nationale*
FLN	*Front Libération Nationale*
FLNC	*Front de Libération Nationale de la Corse*
FLNKS	*Front de Libération Nationale Kanak Socialiste*
FN	*Front National*, National Front
FNSEA	*Fédération Nationale des Syndicats Paysans*
FO	*Force Ouvrière*
GATT	General Agreement on Tariffs and Trade
GDP	Gross Domestic Product
HEC	*École des Hautes Etudes Commerciales*
HIV	Human Immunodeficiency Virus
IGC	Intergovernmental Conference (EU)
IMF	International Monetary Fund
INSEE	*Institut National de la Statistique et des Études Économiques*, National Institute of Statistics and Economic Studies
LCR	*Ligue Communiste Révolutionnaire*, Revolutionary Communist Struggle
LO	*Lutte Ouvrière*, Workers' Struggle
MDC	*Mouvement des Citoyens*, citizens' movement
MEDEF	*Mouvement des Enterprises de France*, the leading French major business association
MLF	*Mouvement de la Libération des Femmes*, Movement for the Liberation of Women
MNR	*Mouvement National Républicain*, National Republican Movement
MPF	*Mouvement pour la France*, Movement for France

NA	National Assembly
NATO	North Atlantic Treaty Organisation
NSM	new social movements
PCF	*Parti Communiste Français*, French Communist Party
PM	prime minister
POS	political opportunity structures
PR	proportional representation
PR	*Parti Républicain*
PRG	*Parti Radical de Gauche*, Radical Left Party
PS	*Parti Socialiste*, Socialist Party
QMV	qualified majority vote
RASN	*Réseau pour un Avenir Sans Nucléaire*, Network for a Non-Nuclear Future
RCPR	*Rassemblement pour la Calédonie dans la République*, Rally for France in the Republic
RMI	*Revenu Minimum d'Insertion*, minimum income
RPF	*Rassemblement du Peuple Français*, Rally of the French People
RPF	*Rassemblement pour la France*, Rally for France
RPR	*Rassemblement pour la République*, Rally for the Republic
SDF	*sans domicile fix*, without fixed address (homeless)
SGCI	*Secrétariat Général du Comité Interministériel pour les Questions Économiques Européennes*, the General Secretariat of the Interministerial Committee for European economic matters
SE	*Syndicat de l'Enseignement Supérieur*
SEA	Single European Act
SEM	Single European Market
SFIO	*Section Française de l'Internationale Ouvrière*, French Section of the Workers' International
SIDA	*Syndrome Immunodéficitaire Acquis*, AIDS
SMIC	*Salaire Minimum de Croissance*, minimum monthly wage
SNA	subnational authorities
SNES	*Syndicat Nationale d'Enseignement Supérieur*
SNI	*Syndicat Nationale des Instituteurs*
SPD	*Sozialdemokratische Partei Deutschlands*, Social Democratic Party of Germany
STS	*Sections de Techniciens Supérieurs*
TER	*Trains Express Régionaux*
TEU	Treaty on European Union (the Maastricht Treaty)
UDF	*Union pour la Démocratie Française*, Union for French Democracy
UDR	*Union pour la Défence de la République*, Union for the Defence of the Republic
UER	*Unités d'Enseignment et de Recherche*
UFR	*Unités de Formation et de Recherche*
UMP	*Union pour la Majorité Présidentielle*, Union for the Presidential Majority

UMP	*Union pour le Mouvement Populaire,* Union for the People's Movement
UNEDIC	benefit centres
UNR	*Union pour la Nouvelle République*
USSR	Union of Soviet Socialist Republics
VAT	Value Added Tax
WEU	Western European Union

1

CONTINUITY AND CHANGE: THE EVER-LASTING PAST

When I consider this nation in itself, I find it more extraordinary than any of the events in its history. Has there ever been any nation on earth which was so full of contrasts, and so extreme in all of its acts, more dominated by emotions, and less by principles; always doing better or worse than we expect, sometimes below the common level of humanity, sometimes much above it; a people so unalterable in its basic instincts that we can still recognize it in portraits drawn of it two or three thousand years ago, and at the same time so changeable in its daily thoughts and tastes that it ends up offering an unexpected spectacle to itself, and often remains as surprised as a foreigner at the sight of what it has just done; the most stay-at-home nation of all and the one most in love with routine, when left to itself; and, when torn despite itself from its hearth and its habits, ready to go to the ends of the earth and risk all; insubordinate by temperament, and always readier to accept the arbitrary and even violent empire of a prince than the free and orderly government of its leading citizens; today the declared enemy of all obedience, tomorrow attached to servitude with a kind of passion that the nations best-endowed for servitude cannot match; led on a string so long as no one resists, ungovernable as soon as the example of resistance appears somewhere; thus always tricking its masters, who fear it too much or too little, never so free that one must despair of enslaving it, or so servile that it may not once again break the yoke; capable of everything, but excelling only at war; a lover of chance, of strength, of success, of fame, and reputation, more than of true glory; more capable of heroism than of virtue, of genius than of common sense, ready to conceive vast plans rather than to complete great tasks; the most brilliant and most dangerous nation of Europe, and the best suited for becoming by turns an object of admiration, of hatred, of pity, and of terror, but never of indifference?

France alone could give birth to a revolution so sudden, so radical, so impetuous in its course, and yet so full of backtracking, of contradictory facts and contrary examples. Without the reasons which I have given, the French would never have made the Revolution; but it must be recognized that all these reasons together would not succeed in explaining such a revolution anywhere else but in France. (Alexis de Tocqueville 1998: 246–7)

THE FRENCH AND THEIR PAST

It is difficult to overestimate the importance of the past and of perceptions and interpretations of that past (in other words, memory) for contemporary French society, politics and culture. A grasp of collective understandings of the past is important for getting to know any contemporary society, of course. But France is a case apart. One can adduce several reasons for this, but the main reason for the peculiar significance of the past and interpretations of the past in French society is related to the French Revolution. That series of events and processes was so dramatic, so abrupt, and so influential that it imposed its shadow on French society for at least the following two centuries. A senior Chinese politician was asked once, in the second part of the twentieth century, whether he thought the French Revolution had been a good thing for human history or not. He replied that it was too early to know. In the same way, it may be too early to know whether the French Revolution's legacy of acrimonious and often violent confrontations in subsequent French history (the *guerres Francofrançaises*) is over, as most analysts in France tend to think since the 1980s. But, independently of that, its legacy is deeply imprinted in French culture, society and political culture. The very terms 'right' and 'left', used to describe political forces or camps, come from the French Revolution (due to the seating arrangements in the first assemblies of the revolutionary years); so do words like 'conservative', 'progressive', 'reactionary', to name but a few. To cut a long story short, a disproportionately great part of French political debate during the two centuries that followed the outbreak of the French Revolution has been dedicated either to rehearsing the same battles, arguments, passions, or to interpreting them, trying to make sense of the revolutionary experience, and trying to make France a 'normal' country again, a country reconciled with itself, not divided by the profound cleavages and wounds left by the extraordinary experience of the French Revolution. Every political or cultural debate in France during the last two centuries has been conducted in terms containing direct references or bearing the imprints of the revolutionary experience. Thus, the first thing to remember about French politics and political culture is that this is a profoundly historicist political culture, revolving around past events and debates and interpretations thereof, much more than that of any other major western country. To put it simply, there is no way one will understand what the French are talking about today when they debate something if one does not have at least an elementary conversance with French history. Historical references constitute the very vocabulary of French contemporary debates.

Thus, in the first place, when French public figures want to make a point, they more often than not find it expedient to make it by invoking some historical example, event, parallel, or some personality from the past. A striking instance can be provided by the debate that took place among French intellectuals and politicians over the issue of the 'Islamic headscarf' (*affaire du foulard islamique*) between November and December 1989 (see also Chapter 5).

Quite characteristically, both manifestos on the issue signed by intellectuals with diametrically opposed views on the appropriate course of action in this case have recourse to powerful evocative metaphors from the past in order to make a point. Thus, the first manifesto of intellectuals (including Élisabeth Badinter, Régis Debray, Alain Finkielkraut), which came to condemn the education minister's (Lionel Jospin's) statement that, if the students insisted, they should be allowed to wear headscarfs in the classroom, denounced what it called *le Munich de l'école républicaine* (*Le Nouvel Observateur*, 2 November 1989) (making allusion to the Munich agreement of 1938 through which, by making concessions in an attempt to appease Hitler, the western democratic powers turned out to have encouraged him to become bolder). A week later, those who disagreed with this view and argued that Muslim students should be allowed to wear headscarfs in the classroom if they wished (intellectuals including sociologist Alain Touraine), in their own manifesto, denounced what they called *le risque d'un 'Vichy de l'intégration des immigrés'* (*Politis*, 9 November 1989) (this time the allusion being to the intolerant and anti-Semitic extreme right-wing government of Marshal Pétain during the Second World War).

In the second place, contemporary political alignments and divisions and, even more, perceptions of these alignments and divisions, tend to be decisively influenced by references to and attitudes towards past events, divisions and personalities. We will have several instances of this in the following sections of this chapter, but an example may help illustrate the point at this stage. When, in 1998, the Socialist prime minister Lionel Jospin's left-wing government (elected in June 1997) was in serious difficulties due to a combination of strikes, student revolts and unemployed people's occupation of university buildings in Paris, a minister had been questioned in the National Assembly on some issue by an opposition right-wing deputy. Normally it should have been left to the minister in question to reply. However, Prime Minister Jospin took it upon himself to rejoin. Leaving the concrete issue concerned to one side, Jospin delivered a passionate attack on the conservative right in general, drawing a sharp dividing line between 'us', the left, who have always been on the side of progress and justice, as in the case of the Dreyfus Affair of the late 1890s (see more in Chapter 6), and 'you' of the right, who have always been on the side of reaction and darkness, as in the case of Dreyfus, when the right wing was in the anti-Dreyfusard camp, and so on.

Obviously, as political commentators in Britain were quick to notice, Jospin chose that topic at that particular moment in a desperate attempt to divert attention from the pressing crisis surrounding his government, and to polarise the political atmosphere along the traditional division between left and right by appealing to the French public's traditional, historically determined, reflexes (thus hoping to lure striking workers, revolting *chômeurs* and students to close ranks around his beleaguered government by opposition to the common enemy, the 'reactionary' right). First of all, it is interesting that Jospin chose to do this, because it means he believed it might work. However, what is much more interesting is the reaction Jospin's speech provoked.

The prime minister was heavily criticised for this speech in France, but not for the same reasons for which a British politician would have been criticised. Instead of attacking him, as would be the case in Britain, for trying to divert attention from current pressing problems by invoking the phantoms of the past in an evidently tendentious way, the French press and commentators attacked him, rather, for getting his history wrong. They did not criticise the very fact of invoking events and situations of no less than a century earlier which had no obvious relevance to the issue discussed, but rather the fact that he showed himself insufficiently versed in the history of the events he referred to by mentioning Gambetta as the leader of the 'left', while Gambetta had died already in 1882 and he should have talked of Clemenceau instead. Also, historians immediately pointed out that the division of intellectuals between those in favour and those against Dreyfus had not been a clear-cut division of left and right as Jospin had asserted, and so on. For several weeks, magazines were dedicating articles by specialist historians to the issue, radio programmes were inviting eminent historians to comment on the prime minister's speech, and the whole affair took on dimensions and directions that it would not have taken, for example, in the United Kingdom. This is because in France nobody questions the relevance of the past to contemporary debates in itself. Rather, disagreement arises as to what the right interpretation of the past is, and this is what feeds political debate.

As we have seen, no example of the significance of interpretations of the past is so striking as the divergent interpretations of the French Revolution which have fed passionate debates for two centuries and which were ceremoniously rehearsed on the occasion of the bicentenary of the French Revolution in 1989. And few people have exercised as much influence on political and intellectual developments in France in the last quarter-century as the historian François Furet, not least through his revisionist interpretation of the French Revolution. The examples could be multiplied indefinitely. Obviously, the thing to retain is that, in France, the past is not an affair of the past, left to historians to debate, but part of everyday discourse. As has been said of the bitter legacy of collaboration and the Vichy regime during the Second World War, it is *un passé qui ne passe pas*. This is the reason why contemporary France has developed a number of distinctly French political traditions.

FRENCH REPUBLICANISM

French republicanism is, if possible, even more rooted in France's turbulent history than the other political traditions. This is because it owes its emergence to the turn of events during the French Revolution and its subsequent character to reactions to those events and divergent interpretations of them during the next two centuries or so. This is also the most complicated of French political traditions, because of the way in which what was initially the ideal of a (sometimes smaller, sometimes larger) faction or party, 'the republic', came to be accepted as the legitimate political regime of France, subscribed to by all mainstream political parties and forces. Due to this evolution of attitudes towards the republic, being republican means different things to different people in France today, and this was the case during much of France's modern history. As the major historian of the meaning of the republican idea during the most crucial period of its consolidation, Claude Nicolet, has put it, *république* is one of the *mots voyageurs* of French political vocabulary, meaning different things to different people and at different periods (1982: 16–34). This protean character of 'the republic' makes it difficult to describe the exact meaning of republicanism even during the periods when it was the ideal or ideology of only a part of the political forces of France. Very simply, even when they were very few (in the 1830s, for instance), French republicans were never agreed as to what their ideal consisted in and what 'the republic' meant. Things have become even more complicated today, however, due to the fact that the republic has been accepted by nearly all political forces, including the direct heirs of its former enemies. Today parties and politicians of both right and left proudly – and sincerely, to the best of one's knowledge – call themselves 'republican'. Listening to politicians or political commentators speaking of the republic and republicanism today, one is at a loss to figure out what exactly it means. It seems to mean so much that it comes close to meaning nothing. This is because *républicain* tends to be used to describe whatever one considers to be good in politics. To provide a felicitous example used recently by historian Maurice Agulhon (1998: 128), it can happen that a minister of the interior (France's equivalent to the Home Secretary), determined to maintain order and wishing to affirm his resolution to do so, exclaims 'that he will re-establish order', but it very often happens that, in order to give emphasis to his statement and be more listened to, he declares that he will 're-establish the republican order'. Or he may want to say that laws should be applied, but, in order to stress his statement, he is more likely to say that 'the laws of the republic have to be applied'. As Agulhon correctly remarks, this is unnecessary emphasis, or rather tautology: in the French Republic (France's official name) order and the laws are 'republican' by definition. Yet, calling them 'republican' is assumed to give them the power attached to the idea of citizenship. Therefore, this kind of language is used by all political camps.

But what does this republic that seems to unite all the French political forces these days stand for? Here we have to search for the minimum common denominator. Well, being republican today means, not being a monarchist, not desiring the restoration of either one of France's two royal families (Bourbon and Orléans) or of the Bonapartist empire. It also means not being in favour of any kind of dictatorship of one person maintaining themselves in power in opposition to recognised rules. And, in the third place, it means not being anarchist either, as the republic is strongly connected with the power of the state, while the latter is anathema to anarchists. In this sense, almost all French men and women are republicans today (although this was not the case a century or so ago). The French people today accept the fundamental rules of the political game, the fundamentals of the constitutional framework of their country, which, in the case of France, is a republic, headed by a non-hereditary head of state (whereas in the UK it is a constitutional monarchy, as the head of state is a hereditary monarch, the first-born (male) of a royal family). Around this 'republic' have clustered a number of principles and values concerning which there is a general consensus in France today (a consensus that has grown gradually, and was not complete before the 1970s–1980s). Except for a few hundred people who assemble every year to remind their countrymen of their monarchical past, most French people accept today as legitimate the fact that their country has a non-hereditary head of state, elected by the rest of his fellow-citizens to be their president. A large majority want their state to function according to the law, without violence and arbitrary power exercised over anybody. They want power in their country to have a democratic origin, to emanate, that is, from an electoral body that is composed by all adult citizens. And they want their state to protect their freedoms (such as their right to assemble and associate), to allow a free press to operate and help citizens form opinions, and to refrain from recognising any privileges consecrated by law. In other words, French people today have come to form a consensus around the political system of what is usually called liberal democracy, whose historically consecrated form in France is the republic (Agulhon 1998). And yet, consensus on all these things does not mean that the French and their politicians are united. Despite their (real yet tacit) consensus on the basic institutions, there are French republicans who do not like at all other French republicans. On the contrary, parties of the 'right' and parties of the 'left' try assiduously to convince their supporters to fear and loath each other. Allowing for tactical motivations and individual political ambitions, one additional major reason why such political categorisations and animosities still exist in France among political forces which all call themselves 'republican' is that they do not all define in the same way the 'republic' that is their apparent common reference. The significant divergences in the definition of the republic that are conspicuously present today are due to their respective pasts, to their history. It is imperative, therefore, if we are to understand what republicanism means, to consider the way in which the idea of the republic and republicanism evolved in France during the last two centuries.

Before the French Revolution, for the educated members of French society, the republic referred to the remote historical experiences of Athens and Sparta in ancient Greece, and then of Rome. There was great admiration on the part of many Frenchmen for what they understood as the public spirit and the civic virtue that characterised those societies, where the *res publica* was the common concern of all citizens. To this admiration for the civic virtue of ancient republics came to be added, from 1776 onwards, fascination for the rumoured public-spirited achievements of another republic, this time modern and on a large scale: the American republic of Franklin and Washington. This admiration was not at first translated into any desire or intention to dethrone the Bourbon kings and try the experiment in France. 'Republican' was simply a synonym of the virtuous in politics, of the good citizen who possessed and displayed civic virtue. However, once the French Revolution broke out in 1789, and following the dethronement of King Louis XVI and the installation of a republic (the First Republic) in 1792, this was to change. By 1830, the vast majority of militant republicans were not republicans out of admiration for the ancient Greek or Roman heroes portrayed in Plutarch's books, but rather because of direct inspiration from the First Republic of 1792–4, along with the rest of the Revolution (Agulhon 1998).

It is its close association with the legacy of, and disputes over, the French Revolution that has made the republic in France such a protean and disputed notion. For most of the last two centuries, the republic has meant much more than just a regime where the head of state is non-hereditary but rather an elected president and which possesses the main attributes of a modern constitutional liberal democracy – which is, roughly, what it can mean today to those who accept what historian Maurice Agulhon has recently called the 'minimal' definition of the republic in France. Because of the specific course of French history, the idea of the republic has come to acquire, in the eyes of the political left, a number of features which represent so many additions to the common-sense, minimal definition of the regime. The left has come, accordingly, to entertain what Agulhon calls a 'maximalist' definition of the republic (1998: 122). To understand all this, an excursion into the past is indispensable.

The republic, which was first tried in France in 1792 (First Republic) – and again tried briefly in 1848–51 (Second Republic) – was for the first time relatively consolidated at the end of the 1870s, almost a decade into the life of the Third Republic (which lasted between 1870 and 1940). In other words, it took a bit less than a century of struggles between those who wanted a republic and those who did not want one. Why was this? To understand the bitter and bloody history associated with the idea of the republic and the struggles between its supporters and enemies, we have to remember the French Revolution and its significance for subsequent French history. The French Revolution that started in 1789 was not, initially, a republican revolution aiming at replacing the king by an elected head of state and introducing a republic. Events developed their own dynamic once the revolution had started, and most of what happened went far beyond original intentions or expectations. The system that was tried initially, with the Constitution of 1791, was a constitutional monarchy, which kept the king as head of state but put his reign under constitutional limitations and rules that did not exist before. However, given the failure of this system very shortly after it was installed, a republic was put in place in late 1792. This republic has been associated in history and memory with one of the least attractive features of the whole revolutionary period, the so-called Terror. Under the leadership of the Jacobins and particularly Maximilien Robespierre, the new republican regime imposed a cruel reign of terror, purporting to impose 'virtue' by violence, eliminating all those suspected of not being 'patriotic' enough, all the suspected enemies of the revolution or even people simply considered not sufficiently loyal to the revolution (or rather to the new constellation of power).

Robespierre was assassinated in 1794 and a new regime called the Directory was installed, to govern France until Napoléon Bonaparte's *coup* in 1799. That regime was also formally a republic, as it had a non-hereditary head of state. The Directory was a much more moderate and constitutional regime than the reign of Robespierre and the Jacobins had been, but the memory of the first republican experiment in France was indissolubly associated with the period 1792–4 and with the Terror. This is why many French people were scared at the very mention of the word 'republic' through most of the nineteenth century. On the other hand, despite its association with that controversial period, the republican idea was, in the eyes of most of its supporters, associated with the legacy of the whole French Revolution, not just the Terror and the First Republic. In other words, although the first years of the revolution saw France under a monarchy constrained by representative institutions rather than under a republic, subsequent French republicans identified with the achievements and – even more – with the aspirations of that earlier period of the revolution at least as much as (and, most of them, even more than) with the achievements or aspirations of the specific and limited period of the First Republic itself. (One of the latter, which was to remain in the agenda of republicans throughout the subsequent decades, was universal manhood suffrage, the granting of the vote to all adult males, stipulated by the constitution of the First Republic in 1793, a constitution that was never put into practice.) The most characteristic way out of the potential contradictions and dilemmas posed by the differences in the legacies of the different phases of the revolution (particularly the 1792–4 period) was offered by the republican leader of the Radical Party, Georges Clemenceau, at the end of the nineteenth century when he argued, in a debate in the Chamber of Deputies, that *'La Révolution française est un bloc'*. The implication was that there was an incontestable continuity between 1789 and 1793, that the sort of contract imposed on the monarchy during the first phase of the revolution was only the first episode in the fall of the monarchy and that the guillotine that killed the king and queen in 1793 had as its only object to preserve the conquests of the Declaration of the Rights of Man and Citizen of the previous period. In other words, independently of what was actually the case in terms of historical fact, in the narrative and mythology that sustained the republican tradition in France after the French Revolution a kind of modernising determinism had been at work, which had led inexorably from the assertion of popular sovereignty to the subsequent abolition of the monarchy, relic of the old system, and the installation of the republic, the ideal regime for the modern era. The upshot of all this is that, although many of the subsequent republicans had their reservations about the cruel methods, bloodshed and overall experience of the years 1792–4, the French Revolution as a whole, from 1789 until 1799, was seen by French republicans as their main historical reference, the point of departure of French republicanism, their source of inspiration and legitimation (Agulhon 1998).

On the other hand, the onslaughts of the French Revolution on the Catholic Church's privileges and property, and, even more, the fact of regicide: the fact that, in the beginning of 1793, the revolutionaries killed King Louis XVI (appointed by God, according to Catholics) and Queen Marie-Antoinette on the guillotine, resulted in the implacable hostility of the vast majority of loyal French Catholics to the whole revolutionary experience, to the whole 'bloc', to use Clemenceau's term. Catholic conservative political thinkers, starting with Joseph de Maistre and Louis de Bonald, attacked the whole revolutionary experience and established a long tradition of Catholic hostility to the legacy of the revolution.

Thus, one of the things that distinguished the republican founders of the Third Republic (Léon Gambetta, Jules Ferry, Jules Grévy, Georges Clemenceau and others) from their conservative opponents who were against the republic was that the former, the 'left', took for granted that the republic was a daughter of the revolution and that one could not be a real republican if one did not respect and cherish the revolution (slight divergences over the unpalatable episodes of 1793 notwithstanding). This was the first of the additions alluded to earlier, which made the idea of the republic what it is in the eyes of the left, the 'maximal' definition of the republic.

There were other additions as well. It has come to be taken for granted by the left that the idea of the republic included a strong sense of French patriotism-nationalism. It has also come to be taken for granted that the idea of the republic included a keen concern with 'the people' – *le peuple* – and a solicitude to ameliorate its lot (although serious divergence arose in this respect between those who would go as far as to endorse socialism as a way of ameliorating the lot of the people through radical social reform, and those who were content to try to improve the people's condition by means of moderate liberal reforms – cf. Exhibit 1.1, below). And, far from least, it has come to be taken for granted by the political left that the republic is secular (*laïque*), and anti-clerical, as a direct result of the Catholic Church's espousal, since the early 1790s, of the cause of counter-revolution. (The principal terrain on which this battle between *laïcité* and *cléricalisme* was fought was that of who would control education – the secular state or the Catholic priests. It is not

Exhibit 1.1: A British view of French 'republicanism' at the beginning of the Third Republic

As [the new French Assembly] will be republican, it will have to make the republic; and though its members will be agreed that the government shall bear that name, they will, if they resemble present republicans in France, be agreed on little else. Between the republic of M. Thiers and of M. Gambetta, between that of the moderate left and of the extreme left, between that which is desired for socialist and that which is desired for political ends, there are immense differences. *Though French republicans are united by the accident of a common name, many of them are much nearer to the partisans of other forms of government than they are to one another.* (Walter Bagehot, 'The Prospects of Bonapartism in France', *The Economist*, 30 May 1874; emphasis added) accidental that an episode of this struggle was fought as late as the early 1990s, with conservative prime minister Edouard Balladur being attacked by Socialist president François Mitterrand for having tried to allow more scope to private education, which, in the French context, meant Catholic education. Mitterrand tirelessly repeated in his speeches then, that *'la République est laïque'*. Two different conceptions of what the republic meant were in full display, one being the republic according to the right, and the other the republic according to the left.)

Finally, it had come to be taken for granted by the left that the republic was threatened if there was a strong executive branch in the hands of a popular man. This – like everything else in this conception of what the republic meant – was the direct result of historical circumstances. Had the republic not been subverted and destroyed twice by men who enjoyed great popularity and at some point made a *coup d'état*, abolished the republican institutions which they were supposed to serve, and assumed dictatorial powers as emperors? This was the story of the first Napoléon Bonaparte in 1799, and again of his nephew Louis-Napoléon Bonaparte in 1851. The latter, having been elected with an overwhelming majority President of the (Second) Republic in 1848, used his great presidential powers and his popularity to the purpose of subverting the republic and introducing personal rule as emperor. No wonder, therefore, that, when his Second Empire (1852–70) collapsed due to its humiliating defeat in the Franco-Prussian War in 1870, republicans were determined never again to allow a popular and strong president to be able to use his extensive powers against the republican constitution. This is why they became obsessed with limiting the powers of the executive as well as with making sure to elect rather insignificant and uncharismatic men as presidents throughout the life of the Third Republic. This is why it became the article of faith of republicans that sovereignty and power should be vested in parliament, in the body of the representatives of the sovereign nation, and that no other institution should be in a position to subvert or threaten the power and will of the assembly elected by the people. Thus, in other words, it came to be identified as the 'republican' attitude to insist that the head of the executive should be invested with few powers, and that undivided and unlimited sovereign power should reside with parliament. This is why the Third (1870–1940) and Fourth (1944–58) Republics were parliamentary (as opposed to presidential or semi-presidential) regimes. This historically formed set of attitudes and predilections (respect for the great French Revolution, distrust of the Church and the priests, distrust of great men who could appeal directly to the people and win majorities through referenda) came to be the initial conception of what the republic meant for all republicans in the decisive decade 1870–80. It is this conception of the republic, the 'maximal' definition of what the republic meant, that has been kept and cherished until today by the political left in France.

However, the reason why there is confusion as to the meaning of the republic and republicanism is that there is also another conception of the republic, that of the political right. This latter is (in Agulhon's terms) a 'minimal' definition of what the republic means. The reason why this second, 'minimal', definition of the republic emerged is that, from the beginning of the Third Republic in the 1870s onwards, successive waves of former opponents of the republic from the right wing of the French political spectrum came to rally to the republic for various reasons. These successive groups of *ralliés* came to accept the institutions of the republic, and its liberal democratic framework, but not most of the additions that the tradition of the left had accumulated as part of the baggage of the republic. The first of the *ralliés* was Adolphe Thiers, the conservative-liberal monarchist (Orléanist) veteran politician who headed the republic in its first steps in 1870–71 and who was instrumental in making it acceptable to groups in French society that would otherwise never have accepted a regime called 'republic'. Thiers offered them what he called a 'conservative republic', and argued that the republic was 'the government that divides us least' (*la République est le gouvernement qui nous divise le moins*). These *ralliés* of this first phase of the Third Republic were members of the bourgeoisie and local notables, elected to parliament in the provinces, who – while monarchists in their traditional affiliations – came slowly to accept the republic established by Thiers (and then Gambetta) as rather harmless, and started calling themselves, no longer monarchists or Bonapartists, but rather simply *conservateurs*.

However, this was only the first wave of *ralliés* to the republic. Soon was added to them a new wave, the Catholic *ralliés* who, following the advice of Pope Leo XIII to stop opposing the republican regime but rather join it in order the better to fight against 'bad' laws, came to accept the republic and joined the ranks of republicans. And, finally, there was a third category of *ralliés*, composed of monarchists who, putting their patriotism above any other consideration, came round to the opinion that they would serve France better by serving a regime (the Third Republic) which had given tangible proofs of its patriotism in 1870 (thanks to republican leader Gambetta's fierce resistance to the invading German armies), than by upsetting it indefinitely with plots of doubtful prospects of success. To this category of republicans by resignation and due mainly to national and patriotic considerations, belongs, for example, the most illustrious and most influential of all the *ralliés* to the republic, Charles de Gaulle (Agulhon 1998). Army officer and junior minister by the time of the fall of the Third Republic in 1940, de Gaulle had accepted the republican regime and served it loyally, although he was, at the same time, a staunch Catholic, and he had been a monarchist by tastes and predilections. As he made clear shortly after the Liberation of France in the wake of the Second World War, de Gaulle was also a believer in a strong executive, a powerful president with very excessive powers, standing above parties and parliamentary squabbles, and drawing his legitimacy directly from the people. Thus, from around 1890 or 1900 onwards, due to successive additions of *ralliés* to the republican camp, one could be a sincere republican in the sense of accepting and being loyal to the institutional framework of the republic and being a patriotic Frenchman, while still rejecting the 'maximalist' republicans' anti-clericalism (thus being also a good Catholic), not particularly liking the French Revolution, and preferring a strong executive to the *régime des parties*. In other words, these newer republicans who joined the ranks of the republic from the formerly anti-republican right accepted the regime, its institutional framework (non-hereditary head of state, and so on), and its liberal democratic bases, but did not share the cherishing of the various 'additions' that gave the perception of the republic by the left its 'maximal' definition. Thus, from around the end of the nineteenth century onwards, there existed in France a new phenomenon, a republican right wing (*droite républicaine*). This republican right was not composed only of right-wing citizens (formerly all monarchists of one sort or the other) who at some point rallied to the republic. To these were also added older republicans (original republicans, as it were) who passed to the right, once this right had accepted the republic, due to discontent with their former comrades. The result, in both cases, was the gradual emergence of a republican right.

Now, one would perhaps have expected the left to have triumphantly congratulated itself at the fact that the right came to accept a great part of its own historical baggage by accepting the republic. This, however, did not happen. And the reason why it did not happen is one of the major causes of the continuing confusion surrounding the meanings of the republic and republicanism. Instead of celebrating the conversion of the right to the republic, the two main parties of the republican left during the early twentieth century, the Radicals and the Socialists, tended to reserve the label 'republican' only for themselves and to challenge the sincerity of the right-wing parties' attachment to the republic. It was this republican exclusivism of the left that perpetuated the confusion as to the meaning of the republic.

This exclusivism has gradually disappeared and is no longer one of the Fifth Republic's characteristics. Whatever their differences, French parties of the so-called mainstream (which excludes today the *Front National* and small Trotskyite parties, Bruno Mégret's *Mouvement National Républicain*) do not challenge each other's republican credentials. In fact, to such an extent has the acceptance of the mainstream right and centre-right parties as 'republican' even by their left-wing opponents advanced, that, after Socialist candidate Lionel Jospin was eliminated after the first round of the presidential elections of 21 April 2002, the 2 weeks that followed until the second round of 5 May saw the formation of a so-called *front républicain*, with all the parties of the left joining the mainstream right and centre-right in the campaign to re-elect incumbent president Jacques Chirac (whom they had been openly accusing of involvement in financial scandals up to 21 April) in order to form a 'barrage à Le Pen' (in other words, in order to block the possibility of the election to the presidency of his rival, Jean-Marie Le Pen). It is unarguable, in fact, that the overwhelming show of force against Le Pen – including a demonstration by more than a million people in Paris on 1 May – that took place between the two rounds of the presidential elections was primarily a result of the mobilisation of the left's supporters, rather than of the mainstream right's own making. The result was that Chirac received 82 per cent of the votes cast, an unprecedented result by Fifth Republic standards (one has to go back to December 1848, when Louis Napoléon Bonaparte was elected

President of the Second Republic, for a better result for a president). The implication of all this was, of course, that Le Pen's National Front is considered by the mainstream political parties and the media to be beyond the pale of French republicanism, despite its profession of loyalty to the republic. It is quite interesting in this context that in the electoral rallies for Le Pen during the April–May 2002 presidential elections, roughly half of those assembled to cheer him were carrying the tricolour flag of the French Republic, while the other half were waving the white Bourbon flag, the flag of the *ancien régime* French monarchy – an indication, apparently, that at least those supporters of the *Front National* (FN) do not accept the French Revolution and its result, the republic.

Apart from some of the FN's supporters, however, of the rest of the French it is true that they are 'all republicans now'. What is important to remember, though, is that they are far from agreed as to what this means, and thus arguing that this or that proposal or policy is or is not consistent with 'republican principles' has become commonplace in French politics.

SOCIALISM

France has a distinctly national socialist tradition and was the country where socialism first flourished as an ideology, a current of political ideas and a political movement, in the nineteenth century. The crucial period was the decade of the 1840s, when, in the recesses of secret societies, persecuted by the strict measures against them taken by the governments of the July Monarchy, most socialists coalesced with some important segments of the republican movement and thus prepared the outbreak of what became known as the Revolution of 1848. During the years before the 1848 uprising, socialist thinkers of various hues had been writing works seeking to find solutions to what was now known as 'the social question', the question of the lot of the ever-increasing masses of urban poor who were the victims of the economic, demographic and social changes that the Industrial Revolution had brought in its wake. Charles Fourier, Louis Blanc and, before them, Henri de Saint-Simon, were among the many thinkers who came up with various solutions to the rapid social changes of the early nineteenth century. Karl Marx, a German exile in Paris during much of the 1840s, was to dub the ideas developed by these thinkers as 'utopian socialism', in contradistinction to his own 'scientific' socialism, as he saw it, based on a robust materialist philosophy of history.

However, although the Revolution of 1848 gave the socialists a prominent position (some of them became ministers in the new republican Provisional Government between February and April 1848), it also discredited them – perhaps fatally – when various proposed solutions to the social problem (such as the infamous 'national workshops'), which were seen as socialist solutions, were proven to fail in practice. The subsequent second revolution of June 1848 (whose immediate cause had been the displeasure of the Paris crowds at the closure of the 'national workshops') led majority public opinion in France (the peasants of the provinces and the bourgeoisie all over the country) to an almost paranoid fear of anything resembling 'socialism'. To cut a rather long story short, by 1848 socialism had raised too high expectations for the rapid resolution of huge social problems. When the chance was seen to have come (with the Revolution of 1848) and the problems remained unresolved – or new problems arose as a result of the proposed solutions – socialism became very unpopular with the vast majority of the country, although it remained the main hope of sizeable segments of the urban workers (*ouvriers*). Socialism had to go underground during the authoritarian years of the Second Empire, but, by the early years of the Third Republic in the 1870s, it was again raised as a possibility. By now French socialism had come to be influenced by Marxist thought. Through a combination of Marxist ideas and the older French tradition of 'revolution' (which had permeated a section of the older republican movement since the early 1830s), a socialist movement emerged, in close cooperation and collusion with the syndicalist (trades union) movement. A socialist party calling itself formally the *Section Française de l'Internationale Ouvrière* (SFIO) emerged by the end of the nineteenth century, and in the early years of the twentieth century it even started being part of governing coalitions. During the first decade of the twentieth century a major battle was fought between two tendencies in the SFIO. On the one hand, there were those, around the independent figure of humanist socialist leader Jean Jaurès, who wanted the SFIO to participate in coalition governments and try to change the system from within through gradual reform. On the other hand, there were the hard-liners, led by Guesde, who rejected any cooperation with so-called 'bourgeois' (non-socialist) parties and wished to remain in opposition and fight the capitalist system. Due to the influence of the international socialist movement (the decision was made at the Congress of the Socialist International in Amsterdam), it was Guesde's line that was adopted, and Jaurès had to comply, so the Socialists left the governing coalition with other leftist and centre parties in 1905. In the years leading up to the First World War (1914) the French Socialists had adopted a militantly pacifist and internationalist line, rejecting calls for war preparations in view of what was seen (since 1905 in particular) as overt German aggressiveness. In the end, Jaurès, the most staunchly anti-war campaigner among the Socialists, was assassinated in late July 1914, shortly before the outbreak of the war. In the event, the Socialists did join in the *Union Sacrée*, the great patriotic rally in August 1914, and supported the French war effort until the end of the war (1918).

After the end of the Great War a new factor had a decisive effect on the position of the French socialist movement. In October 1917 a Communist Revolution had taken place in Russia, and the new rulers of that country (now called the USSR or Soviet Union), the Communist Bolsheviks, headed by Vladimir Lenin, came to pose as the natural leaders of an international and internationalist revolutionary movement against capitalism and 'imperialism', and invited all socialist and anti-capitalist forces and parties all over the world to follow their lead and tread their line. In France this new development was discussed at the Tours Congress of the Socialists (SFIO). An historic split took place, with the majority of members of the SFIO abandoning it to form a new party, the *Parti Communiste Français* (PCF), which was to follow Moscow's lead – too closely, according to its critics, until the very end, the dissolution of the Soviet Union itself in 1991. The remainder of the SFIO's members, those who did not want to obey Moscow's rule, continued to be officially called SFIO until the late 1960s, when they came to be called *Parti Socialiste* (PS). The Socialists came to power for the first time in the Fifth Republic's history in 1981 with François Mitterrand's electoral victory in the presidential elections, followed by a victory for the PS and its allies, the PCF, in the legislative elections of the same year. The test of power proved decisive. While in their first 2 years they tried to implement what looked like a radical programme of economic and social reforms, including forced nationalisation of public utility companies, they reached a major dilemma by 1983. Either they would have to reverse the reflationary economic programme or face the prospect of leaving the European Economic Community (EEC), with whose rules much of what they were pursuing was incompatible. In the end, with Jacques Delors (who was later to become president of the European Commission in Brussels) as finance minister, Mitterrand reversed his policies and the Socialist Party had to tacitly accept the realities of market economics. As a result of his inability to implement anything approaching a radically socialist transformation of society, Mitterrand started looking to 'Europe' as the new inspiring myth and vision for his presidency and for France. From then on, and until the end of his presidency in 1995, the Socialists became particularly identified with the urge for further European integration and the 'European project'.

After Mitterrand's departure from the political scene (and his subsequent death), Lionel Jospin, who succeeded him as *de facto* leader of the Socialists, had the difficult task of keeping the different elements and factions of the Socialist Party together, a task in which he was rather successful until his humiliating defeat in the first round of the presidential elections of 2002, after which he retired from politics. With his electoral victory in 1997 the Socialists and their various allies, the Plural Left (*gauche plurielle*), came to power and remained there for the full term of 5 years, in 'cohabitation' with centre-right president Jacques Chirac. What characterised their term in office was a determination not to accept the so-called Third Way promoted by British Labour Party Prime Minister Tony Blair and German Social Democrat Chancellor Gerhard Schröder. Rather, the French Socialists preferred to stick to the traditional left rhetoric and to be seen as not too keen on the operation of the free market (while in practice they partially adjusted to it). It remains to be seen what direction the Socialists will take in opposition following their defeat in the June 2002 parliamentary elections. Most critics seem to agree, however, that it is their traditionalism, their stubborn refusal to see that capitalism has changed, that the whole pattern of labour and employment relations has altered dramatically in the last 20 years, and their insistence upon traditional solutions to social problems that bedevils them the most at the moment (cf. Rosanvallon 2002). It could be said that the verdict on them passed by the late historian François Furet in the 1980s may still be relevant: 'The tragedy of the Socialists [according to Furet] was that they remained prisoners "of a historical design that history has the impertinence to contradict". A minimal grasp of reality ought to have convinced them that their very rise to power was made possible by the desiccation of the revolutionary tradition' (Kaplan 1995: 126).

COMMUNISM

We have seen how the Communist Party emerged after the split in the socialist movement at the Congress of Tours in 1920. It was obvious from the start that the PCF would have a peculiarity among French parties, in that it was established by definition as the party that would follow the wishes of the leadership of a foreign country, the Soviet Union, whom it accepted as the vanguard of the international revolutionary movement. Characteristically, Socialist leader (and premier in the first Popular Front government in 1936) Léon Blum has observed of the PCF that they were 'a foreign nationalist party' (alluding to the widespread perception that they paid their supreme allegiance to the Soviet Union and its national interests, rather than to France and its national interests). In a striking manner, at several points before, during and after the Second World War, the PCF changed its line completely, making a full U-turn in compliance with new orders from Moscow. Notwithstanding this, the widespread perception that they had played the major role in the resistance movement within France during the German occupation (a perception carefully orchestrated by the PCF), combined with the new-found prestige of the Soviet Union thanks to its role in the victory against Hitler, contributed to their unprecedented popularity after the war, emerging as the single strongest party in terms of votes in the first elections after the *Libération*. The Communists remained a significant force for decades during the Cold War. In some respects, in certain heavily communist *banlieues* of urban centres, the Communists were able to create a sort of communist political subculture, with mutual aid and communal arrangements that made the lives of the members less difficult.

However, while in the immediate after-war years they were indisputably the major party of the left, by the time they joined François Mitterrand's government in 1981 they had become (not least thanks to Mitterrand's machinations) the junior partner in an alliance dominated by the Socialists. Since then they have been almost steadily declining in electoral support. A serious blow to them came after the collapse of communism and the dissolution of the Soviet Union itself in the years 1989–91. Since then, it is difficult not to see them as a kind of anachronism, bound to decline more and more as the older generations of traditional communist voters die out. In the first round of the 2002 presidential elections, the Communist leader, Robert Hue, received less than 4 per cent of the vote. In the legislative elections of June 2002 Hue failed to be elected as a deputy. The PCF vote fell to an historic low of 4.7 per cent and only 22 Communist members won seats in the National Assembly.

GAULLISM

As the word itself indicates, 'Gaullism' is a political tradition that is based on the legacy of one man, General Charles de Gaulle. It is, more than any other of the traditions discussed here, peculiarly French. It has often been said that de Gaulle coveted the mantle of the Bonapartes, and that Gaullism was a modernised form of Bonapartism. There clearly were some striking similarities:

> Bonapartism left in French political culture an idea of how strong yet popular government could be carried out. Like the Bonapartes, de Gaulle was a guarantee of the revolution (against *vichyite* counter-revolution), a guarantee of order (against Communists and the ultra-nationalism of *Algérie Française*), and a symbol of France's greatness. ... Like the Bonapartes, he was able in consequence to play a dynamic and creative role, founding new political institutions and promoting economic modernisation. Finally, like them, he gave the regime a face. (Tombs 1994: 176)

The comparison is felicitous, although it should not be taken too far. What de Gaulle shared with the two Bonapartes (Napoléon I and Louis Napoléon, later – 1852–70 – Napoléon III) was a preference for a kind of plebiscitary-democratic regime, where one man, the leader, is either elected or approved (by plebiscite, in the Bonapartes' case) by the majority of the people and has a direct relation with them, unfettered by constitutional constraints or quarrelsome and divisive parliamentary assemblies. It has to be stressed, however, that times had changed between the Bonapartes and de Gaulle and that de Gaulle did have an unequivocal loyalty to democracy, which the Bonapartes did not. His affinity with the Bonapartes was used often against the General by his critics, who accused him of imperial and dictatorial tendencies. The criticism is unfair to the extent that de Gaulle, while he was a believer in *grandeur* and greatness and strong leadership, did not dream of dictatorial personal rule at any stage. What he wanted was a constitution that would provide France with a strong head of state, as opposed to what he saw as the weak parliamentary systems that led to the instability and divisiveness that blighted the Third Republic and (as he had prophetically warned in his famous Bayeux speech in 1946) the Fourth Republic as well. This is why, when at last given the chance to dictate the terms of his return to power in 1958, he had his followers draft a constitution (of the Fifth Republic) that gave the president very extensive powers indeed.

Independently of his constitutional ideas and legacy to France, de Gaulle has also been identified with certain themes such as the pursuit of the country's *grandeur*, the pursuit of an 'independent' and proud foreign and defence policy, the pursuit of national unity. These are themes that pre-existed in

French political culture, which is one of the reasons for de Gaulle's success and the strength of the Gaullist legacy. He managed to incarnate certain profoundly held views and wishes of the French people, and to have them identified with himself. It is a striking indication of the extent to which the French are 'all Gaullists now' that politicians of all parties (including Socialists) have tried and are still trying to imitate de Gaulle's style, to appropriate his themes, even to plagiarise his figures of speech. Thus, while the so-called neo-gaullist party founded by Jacques Chirac (the RPR, Rally for the Republic, *Rassemblement pour la République*) may or may not have much in common with the general's concrete policies on issues such as France's relation with the European project, for instance, Gaullist themes and overtones have become national patrimony, diffused throughout the political spectrum.

LIBERALISM

Le libéralisme is, as a general rule, a dirty word in the French political vocabulary. Whereas in Britain, the United States and a number of other western countries there is a 'liberal' consensus (although different things are understood by 'liberal' in each of these countries), in France very few people admit to being liberal. The only political party that openly brandishes its 'liberal' credentials is Alain Madelin's *Démocratie Libérale*. With 3.8 per cent of the vote in the first round of the presidential elections of 21 April 2002, M. Madelin is not exactly at the top of French voters' preferences. So, what then of the rest of the parties, the parties the vast majority of the French voters have given their preferences to; are they all anti-liberal, or illiberal? Things are not as simple as that. What complicates the discussion of the place of liberalism in French political culture is a striking confusion, in France, between two different senses of 'liberalism', the economic and the political-philosophical. Alain Madelin's party is the only party which openly advocates *economic* liberalism as the best way of running a society and as the way forward for solving France's economic and social problems. In other words, it advocates more free-market economics, less state intervention in the economy, more deregulation. This approach to economics is indeed called 'liberal' and it is deeply unpopular in France, as any mention of it raises the spectre of insecurity for the large segments of French society who think they benefit from the *état-providence*, the welfare state that M. Madelin's policies would threaten. But 'liberalism' also refers to a political philosophy and a political ideology and tradition based (in some cases more loosely than in others) on certain political-philosophical fundamental assumptions about how best to organise a society and the relationship between society and the state. Based on the successive and cumulative influence on the English-speaking world and then on other countries of political thinkers such as John Locke, Jeremy Bentham, John Stuart Mill and others, liberalism emerged as one of the two major political forces (in the shape of the Whig Party, later succeeded by the Liberal Party) in nineteenth-century Britain. By the first decades of the twentieth century, however, liberalism had ceased to be the doctrine or programme of one party only (in fact, the Liberal Party itself declined and was replaced by Labour as the second major force of British politics, the other being Tory conservatism); rather, it had come to permeate the whole political culture of Britain (as well as America, in a different context and in different ways) and to have somehow attained the status of a national 'frame of mind'.

There has been, since the beginning of the twentieth century at least, a considerable degree of consensus about some of the fundamental tenets of liberalism in Britain. What are these tenets or doctrines? It is extremely difficult to give even the most elementary gist of a tradition as rich and multifarious as liberalism, but the effort has to be made. Liberals tend to believe that certain fundamental securities (some – most today – call them 'rights') should be given by a supreme law, a constitution, to individuals, guaranteeing a number of domains in which individuals should be left free to pursue their lives and aims in the ways they see as best, provided they do not harm other individuals or society as a whole and do not interfere with other people's equal entitlements to the same securities or rights; that all human beings are born equal and have equal moral worth, and that, consequently, distinctions and hierarchies should be based on merit rather than birthright; that sovereignty and power should never be concentrated in the hands of one person, government or even an elected assembly, but rather should be divided, split into separate branches which can control each other. (There are several theories and versions as to how this can be best achieved in practice, the most influential having been the theory of the 'separation of powers' – for example, in legislative, executive and judiciary branches – and the theory of the advisability of there being mutual 'checks and balances' between the different branches or bodies of government.) More generally, a considerable degree of suspicion of power, and therefore of resistance to concentration of power, leading to a vigilance against government or 'the state' increasing their functions, as well as against administrative centralisation, has been characteristic of most classical liberals. Toleration of different or even opposite viewpoints, religious loyalties and attitudes to life is regarded as a good thing, and most liberals hold that societies should tolerate difference and refrain from persecuting or penalising those who differ from the majority's norm. Although there are exceptions, many liberals tend to even think that difference should be positively encouraged, because they see diversity of various sorts as conducive to freedom and the encouragement of individuality. Now, although this short enumeration of some fundamental tenets of most liberals is bound to be schematic, it is to a great degree true that the political cultures of Britain and the USA have come to accept most of these shibboleths of liberalism as more or less self-evident values or principles from which arise a number of almost sacrosanct rights, and have developed their institutions, their political constitutions and their legal systems in ways that reflect this acceptance.

The question that arises in our context is, can the same be said of France? The answer to this question has to be a qualified 'no'. For a number of complicated (and still disputed) historical reasons, France did not develop a political culture that had the same degree of regard for these principles that the English-speaking countries (*les anglo-saxons*, as most of the French still call them) and some other western societies did. Although in some respects things are slowly changing in France, France is seen, both by many foreign observers and by some of its most distinguished analysts, as possessed of an 'illiberal' political culture (see Rosanvallon 2001). France became from quite early on a highly centralised and bureaucratised country, where the institutions that constituted 'the state' became extremely powerful and influential. (As General de Gaulle was to put it later, 'France exists thanks to the state alone'.) The kings of France and their governments managed (to an extent never achieved by their counterparts *outre-Manche*) to subdue and domesticate the local aristocratic magnates, and neutralise their potential for resisting the incursions of the state and its tax collectors (the latter needing to collect more and more taxes, more and more efficiently, if the French monarchy's constant wars were to be financed). Thus, as French liberal thinker, politician and historian Alexis de Tocqueville was to say in his celebrated work *L'Ancien Régime et la Révolution* (1856), it was not the French Revolution that destroyed the power of the aristocracy in France (and thereby, in his opinion, also the local foci of resistance to state power and its potential for tyranny), but rather the French kings who had gradually centralised France and made it a country consisting of an all-powerful state and a society composed of isolated individuals.

Thus when the French Revolution came, and after the initial ideological battles to determine its orientation had been fought in the assemblies, it was another set of centralisers that prevailed – culminating in the period of Jacobin rule. What happened in the end was that the absolute and undivided power earlier possessed by the king was now transferred to the body purporting to represent the people, the Assembly (or the various groups that emerged through the internal squabbles of the assemblies, claiming to speak for 'the people'). The crucial thing about all this is that the idea that sovereignty should remain undivided and unfettered by checks and balances survived the fall of the monarchy. It was thought that, once power was in the hands of the legitimate and genuine representatives of the people, there would be no reason to fear its abuse; the people could not tyrannise itself. This thinking was premised on the assumed existence of a united (and somehow undifferentiated) 'people', whose interests or wishes could be safeguarded if only the people had the power to decide who would govern them. Much of this was a result of the influence of Genevan-born eighteenth-century *philosophe* Jean-Jacques Rousseau, modified by some of the revolutionaries (like the Abbé Sieyès) to fit the needs of a country as large as France through the device of representation. (Rousseau himself was no enthusiast for representative government and preferred direct democracy.)

The problem with this way of thinking (particularly the insistence that sovereignty should remain undivided and unfettered by constitutional constraints and guarantees) turned out to be that 'representatives of the people' could and indeed did tyrannise the people, or some of the people at any rate. Also, it became clear to some liberal thinkers in the nineteenth century (through close observation not only of French but also of contemporary American experience) that, even if the people's representatives did genuinely and loyally implement the people's will and wishes, there was an even more insidious danger: it was, as Alexis de Tocqueville put it memorably in his celebrated masterpiece, *De la Démocratie en Amérique* (1835, 1840), the 'tyranny of the majority' which could prove fatal to liberty.

Perhaps paradoxically, though, for a country of which we have said that it never warmed up to liberalism as much as its neighbour on the other side of the English Channel, France can boast a remarkably distinguished and illustrious constellation of liberal political thinkers, some of whom have emerged as luminaries of the western liberal tradition more generally, with great influence far away from their country and long after their lifetime. To start with early forefathers, the very theory of the separation of powers (one of the fundamental principles on which the American Founding Fathers based the constitution of the USA) was the work of an eighteenth-century French aristocrat, Montesquieu (in his celebrated *De l'esprit des lois* of 1748). But, even more significantly, it was in the early nineteenth century that French political debate and reflection produced some of the best liberal thought ever produced anywhere. Unlike most English-speaking political thought, then or since, which has a tendency to discuss political and philosophical issues somehow *in abstracto* and, to a certain degree, in an ahistorical manner, French political thinkers in the first half of the nineteenth century had to deal with very concrete and very pressing problems and questions affecting the most fundamental aspects of their social existence. Following the French Revolution with its various breathtakingly short-lived successive phases, the emergence, through the revolutionary experience, of Napoléon, the forced restoration of the Bourbon monarchy after Napoléon's defeat in the battleground, and the experience of the July Revolution of 1830 and the subsequent (failed) attempt to establish in France something resembling the British system of constitutional monarchy, French political thinkers of the period had a lot of food for thought. Some of them acquitted themselves admirably, and produced some of the most remarkable classics of the liberal tradition, often more influential or celebrated in the USA or Britain than in France itself, at least before the so-called liberal revival that started in the 1980s in the realms of political philosophy as well as historiography. Benjamin Constant, Alexis de Tocqueville, François Guizot (and a number of the other so-called *Doctrinaires*) all wrote important works of political thought from a liberal perspective and their thought is more and more recognised as having significantly enriched the overall western liberal political tradition. Besides Tocqueville's monumental anatomy of modern democracy already mentioned, Benjamin Constant offered the most influential distinction between two different kinds of liberty (liberty of the moderns and liberty of the ancients). What distinguishes this liberal output (starting with the extremely important contributions of the so-called *Doctrinaires*) in comparison to most English-speaking liberal thought is its attentiveness to the sociological background and requirements of political practice. They had found out, through painful experience, that introducing certain political institutions was not enough to achieve certain results. The institutions had to be appropriate for the society in question, and plans to change them in the direction the legislator wished had to take into account social realities (it is quite characteristic in this respect that the term 'class struggle', which most people tend to associate with Karl Marx's sociologically inclined way of thinking about politics, was first used by Guizot in his historical writing).

Characteristically for a country whose political and intellectual culture is, as we saw earlier, profoundly 'historicist', it was through the historical study of the works and thought of such nineteenth-century liberal luminaries that liberal reflection has come to emerge again in France to a remarkable degree and with some impressive results in the domain of the history of political ideas as well as contributions to contemporary political theorising. Through a more or less close circle of people associated with the historian François Furet (president of the prestigious *École des Hautes Etudes en Sciences Sociales* from the late 1970s), and including people like Pierre Rosanvallon, Marcel Gauchet, Pierre Manent, Bernard Manin and others, the study and resurrection of the political thought and activity of the most important nineteenth-century liberal thinkers became a direct or indirect way to contribute to and – in the cases of some of the scholars–intellectuals concerned – to shape contemporary French reflection on issues of democracy, its relation to liberty, the nature of liberty, and the crucial issue of sovereignty. (It is not accidental that one of the most influential members of this circle, Pierre Rosanvallon, having rehabilitated Guizot as a serious thinker with his 1985 book *Le Moment Guizot*, and having then produced a valuable trilogy of books charting French reflection on universal suffrage, representation and sovereignty, has recently promised a future work of normative political theory proposing a theory of what he calls *souveraineté complexe*.)

Although the influence of such intellectual developments is not directly traceable in electoral terms and party politics, this so-called liberal revival in France should not be underestimated. It has completely changed the intellectual landscape since the 1980s. It is not an exaggeration to say that de Tocqueville replaced Marx as the one most influential and revered figure in French political reflection. The post-structuralist and post-modernist writings of some French writers may still fascinate some people in American university campuses, and Michel Foucault may still be a hero there, but in France itself the political thought debate has moved decisively away from these fads for at least the past 20 years or so. To what extent and in what ways such developments in the intellectual landscape do or will affect party politics, programmes and electoral results is another story, particularly because it is too early to say. Such transformations at the level of an entire political culture happen slowly and surreptitiously, and their results are rarely if ever directly or immediately traceable. But a visit to some central Parisian bookshops, and a look at what is being published since the 1980s and 1990s (including an impressive wave of translations of works of Anglo-American political philosophy) compared to what was the case earlier, leaves one in no doubt that a silent revolution has taken place starting some time around the decade when France celebrated the bicentenary of the other French Revolution, that of 1789. Thus, paradoxically for some, France has an ambivalent relationship with liberalism as a political tradition. On the one hand, liberalism has not (not yet, at any rate) been accepted as an undisputed set of values and principles that permeate the whole political culture (as it was accepted in Britain long ago). On the other hand, however, through rediscovering, republishing, and commenting on an illustrious older French liberal tradition, French political thinkers, historians of political thought, philosophers and intellectuals (capacities which usually go together, in France, in any case) are at the same time making a valuable contribution to debates about the nature of liberalism, its value in today's societies and its future.

One should not overestimate the unity of cohesiveness of the group of academics or intellectuals that could be referred to as 'liberal', however. A serious controversy leading to apparently fundamental realignments within circles previously seen as 'liberal' has begun since the publication of a short book by Daniel Lindenberg (2002). See Exhibit 1.2.

Exhibit 1.2: The 'nouveaux réactionnaires' controversy: who are the authentic liberals?

A new phase of intense French intellectual debate began in November 2002, following the publication of a short book written by former Marxist Daniel Lindenberg. He argues that many intellectuals of the left had begun recently to defend 'reactionary' and 'illiberal' positions on all sorts of issues, putting on trial the 'culture de masse', the 'liberté des mœurs', the legacy of May 1968, what they call contemptuously 'le droit-de-l'hommisme', Islam, and, not least, equality and democracy itself. According to Lindenberg, the main targets of this 'illiberal' assault are the two sole poles that defend the foundations of an open, pluralist democracy in France today (struggling for a 'société ouverte et pluraliste'): 'la gauche égalitaire' and 'la droite libérale'. The major criticism against the book has been that it lumps together as 'nouveaux réactionnaires' thinkers and writers who have very little in common. Lindenberg's defenders argue that it is true that the older 'anti-totalitarian' alliance (often hailed as a revival of 'liberalism' and as the acceptance of 'l'État des droits' in France) was in fact composed of two quite different groups of people: on the one hand, those who tried to use the revival of de Tocqueville and the rest of nineteenth-century French liberal thought just as an instrument against Marxism, before turning against liberalism itself more recently (the so-called 'nouveaux réactionnaires'); and, on the other, those who, 'loyal to liberalism's revolutionary inspiration, dedicate their efforts to reconciling liberalism with democracy' ('Nouveaux réacs?', Le Nouvel Observateur, 7–13 November 2002, p. 28, authors' translation). These latter are the 'authentic' liberals according to the Lindenberg thesis.

2

FRENCH SOCIETY TODAY

For Jean-Marie Le Pen, the halt is evident and spectacular. Nevertheless, his ability to retain his votes [in the second round of the presidential elections] shows that the widespread discontent whose vehicle he has been for the last twenty years has resisted the splendid republican mobilisation *between the two rounds [of the presidential elections]. It is a proof that the social* malaise *persists; that the cultural and social fracture has become, as they say in the vocabulary of surgery, an open fracture. ... Because France is not going very well: in terms of employment, of production ... The pockets of under-development will not be reduced but by a dynamic economy, a generator of wealth. ... No matter how necessary might have been the pursuit of the beautiful anti-racist burst between the two rounds, we need to persuade ourselves that we will not bring to an end the tumour unless we cure its causes: insecurity, certainly, the degradation of the urban fabric, but also, and moreover, unemployment, failure at school – which is a failure of the school system itself – the progressive paralysis of the public services and the state. ... All this is for tomorrow. We might as well, for one evening, let ourselves indulge in unadulterated joy. Decidedly, this sacred country, as Tocqueville and de Gaulle thought, is not equal to itself except in exceptional circumstances. (Jacques Julliard, Affront lavé.* Le Nouvel Observateur, *9–15 May 2002: 49; emphasis added, authors' translation).*

VERSIONS OF *MALAISE*: FROM *LA FRACTURE SOCIALE* TO *L'INSÉCURITÉ*

French society today seems almost distilled in the above selections from an article written by one of France's most distinguished commentators immediately after the second round of the presidential elections, when Jean-Marie Le Pen had just been defeated and, therefore, '*[d]e nouveau nous pouvons être fiers de notre pays*', as Julliard put it. The French who agreed with Julliard's views could indeed be proud of having avoided what a British newspaper dubbed the 'A Front National' (alluding to the extreme right leader's success in qualifying for the second round after the result of the first on 21 April

2002), by giving a resounding and almost unprecedented 82 per cent of the vote to Le Pen's opponent, Jacques Chirac, in the second round. And France's friends and lovers abroad did shed a tear or two at the result of the second round and the jubilation that followed. Yet, Julliard is no less right in alerting his readers to the deeper causes of the protest vote for the candidate of the National Front: *le malaise social ... la France ne va pas très bien: ... mécontentement diffus ... la fracture culturelle et sociale ... l'insécurité ... la dégradation du tissu urbain ... le chômage ... échec de l'école ... paralysie progressive des services publics et de l'Etat ...* It reads like a compendium of the ills of French society today. Of all these causes of *malaise* usually invoked in contemporary France, none was more *à la mode* during the electoral period from April to June 2002 than *l'insécurité* – in the same way as *la fracture sociale* had captured the mood of the moment during the electoral campaign for the 1995 presidential elections (and, arguably, given victory to Jacques Chirac, who adopted the concept and promised to alleviate the condition described). Many tried to dismiss the fears of insecurity and play down the problem referred to by the term, accusing those who used it of being victims of an *obsession sécuritaire*. Yet, the term was here to stay, it turned out, and those who tried to pretend that the problem complained of did not exist proved to have done so at their peril. Those – primarily Socialist politicians – who tried to dismiss talk of *l'insécurité*, not least out of fear that it could play into the hands of xenophobic racists (who blamed the problem squarely on foreigners and immigrants) did not manage to wish it away. And those (many) who blamed the media for having created Le Pen's relative electoral success by overplaying the theme of insecurity and showing too many grim details of urban delinquency and crime may have to think again whether the problem is the presentation of these unpalatable traits of everyday life in French society on people's television screens and newspaper pages, or rather the fact that they are as prevalent as they appear to be. It is said by many in France that the fact that images of 'papy Voise', an elderly man brutally beaten by his attackers, were shown incessantly on television screens on 20 April 2002 (the day before the first round of the *presidentielles*) may have added to the anxiety felt by the public and increased to Le Pen's vote. But is that really the problem? Is the messenger to blame for the bad news? It seems not. Rather, it is more to the point to accuse politicians who have tried for a long time to suppress debate on issues like crime, juvenile delinquency, the – disproportionately great, according to all statistics – part played in crime and delinquency by immigrant youths and the causes thereof, and the ever-more talked of *incivilité* (another recently coined term) of having unwittingly made Le Pen's bed for him. Most of the politicians in question failed to address such issues directly and straightforwardly – for noble reasons, perhaps, fearing that by doing so they could raise a backlash against foreigners and immigrants, or simply because of considerations of 'political correctness'. However, events have shown that failure to discuss the issues does not lead to their elimination.

Simply, given that the problem is there for great numbers of members of French society to see (and suffer from), it is Le Pen and his party that benefit, as they are seen as the only ones who really care for the victims of crime, the only ones who really 'listen' to the people and their problems. Of course Le Pen's solutions are oversimplistic and often foolish, but this is not immediately evident to people who despair of anyone doing anything for them. It is the lack of any debate among mainstream politicians on the causes of crime, delinquency and *incivilité* that left the field open for the extreme right to present itself as the only hope of many segments of French society. If there had been serious debate, perhaps most of its solutions would have been easily exposed as at best insufficient and superficial, at worst outright dangerous and unacceptable. It is this message that Jacques Chirac seems to have grasped when he declared that he had 'heard' France immediately after the 21 April first round, if one is to judge by the priorities of the caretaking government that he appointed after his victory in the second round 2 weeks later. Jean-Pierre Raffarin's government gave priority to security issues and lavished all sorts of promises for improvements in this domain if elected in the legislative elections. The experiment seems to have paid off, if one is to judge by the landslide victory of the pro-Chirac *Union pour la Majorité Presidentielle* (UMP) in the June 2002 legislative elections. As the editorial of *Le Monde* put it immediately after the second (final) round of that election: 'The French have indeed come out clearly in favour of change; just as they opted for the left in 1997 in the hope that unemployment would be brought down – which it was – they have voted for the right in 2002 in order to halt the breakdown in law and order' (Jean-Marie Colombani, *Le Monde*, 18 June 2002).

FROM PLANNING AND THE *TRENTE GLORIEUSES* TO THE STATE'S IMPOTENCE

How did it come to this? France was a society that had achieved unprecedented rates of development, growth, modernisation, urbanisation and prosperity after the Second World War. What is now seen as a problem – immigrants of foreign descent – was then a necessity and a blessing imposed by the country's rapid industrialisation and the concomitant need for labouring hands. Most of the immigrants were actively sought out and invited to come to France and contribute to its development. France, a traditionally rural society of peasants in its majority, was transformed after the war into a highly urbanised society as a result of a real *exode rurale* by people who sought – and could find – better employment in the urban centres. This was the famous *trente glorieuses*, the glorious thirty years, almost three decades of impressive growth between the late 1940s and 1973. Significantly, this growth had been primarily state-planned and state-sponsored, to an extent unknown in countries like the UK. This is important in terms of understanding contemporary frustrations at the state's inability to promote similar processes and find solutions. The past has created high expectations about the role of the state in France, and today the state is seen as unable to deliver what in

French eyes are its essential obligations to society and its citizens. The idea that the state is not omnipotent and that there are things it cannot do and should not be expected to do, aired more and more – though half-heartedly and with characteristic reluctance – by French politicians these days, meets with a mixture of disbelief, frustration and sulkiness in a population that had been used to other ideas.

A SOCIETY IN PROLONGED CRISIS?

When did things start to go wrong? Such developments and processes are by definition complex and no single factor can explain them. However, the beginning of problems came with the global oil crisis of 1973, which hit France hard. Since then, France has been in a spiral of constant decline and *malaise*. As far as relations between state and society and perceptions thereof are concerned, matters have been complicated by the processes of Europeanisation and globalisation. Although further and tighter European integration was actively promoted by France itself, particularly from the late 1970s until the mid-1990s, the constraints this process imposed and is imposing on the French state's scope for manoeuvre in all sorts of areas have attracted more and more critics, by whom the French state is seen as increasingly impotent. Even more dreaded in France is so-called 'globalisation', regarded by most French people as another name for 'Americanisation' – the imposition of American cultural, social and economic patterns all over the world, and the consequent disappearance of France's distinct identity. The astonishingly rapid consequences of globalising markets and economic and financial practices have dealt a very severe blow to French reliance on and confidence in the French state and its capacity to protect its citizens. Voter apathy, abstention from elections (almost 40 per cent in the June 2002 legislative elections), general indifference to politics and anything resembling a community are some of the consequences. Observers of French society in recent years are struck by the ever-increasing advances of individualism, of people's self-absorbed pursuit of personal pleasures, hedonism and consumerism. In this context it should be noted that *Loft Story*, the French version of the unashamedly voyeuristic television show *Big Brother*, became a great success when it was introduced to France in 2001. This phenomenon provoked endless debates regarding its social and sociological significance, with most participants in the debates criticising the programme, claiming never to have condescended to watch it, meanwhile sounding fairly familiar with what was going on. The most successful and most read novelist in France today is Michel Houellebecq, whose books exhibit a degree of cynicism about politics, a focusing on the pursuit of sexual gratification and personal passions and a self-destructive turn that have shocked many observers, both in France and abroad. Both his admirers and his critics find that his works reflect tendencies of contemporary French society (Marc Weitzmann, 'Houellebecq, aspects de la France', *Le Monde*, 7 September 2001). Such observations are anything but new, of course. They are at least as old as de Tocqueville's and his contemporaries' worries in the early nineteenth century, but de Tocqueville's predictions about what the future held (if nothing were done to prevent the unpalatable aspects of modernisation) seem to have been borne out with frightening accuracy in some respects.

CHANGING PATTERNS OF EMPLOYMENT AND UNEMPLOYMENT, AND THE NEW KINDS OF POVERTY

To turn now to some more concrete data about French society today, let us start with changes in employment and employment patterns. France had in 2000 a population of more than 60 million, a population that seems to be increasing, but also getting older. France has a working population of 24 million people, 88 per cent among whom are wage-earners. Among that working population, 13 million are men and 11 million women. Just over one-fifth of this active population are employed by the public service (*fonction publique*), in other words 5.4 million French people are *fonctionnaires*. It is the wage-earners who seem to be most exposed to unemployment and job precariousness. This question of precarious employment is becoming one of the most serious social problems in France today. According to the statistics of INSEE (*Institut National de la Statistique et des Études Économiques*), in March 2001, 2.2 million among the wage-earners (9 per cent of the active population) were employed in a particular form of work, consisting of fixed-term contracts, interim missions or aided contracts. Interim missions counted for 2.5 per cent of the active population, fixed-term contracts for 3.91 per cent, apprentices for 1.1 per cent, and aided contracts for 1.71 per cent. Now, these forms of employment taken together accounted for only 3 per cent of wage-earners in 1983. Such forms of employment are instruments of flexibility which reduce costs more and more for enterprises. People practising these various temporary forms of work particularly tend to be women, young people and people less qualified than the average wage-earners who find themselves in permanent employment. In March 2001, 16.4 per cent of the active population were working part-time. This category breaks down to 30 per cent for women and 5 per cent for men. Unemployment was, on 31 January 2001, at 9 per cent (2 209 000 people were seeking work). Unemployment is very unequally spread depending on sex, age, studies and qualifications. In March 2001, the unemployment rate for active men was 7.1 per cent, while for active women it was 10.7 per cent. For people between the ages of 15 and 24 years, the unemployment rate was 18.7 per cent; for those between 25 and 49 it was 8.4 per cent; and for those older than 50 years unemployment was 6.1 per cent. It needs to be noted, however, that the relatively low rate for those above 50 can be explained to an extent by the fact that the rate of activity for over-50s is relatively feeble. Moreover, it is they who stay the longest in unemployment: in March 2001 the average length of time in unemployment for those over 50 was 24.5 months, against 14 months for people between 25 and 49, and 7 months for the younger group. Even more than age, it is qualifications that seem to be a determining factor. Those without a diploma in unemployment in March 2001 were 14.1 per cent; those with a 'bac +2' (two years of post-secondary education) were 5.2 per cent; while those with higher-education qualifications were 4.9 per cent. Finally, there is serious disequilibrium depending on socio-professional category: in March 2001, the unemployment rate of workers and employees was 11 per cent, against 3.1 per cent for higher staff (*cadres*) and the *professions intellectuelles supérieures* ('Les France de 2002', *Le Monde*, 10–11 March 2002: 16). It is obvious that some categories of the population are more vulnerable than others.

Up to the 1970s, poverty and social exclusion touched mostly older people and particularly the rural world. Today, the face of poverty and exclusion has radically changed. It affects new population groups, often installed in major urban centres (*grandes agglomérations*): the young, single-parent families, salaried wage-earners in part-time work and asylum seekers. Another novelty of recent years is the emergence of a new social category, the 'working poor', people who work in low-paid activities, mainly in fixed-term contracts. There are increasing numbers of homeless people who also work: around 30 per cent of those deprived of abode at the beginning of 2001. According to INSEE, 86000 persons were *sans domicile fix* (without fixed address, SDF) in 2001. They either slept in the streets or were offered accommodation by some organisation. The SDF are a group composed mainly of young people and males: two-thirds are men and 36 per cent are between 18 and 29 years old (while this slice of the population represents 23 per cent of the French population) ('Les France de 2002', *Le Monde*, 10–11 March 2002: 16).

FOREIGNERS, IMMIGRANTS AND SCAPEGOATS

Under such conditions of generalised insecurity, accentuated by an overall anxiety about the future of France and its way of life (almost invariably seen as unique and more or less superior to any other), foreigners easily become scapegoats. Among a sizeable part of the population – one in four of the French said in opinion polls after the elections of 2002 that they agree with most of Le Pen's views in general – this takes the form of anti-immigrant feeling, xenophobia and racism directed against foreign immigrants living in France or against French citizens of foreign descent, no matter how remote (see more in Chapters 4 and 5). Another form in which 'the other' and everything that is seen as coming from abroad is rejected is anti-globalisation agitation, which, in France, is at its most organised and vociferous. It remains to be seen how the relationship of France with the European Union will develop in the new environment of EU enlargement eastwards (see more in Chapter 9) but opinion polls already show that the French population is among the most reluctant in the EU.

GEOGRAPHICAL DISPARITIES IN CRIME AND INSECURITY

Another clear tendency in the past 10 years has been for crime-related insecurity to be disproportionately concentrated in Paris. In the year 2000, the
French capital registered the highest rate of criminality, with 139.54 per 1000
inhabitants. The year 2001 saw a sharp rise in the incidence of violent theft,
armed theft and vehicle theft. This is in large part due to another major social
problem: the uneven geographical distribution of wealth and misery. France
is increasingly becoming a country composed of societies apart. There is a sharp
divide between the affluent parts of Paris and the other big cities, on the one
hand, and the poor *banlieues* on the other, with a striking over-representation
of ethnic minorities. These destitute *banlieues* produce much of France's
criminality and delinquency, and there are now parts of Paris and other cities
which are 'no-go zones' for outsiders. One of the major discussions that arose
out of the elections of 2002 has been the very widespread perception that
the main reason why the political elites do not do anything about crime
and *incivilité*, but appear to try to wish the problem away, is that they are
not really fully aware of the problem. One of the major divides in French
society today is between those who feel threatened by crime and delinquency and those who are protected from it (by living in the affluent parts of
the city, among people like themselves, by not having to use the métro, the
trains and other means of public transport, by not living in close proximity
to the criminal, delinquent and disaffected groups of the population). Many
of the people who feel exposed to the dangers of *l'insécurité* express the
belief that those in power are a separate, well-protected and self-protected
elite, who simply do not care about them and do not know anything
about them and their lives. It is in these conditions that populist movements
like that of Le Pen thrive, as they purport to offer the only perceptible
outlet.

ELITISM, *GRANDES ÉCOLES*, *ÉNARCHIE* AND THE PARIS–PROVINCES DIVIDE

The cleavages described above are accentuated by the fact that the vast
majority of the political personnel in important positions of power are a
co-opting elite, educated in the same *grandes écoles*, primarily ENA (*École
Nationale d'Administration*) (see Chapters 3 and 7 for more details). These are
the famous *énarques*, who make the political system of France look like an
énarchie. Chief among the *énarques*, somehow personifying the beleaguered
French political 'establishment' more than anyone else today (having first
become a minister in the Gaullist government in 1968), is President Chirac
himself. In fact, it seems obvious to most commentators that it was because
of this profoundly held belief that the elites rule France without 'listening' to
'the people' that Chirac chose Jean-Pierre Raffarin as his prime minister after

his re-election on 5 May 2002. Raffarin was seen as conspicuously non-Parisian-elite, non-ENA-graduate, as a likeable provincial politician who was close to 'the people'. His major watchword during the campaign for the legislative elections was that he represented *la France d'en bas*. The results of the 2002 legislative elections were strikingly revealing as far as differences between Paris and the provinces are concerned. Although the left was decimated in general during these elections, it did remarkably well in Paris, where it even increased its vote. On the other hand, in the rest of the country Raffarin's campaign for *la France d'en bas* seems to have been particularly appreciated.

WOMEN, GENDER EQUALITY AND FEMINISM

We have seen that women tend to be more vulnerable in the job market. We will explore further in Chapter 4 the role of women in politics, the problem of inadequate women's representation and the attempts to rectify this. Suffice it to say here that, despite efforts in recent years, there are several domains where women cannot be said to have achieved complete equality with men, and France has lagged far behind Northern Europe – and even Britain and the United States – in all aspects of women's rights. What is important to note in this context is the issue of mentalities, cultural attitudes and the nature of French feminism itself. The latter has never been as aggressive and as assertive as its counterparts in Northern European countries or the USA. Among other reasons, one explanation that has been put forward is that the issue is related to the overall reluctance in France to claim any group-specific rights, rights that are not the same for all human beings, or at least all citizens of the republic, but rather are targeted in favour of a specific segment of the population. This, according to many people's perception, is opposed to the republican ethos (see more on these issues in Chapter 5).

CHANGING FAMILY PATTERNS AND SEXUAL MORES

Related to women's rights and place in society is the question of sexual mores and attitudes and changes in these attitudes in recent years. It is indisputable that all sorts of sexual and social behaviours that were not easily accepted in French society a few decades ago are now increasingly common. Thus there has been a sharp rise in the number of single-parent households as well as in single-person households. Paris has the highest percentage of single-person households of any major city in Europe. Mixed marriages between people of different ethnic or 'racial' groups are on the rise as well. There has also been an increase in the number of 'out' homosexuals – the subject of a recent film comedy starring Daniel Auteil – and the social acceptability of homosexuality has markedly increased over the past two decades (see White 2001). Another social phenomenon in contemporary France that has attracted a lot of attention in the British press (the tabloids as well as the 'serious' broadsheet press) is the reported rise of so-called *échangisme* and *échangiste* clubs (wife-swappers' clubs, as the British press puts it). All these phenomena of sexual libertinism should not be seen as completely new, of course. In the eyes of France's insular neighbours *outre-Manche*, Paris was always identified as the capital of pleasure (and used for escapades of this nature as frequently as one's circumstances allowed). But such activities did not always take place as openly as today.

AIDS IN FRANCE

Related to sexual mores and attitudes is the question of *Sida* (*Syndrome immuno-déficitaire acquis*) as the French call AIDS (Acquired Immune Deficiency Syndrome), which is the terminal outcome of infection with the Human Immunodeficiency Virus (HIV). France has a rate of HIV infection four times as high as that of the UK and the highest in Europe – in 1995, the total reported cases reached 36 982, with 60.8 per cent of these having died and four new cases of infection in Paris per day. The discovery of the AIDS virus in 1983 left its impact on human consciousness and irrevocably affected interpersonal contact in most countries around the planet. The reaction in France has been quite distinctive. The French seem to be much more reluctant than their British neighbours to practise protected 'safe' sex. Rather, statistics and opinion polls show a divide between two equally extreme attitudes in this respect. Many people in France, when asked about the dangers posed by HIV and AIDS, reply that, rather than use condoms, they prefer to abstain from sexual activity altogether, or have only one partner, in order to be safe. An equally sizeable group, on the other hand, respond by declaring that they do not take any measures whatsoever, and that, if they are to die 'of love', then so be it. Commentators on the other side of the Channel cannot help seeing this as one more manifestation of Gallic extremism and hyperbole.

A more general problem has been the disturbing levels of ignorance about AIDS which, arguably, the French state has been slow in countering. It was not until 1988 that the first French condom advertising campaign was launched, by the Rocard government. Such material had previously been banned by pro-natalist legislation. The Rocard government also established the *Agence Nationale de Recherches sur le Sida* (ANRS) to coordinate research into the syndrome. Among its various activities to date, the agency launched in 1991 its own study of sexual behaviour in France: a telephone enquiry followed up by a longer questionnaire completed by those reporting sexual conduct believed to put them at risk from HIV. Other developments have also contributed to more general public awareness of the virus, notably the investigations into the infamous contaminated blood scandal (*l'affaire du sang contaminé*). In 1985 it was revealed that hundreds of haemophiliacs had been infected with HIV by blood transfusion stocks which had not been screened for the virus because Ministry of Health officials had decided to delay the launch of American testing kits in order to allow the commer-cialisation of French ones. The lengthy trial of the officials involved in this decision and the great media exposure given to the haemophiliac victims presented the uncomfortable truth about the virus. Arguably, the most successful planned event to increase awareness of AIDS was *Sidaction*, the transmission of a series of programmes about AIDS and those suffering from it on all French television channels on 7 March 1994. This experiment was repeated in subsequent years.

SPORTS, POLITICS AND NATIONAL IDENTITY

An event that marked French society considerably was the astonishing suc-cess of the national football team (*les bleus*, as they are known) in winning the World Cup in 1998. The Cup was hosted by France that year and, after a dra-matic final against the favourites, Brazil, *les bleus* set the whole of France shivering with enthusiasm and national pride. Besides the boost this gave to French self-confidence, what was remarkable was that the team that had made France so proud was a multiethnic, multicolour team. Moreover, the hero of the World Cup victory was Zidane, the son of Algerian immigrants, something which put wind in the sails of those promoting a more inclusive, multicultural France. (The picture, unfortunately for the French, was very different in June 2002, when the world champions were defeated and elim-inated very early on in the World Cup held in Japan and South Korea. Fol-lowing as closely as it did the success of Le Pen in making it to the second round of the presidential elections, this sporting failure added considerably to the sense of *morosité* among the excitable and easily disappointed popula-tion of France.)

While the World Cup victory in 1998 seemed to boost the chances of inte-gration and multiculturalism in French society more than a thousand dia-tribes and dissertations by sociologists and political philosophers, another sporting event exposed the limitations and weaknesses of integration *à la française*. In September 2001, in the *Stade de France* in Paris, a football match (the first ever since Algerian independence) took place between the national teams of France and Algeria. Among the spectators were thousands of young *beurs*, children born and raised in France by North African parents (Algerian primarily, but also Moroccan or Tunisian). To the great shock of the wider French society, these youths consistently throughout the match hissed the French players, overtly supporting the 'foreign' team and even – horror of horrors – booed when the national anthem of France, the *Marseillaise*, was being played. To those who needed reminding – most people in France, it turned out, judging from their surprised reactions in the press afterwards – this was striking and painful evidence that 'integration' had not been such a great success after all. It was shocking for most of the non-*beur*, non-Muslim French population to have such a tangible and indisputable indication that thousands of their fellow-citizens, young people born and raised in France, possessing French nationality, did not really feel French, and not only would rather support a North African team, but would express their anti-French feelings in such a striking way.

One of the consequences of the realisation that much had yet to be done if there were to be any chance of successfully integrating *beur* and Muslim youths into French society was the decision (long delayed in its implementation, but firmly taken and agreed upon by the main agents concerned) to create a Muslim Council in France, which will coordinate with the French state in attempts to promote integration and counter religious extremism (often referred to as 'Muslim fundamentalism'). Moderate Muslim leaders and clergymen as well as social scientists specialising in issues of immigration and the integration of immigrants (including, notably, Patrick Weil) argue that the creation of such an institution is necessary and might prove very instrumental in curbing the growth of extremism among disaffected Muslim youths in the poor *banlieues*, who currently do not see French society as their own. (It was no less shocking for French public opinion to be informed that one of the suspected members of the Al Qaeda organisation that planned the attacks on the Twin Towers in New York and the Pentagon in Washington, DC, on 11 September 2001 was a French Muslim.) The need to integrate these people and make them feel that France is their country as well as making all the non-Muslim French people (so many of whom voted for Le Pen in April–May 2002) regard them as their fellow-citizens seems to be one of the most pressing challenges facing French society today.

3

THE SURPRISINGLY STABLE
FIFTH REPUBLIC

To some the Fifth Republic represents the successful culmination of attempts to combine the authoritarian and revolutionary traditions of France, while to others it amounts to a 'permanent *coup d'état*' of excessive executive authority, weakening the parliamentary element of the republican tradition. Whatever the view, the Fifth Republic clearly differs considerably from previous constitutional arrangements. Despite its relative – and, most would argue, surprising – stability over the past four decades there remains the question whether the institutional make-up of the Fifth Republic can survive intact into the twenty-first century. In this chapter we first explore why and how the Fifth Republic has so far been the most stable of all the republics. We then examine several of the core elements of the republic in more detail: the powers of the political executive (notably the president), the weakened role of the French parliament, the power of the French administration – including a diversion into the training ground of the French elite, at the *École Nationale d'Administration*. At the same time, the Fifth Republic has experienced change which has not yet succeeded in undermining stability. Three periods of cohabitation since 1986 – that is, periods during which the government must share power with a president who comes from one of the opposition parties – have changed the way in which political scientists look at the roles of the two elements of the bicephalous French political executive. However, they have not – again to the surprise of many observers – weakened the stability of the Fifth Republic and indeed have not met the disapproval of the majority of the French population. The three periods of cohabitation are explored in a dossier on pp. 44–5. The decentralisation reforms of 1982–4 have strengthened local government yet not fundamentally undermined the principles behind the 'one and indivisible republic' nor significantly reduced the pivotal role of the French prefect – the chief representative of central government in the regions. The French party system – despite some fluctuation over the past 40 years – remains a key element in the stability of the Fifth Republic. It is a reflection of the electoral system and the presidentialisation of French politics.

DE GAULLE, THE FOUNDER

In order to understand the intellectual roots of the Fifth Republic's constitution, at least in so far as it differed from that of the Fourth Republic, it is essential to examine the ideas of General Charles de Gaulle, the founder and first president of the Fifth Republic. These ideas were gradually fleshed out during the Second World War and under the Fourth Republic, particularly between 1946 and 1953. De Gaulle presented his ideas to the country in a series of speeches, of which the most famous was given in Bayeux on 16 June 1946. He emphasised the idea of French greatness (*grandeur*), the theme of national unity and the need for a strong state. While de Gaulle accepted pluralism, he did not allow the possibility of calling into question, in the name of an ideology, what he saw as the major options corresponding to the nation's higher interest. Only a strong state could guarantee this higher interest: that is, a respected state, independent of party factions and able to unite all the French. De Gaulle argued that it was necessary to avoid a return to the debased practices of a parliamentary system – which he thought weakened France in the Third and Fourth Republics – and, above all, to correct, through the appropriate mechanisms, the harmful effects of French individualism.

De Gaulle believed that it was essential for the state to have a single leader: the President of the Republic, provided with prerogative powers. Situated above the fluctuations and accidents of political life, he should represent France. He should be the supreme arbiter: 'the man of the nation'. He should also be independent of Parliament, with power emanating directly from the people. Below him, the executive, legislative and judicial powers should be clearly separate and effectively balanced. The National Assembly, elected by universal suffrage, should pass legislation and the budget, and supervise the action of the government appointed by the president. However, it should not be allowed to destabilise governments with 'excessive' interference. A second assembly representing local authorities, social, economic and familial organisations should constitute a chamber of reflection and initiation, counterbalancing the influences of the lower chamber.

The worsening of the Algerian crisis gave de Gaulle the opportunity to put his constitutional ideas into effect. On 13 May 1958 an army revolt in Algiers seized government buildings and declared a committee of public salvation (*comité du salut public*) to assume control of Algeria against interfering French governments that were seen as moving to a negotiated solution with the Arab liberation movement (the FLN) which sought an independent country under majority rule. This followed several years of army activity that seriously undermined the credibility of Fourth Republic governments. The government turned to de Gaulle to control the army, bring an end to the Algerian crisis and preserve a form of liberal democracy. De Gaulle agreed, providing he could impose several conditions including the creation of a new Fifth Republic. On 1 June 1958 de Gaulle was elected prime minister by a majority of the National Assembly.

Under the chairmanship of Michel Debré, whom de Gaulle appointed as minister of justice, a group of experts drew up the articles of the new constitution. This was adopted by a large majority of the National Assembly and the Senate on 28 September 1958. With the exception of the Communists, all the political parties advocated a 'yes' vote in the subsequent referendum. Several of the parties did not approve of the creation of a strong executive, but in the context of the Algerian crisis and military revolt, their priority was the establishment of stability. Nearly 80 per cent of the voters in metropolitan France approved the new constitution and the Fifth Republic came into being on 4 October 1958.

THE POLITICAL CONDITIONS OF STABILITY

The formation of a stable political system and institutional structure through constitutional change is inherently problematic. The real basis of such stability is rooted in political culture – the party system, history and socio-economic realities – rather than in constitutional rules. However, such rules can clearly enhance or promote stability. The key factor which explains the stabilisation of French politics during the Fifth Republic is the existence of stable majorities or coalitions in the National Assembly. This has little to do with the 1958 constitution *per se*. It might be argued that the existence of stable majorities is linked to the new two-ballot majority electoral system – adopted in 1958 but outside the constitution – which discriminates against smaller parties and encourages alliance-building and bipolarisation. However, the principal reason for the bipolarisation which has contributed to the formation of stable majority government was not the two-ballot system, which, after all, existed in the relatively unstable Third Republic (1872–1940), but chance political factors. After the resolution of the immediate threat to republican government in 1958, political parties, and the French population more generally, divided into two groups: those who supported the new constitution and the political institutions of the Fifth Republic, and those who did not. The division into camps supporting and opposing de Gaulle's leadership also corresponded roughly to a right/left split. Although there were left-wing Gaullists, most of those on the left of the spectrum opposed the institutions of the Fifth Republic. The result was the destruction of the previously dominant centre of the Third and Fourth Republics. After de Gaulle's departure, the bipolar party system continued with only occasionally debilitating hiccoughs. De Gaulle as president contributed considerably to this stability. The institution of a presidency with real powers did not. If the president is not the leader of the party or coalition of parties in government, there may be conflict in certain areas of policy making. However, the three periods of cohabitation have shown that this does not necessarily have an impact upon the stability of the regime.

To argue that French Fifth Republic politics has become more stable implies that politics in the Fourth Republic (1946–58) was less stable. When authors describe unstable Fourth Republic politics they usually refer to a parliament dominated by small parties over which unstable and oft-collapsing coalition governments consisting of several medium-sized and small parties attempted to govern. A principal criterion for stability can be drawn from this description: that is, a form of government in which the governing party or parties can stay in power with a majority of the seats in parliament for the full 4 or 5 years until the next legally required election and avoid having to call repeated elections or restructure the coalition due to votes of no confidence. This means that it is necessary for parliament to be dominated by a small number of relatively large parties which can form the government either on their own or in cooperation with other parties in order to direct the implementation of policy and pass bills in the National Assembly. Other factors, in addition to the precise form of government, can also affect the ability of the government to decide and direct the implementation of policy.

In addition to bipolarisation, stability in the Fifth Republic owed very much to the popularity of de Gaulle and the relabelled Gaullist party, the UNR (*Union pour la Nouvelle République*, Union for the New Republic, changed to UDR, *Union pour la Défence de la République*, Union for the Defence of the Republic, following May 1968). The UNR became the most electorally successful political party in the history of French democracy, winning a near majority of National Assembly seats in 1962 and a full majority in 1968. However, the potential for instability remained as long as half the political spectrum was opposed to the institutional make-up of the Fifth Republic. The Fourth Republic was unstable above all because two of the largest parties, the Gaullist RPF (*Rassemblement du Peuple Français*, Rally of the French People) and the Communists (PCF) were fundamentally opposed to its existence and refused to participate in governments. In the Fifth Republic, opposition to the regime on the right dwindled. However, on the left, the Communists and Socialists and some centrists proclaimed the system illegitimate – de Gaulle's 'permanent *coup d'état*' – on the grounds that it both excessively weakened France's parliamentary tradition by permitting a dangerously strong president (the Bonapartist precedent of 1852 in mind) and discriminated against the left (the Communist party, for example, lost seats because of the switch from proportional representation (PR) to the two-ballot system). Long-term regime stability relied upon increased support for the Socialist Party, which began to overtake the Communists in the polls in the mid-1970s, and the moderation of Socialist policies. The French Communists – allied to Moscow – were a lingering threat to liberal democracy. The Socialists succeeded in winning the presidency and a majority of seats in the National Assembly elections of 1981, promising considerable change. The Socialist-led government (which included Communist ministers) pursued a significant reform agenda. However, the Socialist victories also brought about acceptance of the institutions of the Fifth Republic, which were no longer seen as opposed to the interests of the left. Moreover, apart from the nationalisation of several banks and companies, there was no fundamental change to the economy. By 1982 the government had already introduced austerity measures to bring inflation under control, and by March 1983 President Mitterrand had committed the government to the constraints of the European common market and exchange rate mechanism.

There are specific ways in which constitutional provisions contributed to the stability of the Fifth Republic. Notably, the political executive was greatly strengthened in relation to the parliament. Ostensibly, this had been the most important reform sought by de Gaulle to improve stability. The aim was to prevent parliamentarians from undermining the credibility and legitimacy of the government by delaying legislation and through excessive scrutiny. These reforms had a substantial impact upon the institutional make-up of French liberal democracy. However, it is problematic to claim that they significantly strengthened the government. The crucial factor remained the existence of stable majority governments.

THE DUAL (BICEPHALOUS) POLITICAL EXECUTIVE

Ironically perhaps, one of the principal institutional innovations of the Fifth Republic generated the potential for instability. The creation of a dual political executive with a stronger presidency was one of de Gaulle's main objectives. However, the constitutional provisions allowing for this were not clear as those drafting the constitution watered down de Gaulle's vision. On most matters, powers are shared between the president and the government (led by the prime minister), so the potential for conflicting interpretations and battles is great. Serious conflict was largely avoided under the first two presidents – de Gaulle and Georges Pompidou – because of the dominance of the president within the party that controlled the government and the clear subordination of the prime ministers. Instability remained a distinct possibility, however. First, the president might have to share power with a coalition government in which the president's party formed only one element and did not dominate. This happened under President Valéry Giscard d'Estaing. Although there were political difficulties, leading to the resignation of the Gaullist prime minister Jacques Chirac, who refused to accept certain policies that Giscard sought to impose, the conservative coalition partners continued to work together to govern the country. More destabilising yet was the possibility that the president would have to share power with a coalition from which the president's party was entirely excluded. Under this form of cohabitation, which we have already discussed, the president must govern when the president's own party is in the political opposition in the National Assembly. Such cohabitation was a matter of grave concern to many politicians and political scientists on the grounds that it might lead to deadlock in the political executive and even regime collapse. However, the three periods of cohabitation to date – 1986–8, 1993–5 and 1997–2002 – have demonstrated the stability of the Fifth Republic as well as clarified the grounds upon which democratic legitimacy is derived. De Gaulle strengthened the legitimacy of the presidency by holding a referendum in 1962 to bring about direct presidential elections. However, the basis for the legitimate expression of power remained the support of the majority in the National Assembly. Cohabitation demonstrated that without this support, the president's powers are limited to those which are explicitly enumerated in the 1958 constitution, and even here the president's room for manoeuvre is severely constrained by the government's powers.

The Fifth Republic has been marked by a strong president for all but nine of its 46 years to date. France is one of a small number of countries in the world with a dual (bicephalous) political executive. Most liberal democracies are either parliamentary regimes led by a prime minister (with a largely powerless head of state) or presidential regimes with a directly elected head of state. France can be labelled a qualified (semi-) presidential regime: if the president has the support of the government (majority of members within the National Assembly), he is very powerful and the constitution reinforces his power. If the president does not have this support, he is weak and it is the government, headed by the prime minister, that determines most of the policies of the country, with little interference from the president except in a few areas specifically enumerated in the constitution. There are several factors which have determined the power of the French president in relation to the government over the past four decades. These can be labelled the *five Ps*: powers guaranteed in the Fifth Republic's constitution, personality, prestige, patronage and party. First, the French constitution is the necessary but not sufficient source of presidential power. At de Gaulle's insistence, the 1958 constitution gave the president several explicit powers, including:

- emergency powers (article 16)
- powers over defence (the president is head of the army)
- powers over foreign affairs
- power to dissolve the National Assembly
- power to appoint the prime minister (thus establishing a clear hierarchy between the two)
- power to call a national referendum (initiated by the National Assembly)
- power to sign certain governmental decrees (*décrets*) and ordinances (*ordonnances*) (legal devices that do not have to be approved in Parliament, usually involving a specification within an existing law)
- power to nominate three members, including the president, of the Constitutional Council
- power to question the constitutionality of government acts by calling upon the Constitutional Council. (Until the mid-1970s only four people could call upon the Council to examine the constitutionality of legislation: the president, the prime minister, the president of the National Assembly and the president of the Senate. The Council was thus initially created as a tool of the political executive.)

- power to accredit all ambassadors (the president is the first port of call for all visiting dignitaries, even during cohabitation, which strengthens his foreign affairs role).

By personality, the second P, we are referring principally to the strong personality and will of de Gaulle. De Gaulle set the precedent of strong presidential leadership in the *domaine réservé* (defence and foreign affairs), even though these powers are shared with the government in the constitution. Crucially, de Gaulle misused the referendum power granted to him in the French constitution by ignoring the National Assembly's refusal to initiate the referendum on the direct election of the president. He thus assured the direct presidential elections, which greatly strengthened the president's legitimacy. The personal policy interests of subsequent presidents determined the sphere of presidential intervention: Pompidou directly intervened in economic affairs, as did Giscard; Giscard became actively involved in social policy, while Mitterrand also became actively involved in cultural affairs. Given the president's position, he can withdraw from the details of government and focus on the 'big' questions.

The third P is the prestige of the president, which attracts considerable media attention. The president is the only member of the core executive directly elected into office by the population; he is a well-established politician, with a very familiar face.

The fourth P is patronage (implied by the constitution, but an important precedent was established here by de Gaulle). In 'normal' (non-cohabitation) periods of government the president has considerable power of patronage (shared with the prime minister), and this ensures support for the president in top levels of the administration even during periods of cohabitation. The small size of the president's own administrative staff does not reflect his potential power.

The fifth and most important of the Ps is party. Except during periods of cohabitation, presidential power depends principally upon the support of a party in government. The president can only get elected into office (and stay there) with the support of a party machine. The election of Giscard d'Estaing in 1974 was an exception, but his defeat in the 1981 and 1988 elections was owing in part to his failure to build a substantial party machine around him. The president is normally the leader of his party or has a great deal of influence in the party.

Like that of the president, the role of the prime minister and the government in relation to Parliament was strengthened by the Fifth Republic's constitution. Article 20 gives the government the power to determine and run the policies of the country. Articles 37 and 38 authorise the government to make laws, ordinances and decrees and, in particular, assign power to the prime minister, who must sign most decrees and ordinances. The prime minister has powers of management and administration: he is the final arbiter within the government in most cases (except, during 'normal' non-cohabitation periods, when the president wants to intervene and the prime minister is

Table 3.1 The five presidents of the Fifth Republic and their serving prime ministers

President (and dates)	Prime ministers (and dates)
Charles de Gaulle (1959–69)	Michel Debré (1959–62), Georges Pompidou (1962–8), Maurice Couve de Murville (1968–9)
Georges Pompidou (1969–74)	Jacques Chaban-Delmas (1969–72), Pierre Messmer (1972–4)
Valéry Giscard d'Estaing (1974–81)	Jacques Chirac (1974–6), Raymond Barre (1976–81)
François Mitterrand (1981–95)	Pierre Mauroy (1981–4), Laurent Fabius (1984–6), Jacques Chirac (cohab.) (1986–8), Michel Rocard (1988–90), Edith Cresson (1990–1), Pierre Bérégovoy (1991–3), Edouard Balladur (cohab.) (1993–5)
Jacques Chirac (1995–?)	Alain Juppé (1995–7), Lionel Jospin (cohab.) (1997–May 2002), Jean-Pierre Raffarin (May 2002–?)

Exhibit 3.1: The five 'Ps' of French presidential power

Powers: those enumerated in the constitution
Personality: de Gaulle's precedent; policy interests of individual presidents
Prestige: attracts considerable media attention
Patronage: ensures support for the president in top levels of the administration
Party: power depends principally upon the support of a party in government

ready to accept this intervention). Most of the tools of government coordination are also attached to the prime minister's office, including the SGG (the *Secrétariat Général du Gouvernement*) which coordinates most government activities and the SGCI (*Secrétariat Général du Comité Interministeriel pour les Questions Économiques Européennes*, the General Secretariat of the Interministerial Committee for European Economic Affairs) which coordinates French policy on European affairs. The prime minister, or more normally, one of her/his trusted staff, chairs interministerial meetings organised by the SGG. S/he will also chair interministerial committees and commissions on issues of national concern (such as the integration of immigrants). As the head of government, the prime minister must defend its policies, whereas the president has always had more room for manoeuvre. The prime minister chooses with the president the members of his cabinet (*conseil des ministres*). While the president will have a great deal of say over appointments during 'normal' periods, during periods of cohabitation the prime minister has nearly total control. The support staff (*cabinet*) of the prime minister has varied between 18 and 56 advisors and the director of staff (*directeur de cabinet*) and some of the specialist advisors (*conseillers techniques*) will have considerable influence in policy making.

The prime minister is normally the head or one of the heads of the party with the greatest number of seats in the National Assembly. There are occasions, such as with Chirac in 1993, when the head of the party chooses not to become prime minister (Chirac sought to position himself to run for presidency) and can designate someone else (in this case Balladur). During periods of cohabitation the president normally has only very limited choice over who should become prime minister and will bow to the wishes of the head of the party with most seats. During 'normal' periods the president chooses the prime minister from among the leaders of his party. In 1974 the president's party confederation (the UDF, *Union pour la Démocratie Française*, Union for French Democracy) was not the largest in the governing coalition and Giscard was forced to select Chirac as prime minister. However, when Chirac resigned on grounds of differences on macroeconomic policy, the president decided to select a prime minister from his own party even though it was the smaller of the two major coalition partners.

The prime minister will take many more decisions than the president, but the latter can intervene when he wants to and can manipulate the prime minister to decide in a particular way. During periods of cohabitation the prime minister has considerable power and the coordination of public policy becomes more simple. During 'normal' periods, the prime minister will share the choice of the cabinet with the president. Even during 'normal' periods, the prime minister maintains a margin for manoeuvre in relation to the president. This is for several reasons: his/her powers of management; his/her ability to insist upon assuming certain powers at the time of his/her nomination; the fact that s/he is often the head of a faction within the party, the support of which the president needs. In relation to the ministers serving the prime minister, similar considerations apply with regard to the prime minister's powers. The prime minister is *primus inter pares* (first among equals): he is responsible for interministerial coordination and arbitration and thus in the vast majority of cases has the final say. Yet ministers can insist upon certain powers at the time of their nomination and they may be important political figures in their own right, whose support the prime minister needs. Elgie (1993) writes of three groups of factors limiting the overall influence of the prime minister in national affairs: systematic, conjunctural and momentary. The systematic factors include the position of the state in relation to the international political and economic order, the organisation of the state, and the organisation of the political executive. Conjunctural factors include elections: the government is elected every 4 to 5 years, while until 2002 the president has been elected every 7 years. Political debates within the prime minister's party, personality and public opinion are also of relevance. Momentary factors include crises, which weaken the prime minister as the president will normally assume greater control during a crisis.

THE THREE PERIODS OF COHABITATION

The first cohabitation demonstrated four things about the operation of the Fifth Republic and the political executive:

- *the stability and durability of the Fifth Republic's constitution.*
- *the basis of political power in the Fifth Republic*: support of the majority of the National Assembly.
- *the constitutional division of powers* between the president and the prime minister, with the prime minister controlling most. The president continued to possess: a limited influence over the selection of the prime minister and ministers; control in the *domaine réservé* (the president sets the major lines of foreign affairs and defence); power to block government decrees and ordinances; power to make nominations and block certain government nominations; power to dissolve the National Assembly (a weapon of limited use) and call new elections. Moreover, the president retains his presidency of the Council of Ministers (cabinet), thus weakening the importance of this body as the government will not discuss its strategy on politically sensitive matters with the president present. Cohabitation also allowed the simplification of core executive coordination (the president only intervened on foreign and defence policies).
- *the extent to which the president can still intervene in domestic political life* and criticise the government. The president has enough room for manoeuvre to manipulate political situations and get the better of the government. During the first cohabitation Mitterrand manipulated two issues to his political advantage: access to post-secondary education and the treatment of ethnic minorities by the government and police.

The second and third cohabitations showed that each cohabitation changes according to certain factors:

- *the personality and personal situation of the president and the prime minister.* Mitterrand was much weaker as president during the second cohabitation than he was during the first, owing principally to his prostate cancer and to revelations about his involvement in far-right extremism in his youth (by Pierre Péan in *Une jeunesse française* (1994)).

Table 3.2 The three cohabitations

Period of cohabitation	President/party	Government/prime minister
First: March 1986–May 1988	François Mitterrand/ Socialist	RPR-UDF/Jacques Chirac
Second: March 1993–May 1995	François Mitterrand/ Socialist	RPR-UDF/Edouard Balladur
Third: June 1997–May 2002	Jacques Chirac/ RPR (neo-Gaullist)	Plural Left (Socialist-led)/ Lionel Jospin

- *the relationship between the president and his party.* During the second cohabitation, Mitterrand was largely estranged from the PS and several leading PS figures sought to distance themselves from him. During the 1997–2002 cohabitation, Chirac – politically weak and facing accusations of corruption – was abandoned by many members of his own party (RPR).
- *the size of the government's majority* and the weakness of the president's party in opposition. Given the overwhelming defeat for the Socialists in 1993, it would have been difficult for Mitterrand to claim great legitimacy to oppose government policies: 'the people had spoken'.
- *the popularity of the government or certain policies,* which the president can manipulate to his advantage.
- *the proximity of up-coming presidential and/or National Assembly elections* and the ability of the president to run again. Mitterrand was in a strong position in 1986 but in a weak position in 1993. Chirac did not dare organise new parliamentary elections prior to the 2002 presidential elections given the disaster of the May/June 1997 elections which resulted in the surprise victory of the Plural Left. Nonetheless, Chirac was in a surprisingly strong position in his relations with the government thanks to an impressive public approval rating – despite numerous allegations of his prior engagement in corrupt activities.
- *the degree of divergence between the president's policies and those of the government.* For example, during the 1986–8 cohabitation the difference was greater than during the 1993–5 and 1997–2002 cohabitations. There has been an ideological shift in the Socialist Party in government towards the centre, while most of the conservatives oppose unqualified liberal economic policies. Differences do remain – for example, Chirac opposed Prime Minister Jospin on the introduction of a maximum 35-hour working week – but policy positions have been pushed to the centre in the most recent presidential election campaign.

The 'Yes' vote in the September 2000 referendum on changing the presidential term from 7 years (septennat) to 5 years (cinquennat) may spell the end of cohabitation as National Assembly elections will regularly follow May presidential elections every five years. The coat-tails effect is likely to be strong – as indeed was demonstrated in the 2002 elections, when the pro-Chirac *Union pour la Majorité Presidentielle* (UMP) won a massive majority in the lower house.

THE WEAK PARLIAMENT

Another way in which de Gaulle and Debré attempted to bring about greater stability in the Fifth Republic was to weaken Parliament's control over the political executive. The constitution reverses the traditional principle whereby the government can make decrees in only a specifically limited number of areas and all other matters must be subject to legislation and, therefore, parliamentary involvement. Article 34 defines the few spheres in which Parliament can legislate while Article 37 states that everything which does not expressly come within this sphere is the government's responsibility. The constitution also authorises the government to intervene extensively in the procedure for drawing up legislation in order to get its bills passed or prevent private member's (parliamentary) bills from being carried. Thus the government can be involved in the initiation of bills, the discussion stages and at the final vote (as it can make the vote on a bill an issue of confidence). Even after the vote, the constitution provides for a final check: that of a bill's constitutionality. The Constitutional Council (*Conseil Constitutionnel*) was entrusted with the task of confining Parliament within its sphere and preventing the legislature from encroaching on that of the government. Only the political executive – the president and prime minister – and the presidents of the Senate and National Assembly were given the power to challenge the constitutionality of legislation. The Constitutional Council could only engage in abstract review of legislation (that is, prior to the promulgation of laws), not concrete review. In 1974 Giscard d'Estaing introduced a reform that allowed 60 members of the National Assembly or Senate to call upon the Council for abstract review. This equipped parliament with an important power which it has used to great effect over the past two decades, enabling the political opposition to delay or entirely block important legislation on constitutional grounds. Furthermore, Parliament asserts its power with regard to constitutional amendments, which are successfully passed only with the consent of two-thirds of the members of both houses sitting together in a special assembly held at Versailles.

The limitation of Parliament's 'checking and supervisory' role was also designed to enhance the government's stability and increase its freedom of manoeuvre. The 1958 constitution allows Parliament only to put questions to the government designed essentially to inform Parliament and public opinion. The constitution abolished the possibility for *députés* (normally sitting in committees) to demand explanations from the government in public sessions (called *interpellation*) and to pass resolutions of a general nature. Also, parliamentary committees of enquiry – previously the principal way for Parliament to investigate government activity – were deprived of the means to be effective. Very strict conditions regarding form and substance were imposed upon the procedures whereby the government can be called to account. Article 49 of the constitution provides for only four possibilities:

1 when the government presents its programme or makes a declaration of general policy
2 the National Assembly can put down a censure motion
3 the government can make the vote on a bill an issue of confidence
4 the prime minister has the right – but is not obliged – to ask the Senate for approval of a statement of general policy.

More important than these constitutional restrictions, the role of the French National Assembly and Senate in legislation and policy making has been limited by political factors: notably, the presence of stable government majorities

Exhibit 3.2: The structure of the French Parliament

The French Parliament is, like most, bicameral (two-chambered). The government is drawn from the National Assembly, the members of which are elected in single-member constituencies in a two-ballot majority vote electoral system and serve an unrestricted number of terms, each of which can last up to 5 years. The upper house, the Senate, has less democratic legitimacy than the National Assembly. It is elected indirectly by the population: by an electoral college consisting of the approximately 87 000 elected officials from all levels of French government (municipal, *département*, regional and national). One-third of the Senators are elected every 3 years and all serve for 9-year terms. The National Assembly has 577 members (including 22 from the overseas *départements* and territories: the DOM-TOM), while the Senate has 321 members, including 13 for the DOM-TOM and 12 representing French expatriates. The Senate has the power to amend and delay the passing of legislation. Its veto, however, can be overridden by the government.

(either single party or coalitions) and party discipline. Moreover, an active presidency since 1958 gained a great deal of power over foreign, defence and other areas of policy making, weakening the position of the government and parliament.

The strength of a legislature, its ability to scrutinise and influence government policy and legislation depends largely upon a well-developed committee system. De Gaulle and Debré greatly weakened the National Assembly and Senate committee systems. The committees have been strengthened considerably over the past 20 years, but they continue to lag behind those of most western systems, notably those of Northern European parliaments. Of all the Senate and National Assembly committees, only the Committees of Enquiry and of Control serve any function in the control of the executive. They can be set up to examine particular decisions by the government in any policy areas. However, these committees have demonstrated their ineffectiveness as instruments of parliamentary control for four main reasons: there must be a majority in the chamber for the motion to set one up and the government can therefore prevent the formation of embarrassing committees; the committee is only allowed a limited period to produce a report; ministers can refuse to cooperate; and committee reports make virtually no impact on public opinion. In France there are no committee hearings remotely comparable in impact to those of the American Congress or, even for that matter, the comparatively weak British select committees. Today, only motions of censure – which require a normally unattainable majority to pass – remain as an option of challenging the government.

The French Parliament is not seen as an arena of national debate. There is nothing like the opposition days or emergency debates which take place in Britain. This is because in the first days of the Fifth Republic, the National Assembly and the Senate drafted their standing orders permitting motions for debates, which could be voted upon, but the Constitutional Council ruled this to be unconstitutional. The closest device to an emergency debate available to the National Assembly is the power to open debates on ministerial statements. The 'Questions to the government' procedure is being increasingly used by *députés* to force the government to discuss policy decisions and the lack thereof. It is likely that, with the help of television, this procedure will draw more public attention to the Assembly and that the *députés* might spend more time challenging government policy. But such developments will have to overcome considerable public indifference to parliamentary affairs. (The televising of Parliament since the mid-1990s has not had much success in this regard.) The other principal tool which the *député* can use to question the government is the procedure of written questions, questions which are raised in the Assembly but which are not followed by a debate, and are answered several days (or even weeks) afterwards. While Parliament's role as a watchdog has been somewhat lacking, the National Assembly and the Senate do make a contribution to law making. Despite the ability of the executive to employ a wide range of mechanisms to force legislation through parliament, a large majority of amendments made in committees are accepted (although this reflects the responsiveness of the government to the political and technical concerns of its own backbench members of parliament, who dominate the committees).

The members of the National Assembly and Senate do not seem to be expected to produce wise words on government policy unless this policy directly affects local constituents. The limited interest of *députés* and senators in many issues of national policy making is due principally to the problem of 'localism' in France. Owing to a system known as *cumul des mandats*, most parliamentarians are local mayors, *département* or regional assembly members (*conseillers généraux* and *régionaux*). Their efforts in Parliament centre largely (although not, of course, exclusively) upon supporting and maintaining their local power bases and clientelist ties with constituents. This takes most of the *députés'* or senators' time and it tends to undermine their role as legislators and controllers of the executive. Absenteeism in the National Assembly and Senate tends to be high. The *député* is turned into a tributary of the executive rather than watchdog.

Some reforms have been undertaken which were intended to encourage greater *député* concentration on Assembly affairs. However, the 1985 law which limited the *cumul des mandats* and reduced to two the number of important elected posts held by *députés* did not significantly decrease this problem. The tradition of combining local and national roles is an important part of French national political culture. At any rate, as already mentioned, when Parliament does debate on most matters, it is generally ignored by the national media, which further encourages members to focus on local concerns.

The increased importance of European law making and policy making in shaping the national legislative and policy agenda further weakened the role of the French Parliament in that it lacked any *a priori* control over French government positions in the EC/EU Council of Ministers. The French Parliament is presented with a *fait accompli*, a national law that has to be modified to conform with a newly adopted European directive or other legal measure. In 1993, in the context of constitutional reform to enable the French to ratify the Maastricht Treaty, Article 88.4 was added to the constitution. This new clause forces the French government to consult the National Assembly on all issues to be voted upon in the European Union's Council of Ministers in Brussels. It was adopted as part of the French government's efforts to address criticism that the European decision-making process was insufficiently transparent and democratic, and as a means of bypassing claims that the European Parliament should be strengthened in order to reduce the so-called democratic deficit in the European Union. Article 88.4 should, however, be seen in the context of the French government's limited interest in strengthening parliamentary control of the European decision-making process, as the National Assembly has no voting powers on European issues, including the adoption of the Community budget. The consultation period granted to the National Assembly is strictly limited, given the time constraints involved in European decision making. Furthermore, the tendency has been to ignore the application of this article, although recent government circulars indicate that the requirement of parliamentary consultation will likely be better respected in the future. This French situation should be compared to that of the Danish *Volketing*, a well-staffed and informed parliamentary committee which actually vets the government's position on any issue voted on in the European Council of Ministers.

REFORMING THE 'ALL-POWERFUL' ADMINISTRATION?

When asked about what they know of the French administration, most *anglosaxons* will mention its massive size and pervasiveness in the lives of French men and women, its apparent resilience to reform, its bureaucratic rigidity, inefficiency and hierarchical nature and its elite networks. Despite this impression, there have been efforts to reform the French administration to make it more efficient and effective in the performance of its tasks. French governments have introduced reforms which are, on the surface, similar to those in the UK and other West European countries, including (Clark 2000):

- the disaggregation of public service organisations into separate units, related by contractual or semi-contractual arrangements
- a shift to greater outsourcing of, and competition in, the delivery of public services
- a stress on private sector styles of management
- explicit standards and measures of performance linked to a greater emphasis on output controls
- a stress on discipline and parsimony in resource use; and a service and client orientation.

However, the logic behind the reforms and the strategies pursued in France are very different from those in the UK, where governments have been motivated by the 'liberalising' New Public Management school (NPM) which advocates the introduction of market principles into the public sector. French reforms have corresponded to well-entrenched French attitudes on the role of the state. Reform has been pursued in the context of an official 'renewal of the public sector' begun by Socialist Prime Minister Michel Rocard in 1989 and continued by subsequent conservative governments under the labels of 'administrative modernisation' and 'reform of the state'. The state, as the 'guardian of the law which seeks to maintain social cohesion' (in the words of the *Picq Report* of 1994), remains very much the leading symbol (despite budgetary constraints). French reforms have focused on redefining so-called 'service missions', strengthening the executive responsibilities of ministerial field offices in the *départements* and regions (through contractualised relations), and improving human-resource management. Even in these areas, central administrative reform seems to have been relatively limited to date, although local authorities appear to be more actively engaged in modernisation (due largely to the process of decentralisation undertaken in the period 1981–6). The introduction of a 'public service charter' in 1992 represents less the development of a consumer-driven charterism (such as John Major's 'Citizen's Charter' of 1992) with improved responsiveness to citizen-consumers with rights of choice and 'managerialism', than a restatement of the 'republican' principles of equal citizenship, legality and due process and the further development of more user-friendly services (Chevallier 1996; Clark 2000).

French reforms have been shaped by existing French institutions. The relatively large size of the French central administration has contributed to its relatively great political weight and extensive territorial penetration (due to the existence of field offices). In France, the central administration has controlled the strategic functions of analysis, forecasting, evaluation and control, while the local field services of national ministries have been responsible for operation and management. However, these field services are regrouped under the control (*tutelle*) of the leading representative of the state in the *départements* and regions: the prefect. This factor helps to explain why French governments have resisted the creation of agencies to manage areas of public policy (as in the UK) and instead have opted for 'participative *deconcentration*' involving the local field services of government ministries (Fabre Guillemant 1998). Legal frameworks have also shaped French reforms. The French system is confronted with rigid statutory and regulatory modes of operation (Ridley 1998). Reform in France has been firmly based on traditional 'republican' notions of public service well rooted in administrative law and entrenched civil-service rights and privileges, which has blocked the development of strong customer-oriented policies and made it difficult for the French state to force through the *responsibilisation* of agents and allow the more autonomous management of dependent local field offices of government ministries (Fabre Guillemant 1998).

A third factor shaping public-sector reform in France is the nature of the political elite and its relationship to administrative elites (which is reflected in and contributes to the political influence of different ideologies). Notably, much of the French top political elite is drawn from the ranks of the *énarques*, graduates of the training academy of top-level civil servants, the *École Nationale d'Administration*. In mid-2000, for example, the prime minister, seven of the most important ministers – finance, justice, foreign affairs, employment, defence, culture and administrative reform – two junior ministers and three secretaries of state were *énarques*, in addition to the president, Jacques Chirac. The separation between the political and administrative spheres is relatively porous: administrative law grants public officials the right to stand for political office, while civil servants also exert considerable influence over political officials from within larger ministerial support staffs. The nature of the training of the *énarques*, which emphasises state-led responses to various economic and social problems and reinforces public-service ideals, is reflected in dominant political perceptions. Leading members of two of the most influential *grands corps* (elite networks) of the French administration – the Council of State (*Conseil d'État*) and the Court of Auditors (*Cour des Comptes*) – played key roles in developing the 'public-service renewal' project. It is thus not surprising that reform in France has assumed more of a businesslike managerialism which emphasises increased professionalism. Other political factors can be considered. For example, the comparatively strong presence of trade unions (notably *Force Ouvrière*) in the French public sector has worked as a relatively important check on ambitious reform developments (see Clark 1998).

Finally, dominant institutionally embedded cultures and ideas have shaped reforms. The French model of public administration is more authoritarian and less favourable to the consensual types of change that are recommended by NPM (notably, contractualisation of relations, responsibility of agents, autonomy of management). The French administration is based largely on a logic of 'supply', with services organised *a priori* and in a rational manner in relation to general principles of law (such as equality of access of citizens, free provision of services). There has also been a stubborn French opposition to the logic of consumer demand. French arguments typically run as follows: public services are in a situation of monopoly and this offers little choice to 'consumer citizens'. Moreover, these services were created to fill the gaps in the market and many concerns obey a radically different logic from that of the market (for example, social aid).

French administrative power is reflected in the traditional prestige of the state-run *grandes écoles* (elite post-secondary institutions or training schools), including the national administrative school, *École Nationale d'Administration* (ENA). Here we focus specifically upon ENA because the graduates of this school (*énarques*) have traditionally gone on to direct much of the French administration (often labelled *l'énarchie*), have led much of the historically huge public economic sector and, as noted above, have come to dominate the top ranks of the French political elite as well. ENA is unique in the western world in the extent to which it is a funnel for prospective entrants into the elite ranks of the civil service. The school is also unique in that it is the only school that is also a part of the prime minister's office.

THE *ÉNARQUES*: THE FRENCH ELITE

ENA was established by a 9 October 1945 ordinance of the French provisional government. It was the brainchild of Michel Debré, the close aide of General de Gaulle and a future prime minister, who subsequently outlined five reasons for the school's creation. First, the existing bureaucratic elite was largely discredited, having been associated with the defeat of 1940 and the Vichy regime. Second, the school was the fulfilment of a republican ideal of rationality and meritocracy. The objective was to demonstrate to the French population that any citizen could, on the basis of merit, enter into the upper echelons of the French administration. The administrative elites in what are called the *grands corps* (that is, elite groups within the French administration) had previously been selected by competitive examinations, but less meritocratic criteria played an important role in the process and certain families had succeeded in colonising the different corps. To take an extreme example, the selection for the diplomatic corps included oral examinations for which candidates were expected to dress in coat and tails, and a cocktail party at which candidates were judged according to their ability to pick up a woman's handkerchief while holding a flute of champagne in one hand and a cigarette in the other.

The third reason for its creation was that ENA was established in the context of public expectations with regard to the role of the state in the French economy and the establishment of the welfare state. The post-war French government needed well-trained, competent officials to manage the new and increasingly complex welfare state as well as the various banks and companies that were nationalised in the immediate post-war period. Previously, the administrative elite had been trained for the most part at four of the *grandes écoles*: the *École Normale Supérieure*, the *École Polytechnique*, the *École des Ponts et Chaussées* and the *École des Mines*. The *École Normale* is the institution for the study of the humanities whereas the other three are technical schools for engineers (see Chapter 7). France therefore lacked a training institution which focused upon the particular problems of administration and the development of public policy.

A fourth reason for the creation of ENA was that prior to 1945 each of the five *grands corps* (that is, the diplomatic corps, the prefectoral corps, the Financial Inspectorate, the Court of Auditors and the Council of State, which is the highest administrative court in the country) had its own recruitment procedures. A student was therefore normally encouraged to choose at a very young age a particular stream which would prepare him or her for the entrance examinations for the corps of his or her choice. This resulted in a structure of rather cloistered administrative elites and a very limited degree of horizontal mobility. One objective in establishing ENA was to introduce a unifying element into this segmented elite, a common educational base, and a sense of camaraderie which would persist during the career of the *énarque* in spite of allegiance to the corps.

Finally, the creation of ENA should also be seen in the context of General de Gaulle's scepticism with regard to rule by the chattering political classes. De Gaulle believed that in the context of the parliamentary and party system of the Third Republic, politicians were too preoccupied with party politics to develop policies which best served the interests of the country as a whole – hence his belief in the need for a well-trained technocratic elite which would direct policy not only from within the bureaucracy but also within the support staffs of French ministers (which are called *cabinets*) and even the ministerial *cabinet* itself.

Given the important role of the state in post-war French society and the economy, ENA, as the established method of selecting the administrative elite, was recognised very quickly as the most prestigious educational institution in the country. The prestige of the school – it is important to point out – had nothing whatsoever to do with the quality of the education that its students received, but rather the quality of the students who succeeded in getting through the gruelling admission examinations, the usually interesting posts in the French administration that graduates could enter, and the very important positions that its alumni began to assume as early as the 1950s. *Énarques* soon began to enter the top managerial positions in the nationalised banks and industry and some even moved temporarily or permanently into the private sector, a process that has been labelled *pantouflage*, that is 'slipping out' of the administration. By the start of the 1980s, *énarques* were to found in the executive boards of the vast majority of the largest French companies and banks. Following the privatisations of the 1980s and 1990s, their presence diminished somewhat but nonetheless remained extensive.

To foreigners and many French people, ENA is often thought of as a school for politicians. It is true that many top French politicians were educated at ENA, including five of the 1995 presidential candidates, six of the last eight prime ministers (including Jospin) and two presidents (including Chirac). Moreover, the right of administrators to run for office and the practice of appointing top bureaucrats to ministerial positions does encourage their political engagement more than in other countries. However, it must be stressed that the vast majority of *énarques* never run for public office, do not engage in *pantouflage*, and remain in the bureaucracy all their working lives (64 per cent in the mid-1990s according to the school's own figures, but this increases to 86 per cent when state-owned industries and banks and various public establishments are included). Only just over 4 per cent of the *énarques* have held public office and only 2.5 per cent at the national level. While 22 per cent have worked in a public company or bank, only about 14 per cent have entered the private sector at any point in their career, although this percentage is considerably higher among *énarques* who enter the Ministry of Finance (in particular the elite Treasury division) and the elite corps of the Financial Inspectorate.

Because the school and its students are the subject of so much admiration but also contempt there is a great deal of statistical information about the student body. Since the school was established there have been over 6000 domestic students admitted by extremely competitive written and oral examinations on diverse subjects. The number of students in each class has ranged from a low of 38 in 1947 to a high of 150 in 1982. The number of students was lowered in 1987 to 80 but since the mid-1990s this has crept up to over 100. At ENA there are four kinds of students: the externs, the interns, the so-called third-category students and the foreign students who are principally foreign bureaucrats, brought to Paris and Strasbourg in order to be taught the ways of the French state. At the time of their admission, the age of the students varies from 21 to the late 40s. The externs are the youngest group and most are drawn from among the brightest students of another prestigious school, the *Institut des Études Politiques* (better known as *Science Po*, or in more elite circles as the *Rue Saint Guillaume*, the street in Paris where the school is located). Over half of all students at ENA have been externs. The large major-ity of the externs come from Parisian professional or bourgeoisie families and they tend to fill a disproportionately large share of the top positions in the final ranking at the school – two issues of some controversy examined in Chapter 7. The interns are the older students – from their late 20s up to their late 40s. The term refers to the origin of these students from within the administration itself. The interns are required to have worked for the state or local government for at least 6 years. They enter ENA either because they want an opportunity to move to a different administration or because they seek more rapid upward mobility in their own administration. The current policy of the school – which was adopted in the 1990s – is to admit the same number of interns as externs. Most of the remaining students have been in a special third category which permits men and women under the age of 40 with at least 8 years' experience in the private sector or as an elected official to enter ENA (the interns and third category were merged in the late 1990s to form one large category for older students). The intake of women has fluctu-ated at around 25 per cent over the past decade.

At the end of their two-and-a-half-year period at the school – one year on internships and the remaining period at their studies – the students are ranked on the basis of their grades. Currently, the top 15 will normally choose positions in the three most prestigious *grands corps*, the Financial Inspectorate, the Council of State and the Court of Auditors. This is the administrative super-elite, an elite within an elite. Even if the students take little interest in the actual work of these three *grands corps*, they will normally choose to enter them because of their prestige and because members of the *grand corps* have many opportunities to enter into other administrations and industry later in their careers. There are, however, a few exceptions. Martine Aubry, for example, the former minister of social affairs and the daughter of Jacques Delors (former president of the European Commission), was the *major* in her promotion, that is, she was ranked first in her class. True to her left-wing prin-ciples, Mme Aubry entered the Ministry of Employment, a post which would normally be selected by someone ranked in the bottom half of the promotion. However, it must be noted that in spite of her initial refusal, Mme Aubry was later admitted into the Council of State. Below the *grands corps*, students choose to become civil and financial administrators, ideally taking posts in the Ministry of Finance and then as other kinds of administrative inspectors. The ranking of students who select posts in the diplomatic and prefectoral corps and the various ministries varies from year to year depending upon the specific posts available. Posts in the Ministry of Education tend to be towards the bottom of the list!

Has ENA fulfilled the missions that were originally assigned to it?

The school has always had three essential missions: to choose the French administrative elite as far as possible on the basis of merit; to widen access to the administrative elite beyond the socio-economic groups that had monopolised it; and to educate students to become effective and efficient administrators. These three missions are essential to the maintenance of legitimacy in the eyes of the French population: the legitimacy of the school, the administrative elite and more generally the state and the active role that it has played in French society and the economy.

The first and second missions, although seen as complementary by the founders of the school, are of course potentially contradictory. With regard to the first objective, the school has succeeded in selecting an elite on the basis of merit, although the specific criteria which the administration of the school uses to determine merit are the subject of considerable controversy. All students must take the same competitive examinations to enter the school and during their studies, and the equal treatment of the students during the programme is strictly, some would argue excessively, maintained. However, concern with regard to the second mission, that is to widen access to the administrative elite, has qualified the application of the principle of merit. While there has never been any established policy of affirmative action to improve the access of any particular group to the school, the creation of the interns in 1946 and more recently the third category – both of which are reserved a set number of places – is, in effect, a kind of affirmative action. The application of the principle of open access on the basis of merit, without any reserved places, would logically lead to the equal treatment of all candidates for admission. However, in practice this would mean that the large majority of places at ENA would be taken by the younger, more privileged students (the externs). Well over 50 per cent of the interns have not come from white-collar professional or educational backgrounds, so the policy of reserving a set number of places for the interns is in effect a means of ensuring that about a quarter of the overall intake into the school does not come from a white-collar background. Initially this qualification of the principle of merit was limited: prior to 1972 just over a third of the places at ENA were reserved for the interns. However, since 1972 the number of reserved places has gradually increased and now equals the number of places available for the externs. Furthermore, it is important to note that the externs, that is the younger students, tend to be in the top half of the class and the interns in the bottom half, even though in every class there are several exceptions. Thus the administrative elite (notably the positions in the *grands corps* and the Ministry of Finance) tends to be dominated by the externs and thus, one could argue, the meritocratic mission prevails, at least in terms of the manner in which merit is perceived at the school.

It is important to look at the concept of meritocracy and openness in a wider sense. According to a study by the French Ministry of Education, in 1955, a child whose father was a farmer, worker, artisan or small shopkeeper had 24 times less chance than a child in higher socio-economic categories to enter the four most prestigious *grandes écoles* (that is the *École Polytechnique*, ENA, the *École Normale Supérieure* and the *Haute École de Commerce*, the business school). Today, she has 23 times less chance. In the meantime, the chance to enter into university has passed from ten times less chance to four. Even taking into consideration the expansion of the middle educated classes since 1955, it is clear that the elite institutions remain closed. However, of the *grandes écoles*, it must still be accepted that ENA has by far and away the most egalitarian admissions policy. (The questionable success of the French education system as a means to improved equality of opportunity and social mobility is discussed further in Chapter 7.)

The third mission is the education of students so that they can become effective and efficient administrators. In theory this mission relates closely to the application of the meritocratic principle: the highest-ranked students should be those who become the most effective and efficient administrators. However, the *énarques* have had to face many critics who question their abilities. Most famously, the sociologist Michel Crozier has called them the 'dumbest elite in the world' (*l'élite la plus bête du monde*). Crozier argues that the education that the *énarques* receive at the school is inadequate to deal effectively with contemporary socio-economic problems in the context of a shrinking public economic sector, international economic competition and heavy public-sector debt. The highest-ranked students at ENA frequently do not turn out to be the most effective and efficient administrators. Indeed, the training covers a broad range of material superficially and students are judged according to a narrow range of criteria (e.g. ability to write an administrative paper addressing a particular problem). The room allowed for creativity at the school is very limited. Another issue is the lack of basic training in office management. For most *énarques* this is not a problem, given that they enter posts in which they manage very few people and will have to work their own way up to senior managerial positions, hopefully learning the necessary management skills as they do so. However, for the members of the *grands corps* – the elite within the elite – most of whom are the young externs, this gap in administrative training is particularly debilitating.

After the final ranking at ENA, the members of the *grands corps* usually spend around 4 years training within their corps and a few years in a minister's support staff before being catapulted into positions of importance either in the bureaucracy, state-owned banks and companies or the private sector. Most members of the *grands corps* therefore do not have the opportunity to develop effective managerial skills prior to holding senior positions. A general characteristic of the members of the *grands corps* is the arrogance of those who know a great deal and work very hard. This arrogance is reinforced by the excessive deference shown to these *énarques* by most of the other bureaucrats, which in turn encourages unilateral action and discourages consultation with subordinates. The problem stems from having a super-elite which is trained essentially according to one criterion alone: the capacity to write a good exam paper. The trials of experience do, of course, have an impact upon the careers of the members of the *grands corps,* but experience is not considered essential for holding senior managerial positions. This has also tended to create feelings of resentment on the part of middle-level managers who, although having competently worked in an administration or a company for many years, are unable to advance to certain posts which are reserved for *énarques.*

This combination of the superficial nature of the studies at ENA, the pedantic arrogance of the *énarques* and their lack of good managerial skills provides some explanation for Crozier's quip. However, it must be said that despite their faults, the *énarques* are a generally competent, well-informed and hard-working administrative elite. Crozier's criticism probably has far more to do with the expectations that the French have of their elite and the role of the state, and the inability of this elite to meet these expectations in a changing economic environment.

Given the traditional omnipresence of the state in French society and the economy, the popular expectation inevitably developed that the *énarques* control everything and are therefore responsible for everything. The number of *énarques* who have become leading political, industrial and banking figures has reinforced this perception. The 30 years of stable post-war economic growth and the expansion of the state sector were associated to a large extent with technocratic power and state leadership. Today, however, the technocrats are unable to cope so easily in the very different economic environment of the international marketplace and capital flows, where their skills and attitudes do not necessarily help them succeed. *Énarques* are not the equivalent of Wall Street whiz kids and were never meant to be. Some suggest that the recent decision to increase the emphasis upon accounting and managerial strategic planning during the studies (*scolarité*) as well as attempts to increase the number of internships (*stages*) in public and private companies indicate that the ENA administration is placing more emphasis on business-related skills. ENA may be trying to imitate business schools in order to strengthen its credibility as a 'school for management' – particularly in the context of the increased prestige of French business schools – but there is no indication that there will be a dramatic transformation of the ENA programme over the next few years. Furthermore, the number of internships in companies, whether public or private, has actually decreased over the past 10 years rather than increased.

Given the important role of the state in mismanaging certain industries during the 1970s and 1980s, several failed efforts to create international champions, the disgraceful mismanagement by *énarques* of one of France's largest banks, the Crédit Lyonnais, and numerous corruption scandals involving former students, criticisms of the *énarques* have a certain legitimacy. It seems that they were simply out of their depth in their efforts to manipulate economic developments, while the state was simply too unwieldy and slow-moving to play a successful competitive role in the international marketplace. Crozier's criticism is therefore valid principally in the sense that the *énarques* have been trained to think that they know more than any other national elite and the respect shown them is such that they are generally able to get away with thinking this. The decision of the Juppé government in 1995 to require all ENA graduates to spend 2 years in the provinces was principally a reaction to public opinion that *énarques* are not in touch with the realities of the French population. However, the decision did nothing to change the image of the *énarques* because it did not address the underlying expectations of what the French state could achieve.

LOCAL GOVERNMENT: THE STATE OF DECENTRALISATION 20 YEARS ON

France has historically been known as one of the more centralised countries of Western Europe with relatively weak subnational authorities (SNAs), which in order of size are the regions, the *départements* and the communes. There are 26 regions (including four overseas which coincide with the geographical areas covered by the four overseas *départements*), 100 *départements* and approximately 35 000 communes and municipalities. The regions range considerably in size and population from the Île de France to Limousin and French Guyana (in South America), as do the *départements* and the communes. The decentralisation reforms undertaken by the Socialist government during the period 1982–6 (named after the presiding minister of the interior, Gaston Defferre) have only somewhat dented this image of France as a centralised state. The reforms did, nonetheless, have a real impact: they involved a significant relocation of governance.

The Defferre reforms represent the culmination of a long history of periodic and largely unsuccessful efforts to strengthen local government in line with the Girondin tradition of the French Revolution, in the context of regimes more inspired by the centralism of the *ancien régime* and the Jacobin revolutionary tradition. In the first few years of the Third Republic in the 1870s and 1880s decentralisation legislation was passed, including the establishment of democratically elected municipal and *département* councils. However, these remained firmly under the control of the central government through its representatives in the *départements*, the prefects. Subsequent legislation until 1982 was minor and always within the confines of the administrative system set up by Napoléon and the administrative organisation of the countryside established at the time of the Revolution. All debates on decentralisation since the Revolution have been subject to the same terms: to what extent are the requirements of national unity and the principles of equality before the law compatible with local liberty and diversity?

It is important not to overstate the French government's reputation as one of the most centralised in the world. From the start of the Third Republic, local politicians and administrators found effective ways of bypassing the formally centralised system to achieve a far greater measure of local autonomy and power than was legally permitted or publicly acknowledged. For this reason, many French political sociologists have considered the Defferre reforms to be of limited real significance, even though most administrative law scholars – focusing on the actual legislation – insist upon their importance. In fact the decentralisation reforms were very significant indeed. The old system was increasingly unable to meet the demands for local democracy and the requirements of the modern welfare state. The Socialist reforms changed almost every aspect of local government, with a dramatic impact on centre–periphery relations and the local balance of political power. Still, in order to build a consensus, the Socialists did not go nearly as far as they had originally intended. They left aside the more innovative reforms in the area of local democracy, social services and local finances and failed to rationalise the basic structures of local government either by merging smaller communes to decrease their total number or by choosing between the *départements* and regions.

Officially, the Socialists sought to make local government more responsible and responsive to the needs of the local population, more efficient and effective in the delivery of services, and less costly. To achieve this, they widened the official duties of the major local actors, thus formalising many of their existing informal powers. Moreover, they changed the system itself, introducing a new kind of transparency into local officials' practice and a new political and administrative pluralism into the institutions and processes of local government. A dynamic new relationship has been created between the prefects – who have lost their controlling *tutelle* yet maintained a vital coordinating function – and the more powerful presidents of the directly elected *département* and regional councils and the mayors of big cities and rural communes.

The specifics of the Defferre reforms

The decentralisation reforms brought about a legal transfer of control over several policy areas and the devolution of managerial responsibilities, finances and personnel to SNAs (see Schmidt 1990). First, the reforms involved the transfer of executive power in the *départements* and regions away from the state's representative, the prefect, and the end of his control (*tutelle*) over the regional and *département* councils and their budgets. For the first time in the Fifth Republic, the presidents of the councils were elected by their members and obtained the same powers as the mayors of the communes and municipalities. The regions and the *départements* thus became full local authorities, like the communes. The councils *départements* had been elected since 1874 but the prefect had always maintained his executive power. The regions were created only as 'public entities' (*établissements publics*) in 1972 – after de Gaulle's failure to create them as fully fledged local authorities in the 1969 referendum that led to his resignation – and the regional assemblies were not directly elected. The decentralisation reforms transformed them into councils elected every 6 years by proportional representation with constituencies based on the *départements*. The communes and municipalities had had municipal councils and elected mayors since 1874 (although Paris did not have its own mayor until 1977). The Defferre reforms granted them additional powers. The prefect obtained an *a posteriori* legal control over the *département* and regional councils and his/her *a posteriori* control over the communes was clarified. Regional courts of auditors (*cours régionales des comptes*, responsible to the national *Cour des Comptes* in Paris) were created. These are crucial to the maintenance of the prefect's *a posteriori* control because they ensure the local authorities' respect of budgetary rules. Likewise, administrative tribunals can be called upon by the prefect to rule on the respect of the law by local authorities. Clear budgetary rules and conditions were established according to which the prefect (alone) can challenge the management of the local authorities at the regional courts of auditors. Notably, the communes, *départements* and regions are obliged to balance their budgets even if since 1982 they are given some right to borrow in order to do this. The role of the *département* office of the Treasury division of the Ministry of Finance (the *Trésorier Payeur Général* (TPG)) was clarified by the decentralisation reforms. The TPGs survey the financial situation of the prefecture (the prefect's office in the *département*) and the local authorities and can present recommendations to the prefect in case of difficulties.

The administrative functions that were transferred by the decentralisation reforms are set out in Table 3.3.

In addition to these powers, the Defferre reforms encouraged intercommunal cooperation which facilitated the legal creation of intercommunal charters. In several areas of policy making, closely linked powers were deliberately divided. All the local authorities were charged with the promotion of some aspect of local economic development, under the overall supervision of the regions. They were also all charged with an aspect of culture, although the state retains greater control in this area. All the local authorities and the state were given powers with regard to ports and waterways (the *départements* and communes had obtained important powers in these areas in the 1980s). Finally, they were all given powers over the construction and maintenance of the institutions of state education (*Education nationale*).

The decision to allow local authorities diplomatic activity (Article 65 of the 1982 reform) enabled them to establish representation (either alone or in groups) at the European level and encouraged the reinforcement of links with regions in other countries. As early as 1986 the Rhône–Alpes region joined with Lombardy (Italy), Catalonia (Spain) and Baden-Württemberg (Germany) to create the Four Motors Group – to encourage scientific, technical and cultural

Table 3.3 The Defferre reforms of French local government (1982–4)

Subnational authorities	Previous powers	New powers
Regions	Regional economic development and planning (and the attraction of external investment), although lacked the means to engage themselves in these areas.	Construction and maintenance of regional autoroutes (regional transport concerns); vocational and professional training; building and maintenance of *lycées* (secondary schools); culture; ports and waterways; environmental policies; trading standards; consumer protection law; health and safety in the workplace.
Départements	Building and maintenance of *collèges* (early secondary schools), ports and waterways.	Organisation of social services and local health; rural and local development and rural infrastructure; *département* transport concerns; construction and maintenance of *département* autoroutes; schoolchildren; public transport; local economic development; culture; environmental policies; trading standards; consumer protection law; health and safety in the workplace.
Communes	Waste management, water; building and maintenance of primary schools and *maternelles* (kindergartens), ports and waterways.	Land use planning, issue of building permits; right to create legally binding intercommunal charters; local economic development; culture; social aid; local transport (both public and private); supply and maintenance of public utilities and housing provision for EU migrants; trading standards; consumer protection law; health and safety in the workplace.

cooperation – with a joint office in Brussels. The expansion of diplomatic activity – including one case of an agreement between the Provence–Alpes–Côtes d'Azur region and the Tunisian state – was sufficiently great to upset some central government officials and politicians, who perceived this development as an affront to the indivisibility of French foreign policy making.

This led to an attempt by the state to place clear limits on local government powers in this area and the clarification of Article 65 by prime ministerial circulars (in 1983, 1985 and 1987) which limited transfrontier cooperation to adjoining regions, subject to government authorisation and without the conclusion of binding agreements. The repeated violation of these rules led to the reinforcement of state control in the 6 February 1992 administrative reform. However, once the agreements with other regions are established, SNAs can act with managerial autonomy.

The division of services has produced continued complications and sometimes overlaps (*chevauchements*) in the services offered to the public by the different levels of government. Some individuals must make demands on two different local authorities or one authority and the state and several different divisions within the same level of government. Take the example of public assistance for handicapped people. The *département* finances their housing, the region manages their vocational training and the state takes care of their employment. Social security (a state-regulated, semi-autonomous fund) provides them a minimum salary. The situation is even more complicated because decentralisation did not go as far as it should have in the reorganisation of the state services transferred to local authorities. For example, the transfer of social services and health services from the state to the *départements* did not lead to a modification of the division of services and thus transferred several administrative and financial problems of which the state wanted to rid itself, which had the effect of worsening them. For education, jurisdiction over buildings and schedules was transferred but the state continues to control education curricula and the payment of professors. There was a transfer of resources (financial, personnel, offices and buildings) to the *départements* and regions to reflect the transfer of powers. In order to ensure the success of this transfer and attract the best candidates to local administrations, the national government voted in a new law on the territorial (local authority) civil service. This reform improved the conditions of employment of local civil servants, permitted mobility between the national and local services and ensured the transfer of competent national civil servants and local services. However, political considerations prevented radical changes.

Local finances were modified in order to cover the cost of new administrative competences of the regions, *départements* and communes. Notably this involved the enlargement of the four local taxes – on property, local enterprises, habitations and land – and the creation of new local taxes (notably on petrol and tobacco). Regions were given the receipts for vehicle registration fees and *départements* were given the receipts from drivers' permits. The financial assistance of the state was also enlarged: notably, state subsidies not linked to obligatory expenditure (in order to cover a certain percentage of expenditure) and the transfer of a fixed percentage of national taxes. As a percentage of total local expenditure, state transfers to local authorities diminished, from 41 per cent in 1981 to 33.3 per cent in 1987. This reduction is significant, although in total terms – given the overall growth in expenditure – reliance on state funding increased. However, the increased importance of state subsidies not linked to obligatory expenditure in local finances increased the financial liberty of the local authorities. In 1970 these non-linked subsidies reached 50 per cent of state assistance, while in 1985 they constituted 80 per cent of the total state subsidy. Local authorities were also permitted access to borrowing, although they are limited by precise rules concerning the percentage of the budget that can consist of borrowed funds.

THE NEW IMPORTANCE OF FRENCH REGIONS

As a case study of the impact of decentralisation, this section examines the new importance of regions and regional elections to French political life. Most of the claims made here apply equally to the increased importance of the *départements* and cantonal elections. Regional elections are organised every 6 years (to date 1986, 1992 and 1998) according to a system of proportional representation (PR) with party lists and with the *départements* as the constituencies.[1] Regions spend their money on vocational training, educational buildings, investment in economic activities and rural development. Their financial and political importance has increased since their creation in 1986. Regions were responsible for the management of 46 billion francs in 1990 and 78 billion in 1997. The increase was partly due to the gradual transfer of competences and financial resources called for in the Defferre reforms but also because the regions have assumed the management of several powers of the state. For example, several regions have taken advantage of the state offer to give them increased control over transport (regional express trains, *trains express régionaux* (TER)) and the construction and maintenance of university buildings. Initially, regions were less interventionist in the economy, but with the rise of unemployment during the first half of the 1990s, they came increasingly to subsidise small and medium-sized companies to stimulate job creation (from 2 billion francs in subsidies in 1986 to 7 billion today). Despite this growing importance, the budgets of regions represent only 10 per cent of territorial public finances (the *départements* control 30 per cent, while the communes – responsible for the bulk of social services – still control the lion's share, 60 per cent). French regions were intended to become the equivalent of German *Länder* and Spanish autonomous communities (without the same power and autonomy) in the context of a Europe of the Regions. Many national politicians and top officials in the Ministry of the Interior would like to eliminate the *départements*, but this has always been too difficult politically.

The regional election campaigns tend to focus upon the environment, employment issues and youth (education and training). The environment has gained importance, especially given the success of the Greens in the

---

1 For their part, half the *département* councils are renewed every 3 years. Councillors at this level of government are elected, as at national elections, in single-member constituencies by two-ballot majority. To be elected in the first round, a candidate must receive an absolute majority of the votes and a quarter of registered electors. To proceed to the second ballot, candidates must obtain at least 10 per cent of the vote.

regional elections, due in large part to the PR (proportional representation) electoral system. Employment and youth are important because most regional expenses are devoted to the *lycées* and to vocational training programmes; these expenses amounted to less than 8 per cent of the regions' budget in 1986 but rose to nearly 43 per cent in 1991. The regional elections, like the cantonal and municipal, are considered principally as a poll of the government in power at the national level rather than of the capacity of the parties and the governments at the local level. The consistent dominance of the right in the regional councils in metropolitan France is due in part to the timing of the elections: the three regional council elections to date – in 1986, 1992 and 1998 – have all taken place when the left was in power at the national level. In 1992 – when the Socialist government was, in its final year in office, deeply unpopular and facing a worsening recession – the right won 20 of the 22 councils. The left did better in 1998 but the right retained control, though in several regions only thanks to the support of the extreme right-wing party, the National Front.

Given the PR electoral system, the regional elections give candidates from the smaller parties a greater opportunity to win seats. This in turn gives the politicians in these parties money, political legitimacy and, in the case of those smaller parties which participate in coalitions, an experience of power. This has been the case notably for the Greens, which held the balance of power in a few regions from 1992 to 1998, and even held the presidency of the Nord Pas-de-Calais region, and the National Front, which has – very controversially – held the balance of power in several regional councils since 1998. The regional elections (and in many cases cantonal and communal elections as well) thus provide the opportunity for an important mobilisation for and against the National Front. The decision by several conservative political leaders (in most cases led by the UDF) to form governing coalitions with the National Front (or govern with their official support in exchange for political favours) rather than allow the left to assume power has set a very controversial precedent and threatens to weaken the credibility of the UDF, both in the regions and nationally.

Politicians tend to accumulate mandates (*cumul des mandats*). A 1985 law limited the *cumul* to two mandates of importance (in a position involving some managerial responsibilities). In France, it is considered politically necessary for national politicians to have a major post in local government (which is completely different to the British tradition). Thus ministers and prime ministers are nearly always the mayors of the larger cities or the presidents of *département* or regional councils. Chirac was mayor of Paris, Juppé of Bordeaux, Fabius of Rouen, Mauroy of Lille. Presidents Chirac and Giscard d'Estaing were both presidents of regional councils. In the 1998 regional elections, former prime minister Edouard Balladur led the RPR list in Île de France. His conquest of the presidency of the regional council was widely considered a necessary step in his political return to national-level politics. Dominique Strauss-Kahn, then the Socialist minister of finance, ran against him. The presidency of the regional council is equally considered as the start of an important political career for some former top civil servants who want to enter national political life. Therefore, for example, Thibault de Silguy, the former advisor to Edouard Balladur and European commissioner responsible for monetary and financial affairs, led the RPR list in Brittany.

There are several other factors which explain the importance of local elections (arguably of greater political significance than the prize of governing the local territory). Local elections are an important opportunity to mobilise the activists of political parties and ensure their continued loyalty. Local elections and in particular the regional party lists provide a snapshot of the divisions within parties: for example, in the Centre region in 1998 there was an official UDF-RPR list and a list of dissidents, for the most part members of the RPR. Local government provides an opportunity for political and administrative training for politicians before they enter national-level politics. Likewise, after regional and other local elections, there are often ministerial reshuffles, as the elections are also a snapshot of the relative support of coalition partners as well as the factions within parties. Moreover, the prime minister must often replace ministers (usually the less important ones) who, choosing not to hold two posts at once, leave the government in order to assume control of the local council; and the prime minister may have to create new junior ministerial posts in order provide assistance for ministers assuming council presidencies.

CORSICA: A NEW SPECIAL STATUS FOR THE ÎLE DE BEAUTÉ

The birthplace of Napoléon has been part of France since 1768. Over the past two decades the Mediterranean island has been plagued by growing levels of violence by terrorist organisations seeking independence – notably the banned *Front de Libération Nationale de la Corse* (FLNC). Most of the violence has been against property – especially that owned by non-Corsicans – and other Corsican separatists. The demands for independence and the outbreaks of violence have been met by the French government with ever-increasing subsidies for the island's weak economy. The various separatist parties succeeded in winning only a maximum of a fifth of the vote in regional and *département* elections in the early 1990s. By the mid-1990s, bitter divisions and fratricidal warfare resulting in several dozen deaths turned much of the Corsican population away from separation. The generosity of the French state, providing almost half of the per capita income of the island through state benefits and a third of the island's jobs, encourages the large majority of the Corsican population to remain French. Another problem for the separatist cause is that a large number of those claiming to be 'freedom fighters' appear to be most preoccupied with material gain through gangsterism. In 1999 the French prefect on the island, Claude Erignac, was assassinated by a separatist terrorist. The Jospin government reacted by arranging a series of talks with island politicians including separatists, leading to an agreement in 2000 called the 'Matignon process', voted into law at the end of 2001. The 'process' was designed to achieve a political solution to the island's problems by first granting tax subsidies and encouraging the teaching of the Corsican language in state schools, then from 2004 – after the necessary revision of the French constitution – by giving the regional and *département* assemblies of the island the right to amend certain national laws and to approve new building on the coasts: rights possessed by no other French regions and *départements*. This sparked off the resignation of the minister of the interior, Jean-Pierre Chevènement, who denounced a special status for Corsica as fundamentally unrepublican – a challenge to the Jacobin tradition and the indivisibility of the republic – and Jospin's mollifying of Corsican separatists as an ineffectual way to end violence. However, the talks and agreement succeeded in substantially lowering the number of attacks on property on the island. In August 2001 Jospin opposed demands by separatist politicians for an amnesty for 40 so-called political prisoners and an end to the manhunt for Yvan Colonna, the suspected killer of Erignac. The sceptics argue that corruption, crime and violence are a well-entrenched part of Corsican life and will not disappear because of devolution. They also argue that the ecological future of the island has been put at great risk, as local politicians are soon to get their hands on the powers to permit building on Corsica's spectacularly beautiful coast.

THE DOM-TOMS: *LES CONFETTIS DE L'EMPIRE*

Legacies of France's former colonial empire, the overseas *départements* and territories allow the country a continuing global presence rivalled by only the United States and Britain. They include the four *départements* (DOM) – which are also regions – of Martinique, Guadeloupe (in the Caribbean), French Guyana (in South America) and Réunion (in the South Indian Ocean). The territories (the TOM) include Tahiti and New Caledonia (both in the South Pacific) and several 'territorial collectivities', including Mayotte (in the Indian Ocean) and St. Pierre and Miquelon (small rocky islands off the coast of Newfoundland, the remains of France's former possessions in North America).

The overseas *départements* are legally part of France and are treated like any metropolitan *département*. Indeed, it is frequently noted that Martinique and Guadeloupe have been part of France longer than Savoie. The territories enjoy a different status but have gained a certain degree of self-government. The *départements* are the legacy of the assimilationist goals of French imperialism, when conquered peoples and former slaves were expected to become fully French. There are few significant independence movements in the far-flung territories, which reflects both the historical success of the assimilationist mission and the impressive generosity of the French state, which provides exactly the same social security provisions as in metropolitan France, the same minimum wage and a large number of well-paid public-sector jobs.

Generosity to the territories is similarly great. However, this favourable treatment has not stopped the rise of a significant separatist movement on New Caledonia and its dependent islands, supported by many of the indigenous Melanesian inhabitants, the Kanaks. In addition to non-violent separatists who participate in the politics of the island, an armed Kanak liberation movement arose in the early 1980s which met the fierce resistance of the French settler population (the *Caldoches*). To combat the growing violence, the French government signed the 1988 Matignon accord with leading New Caledonian political groups. The accord granted a significant amount of autonomy to the islands, divided them into three administrative divisions, two under Kanak control, and provided a lot of financial assistance to the relatively disadvantaged indigenous population. The French government also promised an eventual referendum on a new status for the territory. This political solution was sufficiently successful that the armed liberation movement largely evaporated, although separatist parties continued to win about half the seats in the territorial assembly. In a November 1998 referendum, 70 per cent of the New Caledonian voters approved the May 1998 Nouméa accord which granted the islands greater autonomy, with another vote on independence set for 2014. The main Kanak separatist party, *Front de Libération Nationale Kanak Socialiste* (FLNKS) views the Nouméa accord as a stepping stone to complete independence; while the anti-independence party, *Rassemblement pour la Caledonie dans la République* (RCPR) dominated by the *Caldoches* (white European settlers for the most part from France and former French colonies) argues that a status of 'associated autonomy' is best for the territory. Despite the heavy subsidies, the French government for its part is keen to keep the territory, which is the fourth largest nickel producer in the world and France's largest territory in the South Pacific. It remains to be seen if the Kanaks gain a sufficiently great attachment to generous French subsidies to discourage their support for independence.

THE FIFTH ESTATE IN FRANCE: THE FRENCH MEDIA

The French press has a long history of diversity in both ideology and style, performing a central role in the establishment and maintenance of pluralism vital to the survival of liberal democracy. However, this role has been greatly weakened by a sharp decline in circulation of daily newspapers (*les quotidiens*) since the Second World War and the collapse of numerous dailies, despite an increase in the total French population and a rise in education levels. France today has one of the lowest rates of newspaper readership in the European Union (well under half the adult population and a particularly small proportion of young people (Kuhn 1995, 1998)). Nonetheless, much of the political spectrum remains covered by the daily press: from the Communist *L'Humanité*, to *Libération* on the centre left (a formerly more radical paper created by the philosopher Jean-Paul Sartre), to the Catholic *La Croix* and *Le Figaro* on the centre right, supplemented by business-oriented dailies, notably *Les Echos*. *Le Monde* remains one of the best quality newspapers in the world: attempting to provide a nonpartisan forum for political debate that offers comprehensive coverage of national and international events. However, *Le Monde*'s readership is limited to a small section of French society consisting of the better educated and politically interested.

The decline in daily newspaper circulation has been offset only in part by the increased readership of weekly news magazines (*les hebdomadaires*) and their diversity. These include *L'Express* (on the centre right) and *Le Nouvel Observateur* (on the centre left), *Le Point* and *L'Événement du jeudi*. The satirical weekly newspaper *Le Canard enchâiné* (similar to *Private Eye*) has long published some of the most critical coverage of French politics, providing the forum for government opponents to take aim and frustrated state officials to leak damaging information. The provincial French dailies have generally fared better than their national counterparts. *Ouest France*, covering Britanny, Pays de la Loire and Normandie, for example, maintains healthy circulation figures and a dominant share in its regional market. However, in nearly all cases local and regional newspapers have kept up circulation figures through a depoliticisation of content, with decreasing information on national and international politics, and increased focus on local news, lifestyle and sports topics.

While the French press has a long history of diversity, the French broadcasting media (television and radio) was until recently a state monopoly operating under a legal framework originally established for radio by the Vichy regime during the Second World War and maintained by subsequent governments. *Radio Luxembourg* was a famous exception, broadcasting alternative cultural and political coverage to French listeners from the Grand Duchy.

The rise to power of the Socialists in 1981 started a dramatic shake-up in the media (Kuhn 1995, 1998). The Loi Fillioud of 1982 ended the state monopoly, while the Loi Léotard adopted by the Chirac government in 1986 encouraged further economic liberalisation. These laws led to the creation of numerous new commercial channels and stations, many of the most successful of which – led in 1984 by Canal Plus, Europe's first terrestrial pay-TV channel, and the NRJ radio station, among numerous others – offered only or principally entertainment with little in the way of political and policy information. The impact on political discussion and debate has been mixed. The public gets most of its political information today from TV and then radio – and expresses most confidence in TV as an accurate source of information (Gerstlé 1993) – while this information has invariably been watered down, made more digestible for a mass audience able to switch over to the entertainment offered on other channels and stations.

The initial increase in the number and variety of private local radio stations in the early 1980s was most impressive, covering all the major subcultures in French society, including those – ethnic minorities and gays – who had been largely shut out by the public-sector broadcasting organisations. However, within a few years this rich diversity was replaced by a commercial oligopoly as financial difficulties plagued many of the smaller niche-market stations and a few competitive professional commercial companies arose to dominate the market, offering much less diversity in output and allowing local branches little room for experimentation (Chapman and Hewitt 1992). Regulation was adopted by the state to help protect community radio stations and uphold the principle of radio pluralism embodied in the Loi Fillioud. Nonetheless, today, small-scale operations form only a minority of the 1800 French radio stations (Kuhn 1998).

In TV-land, the Loi Léotard privatised the leading public broadcaster, TF1, while the two remaining public-sector channels, TF2 and 3, were forced to fight for viewers by focusing their programming less on news and more on mass entertainment in an increasingly competitive market with two new commercial stations – La 5 and M6. With mounting debts, La 5 went into liquidation in 1992.

CONCLUSION

Born out of crisis, involving a political design opposed by large sections of public opinion, rocked by the uprising of May 1968 and numerous other demonstrations, menaced by cohabitation and corruption, the Fifth Republic has survived against the odds. France has demonstrated an impressive capacity for political and constitutional adaptation over the past four decades despite claims of *la société bloquée* (see the next chapter) and a lugubrious state. The direct election of the president strengthened the legitimacy of presidential intervention and arguably strengthened the hand of the executive to push through significant reforms which have both reinforced de Gaulle's original objectives but also undermined them. While the Parliament was greatly weakened in 1958 and the Constitutional Council made a tool of the political executive, both have been gradually strengthened to improve their watchdog role, notably through the 1974 constitutional amendment allowing 60 *députés* or senators to challenge the constitutionality of a proposed law. Decentralisation was carried through without the need for constitutional reform and appears set to continue. The recent manifestation of a (decidedly Anglo-Saxon?) pragmatism with regard to Corsica's status demonstrates an impressive willingness to put the sacred cows of Jacobin republicanism (and Chevènement too?) in their place in the name of a negotiated solution to a longstanding political problem. These reforms, among others, demonstrate the surprisingly impressive capacity of the French state to innovate. While many challenges lie ahead which will require continued institutional adaptation challenging the shibboleths of Jacobin republicanism, we are confident that the Fifth Republic is set to outlive the Third.

4

POLITICAL FORCES AND REPRESENTATION

The aim of this chapter is to provide a brief overview of the political forces that have shaped French politics over the past few decades and in doing so to underscore the manner in which the Fifth Republic has both enhanced and constrained the expression of ideas and dissent in the French political system. The chapter begins with an overview of French political parties and the development of the party system and then proceeds with a section on major interests and New Social Movements in the context of France's notorious tradition of protest. We conclude with an examination of one of the most pressing political issues of the early twenty-first century: the under-representation of women and ethnic minorities in France's elected assemblies. The new *parité* law has only partially redressed the problem of female representation, while ethnic minorities continue to face even greater obstacles in a country where the issues of immigration and integration appear to have obscured that of political participation.

POLITICAL PARTIES

The right

In terms of percentage of the vote, over the past 20 years there have been two large parties of the right and one confederation of smaller centre-right parties. The RPR (*Rassemblement pour la République*) is the neo-Gaullist party created in 1976 by Jacques Chirac, the inheritor of the Gaullist tradition following in the footsteps of the RPF (*Rassemblement du Peuple Français*) created in 1947 by Michel Debré, the UNR (*Union pour la Nouvelle République*) created to rally around de Gaulle in defence of the new Fifth Republic in 1958 and the UDR (*Union pour la Défence de la République*), the Gaullists rebaptised by Pompidou in the aftermath of the May 1968 uprising. The RPR – the dominant party on the right in terms of votes and seats – has long been Chirac's own fiefdom.

However, there have always been challengers vying to assume control of the party – especially with Chirac's weakness in cohabitation following the 1997 elections and accusations of his misuse of public funds. During the 1990s, following the Maastricht Treaty (Treaty of European Union, 1992), the divisions within the party became more intense, in particular with regard to the European integration issue, with two leading members, Philippe Séguin (a former social affairs minister and president of the National Assembly) and Charles Pasqua (minister of the interior from 1993 to 1995), attempting to pull the party in a more Eurosceptic direction. They both failed in their challenge to Chirac's leadership: Séguin resigned as head of the party list during the 1999 election campaign for the European Parliament while Charles Pasqua left the party at the end of 1998 to create his own Eurosceptic neo-Gaullist list in the European elections, which performed almost as well as the RPR list. Pasqua's success led him to announce the creation of a new party, the RPF (*Rassemblement pour la France*). He claimed his new party was more faithful to the Gaullist tradition than the RPR, which had accepted too much European integration over the years.

The UDF (*Union pour la Démocratie Française*) is a confederation of smaller centre-right parties, created in 1978 by President Giscard d'Estaing. A very young finance minister and political high-flyer in the mid-1960s, Giscard left the Gaullist UNR in 1966 because of his opposition to de Gaulle's leadership and established his own small centre-right party, the RI (*Républicains Indépendants*), which became PR (*Parti Républicain*) after 1974 and cooperated increasingly with other small parties of the non-Gaullist centre right and traditional right. The UDF was created above all for electoral reasons, an alliance of different parties that sought to maximise their electoral success in relation to the larger RPR and ensure the victory of Giscard in the 1981 presidential elections (and other UDF candidates subsequently). The confederation performs particularly well in regional and *département* elections and has held control over numerous regional and *département* assemblies over the past two decades. Giscard maintained his control over the confederation well into the 1990s but finally stepped down to make way for the Christian Democrat, François Bayrou. The UDF has succeeded in winning collectively more seats than the RPR but has lost and regained component parties over the years and in the 2002 elections collapsed as many leading UDF politicians joined the hastily assembled *Union pour la Majorité Présidentielle* (UMP) to ensure the victory of a stable centre-right government. In November 2002, the UMP was officially transformed into an umbrella party of the mainstream right, the UMP (*Union pour le Mouvement Populaire*) regrouping the RPR, RPF and much of the UDF. However, a UDF distinct from the UMP persists. The UDF's component parties are at odds on most political issues of the day. On European integration, for example, the traditionalist right party *Mouvement pour la France* (MPF), led by Philippe de Villiers, is hostile to any further undermining of national 'sovereignty', and opposed the Maastricht, Amsterdam and Nice Treaties which have pushed integration forward. Bayrou's Christian Democracy, on the other hand, is the most consistently pro-integration party in France. *Démocratie*

Libérale is a small former component party of the UDF led by Alain Madelin. It is noteworthy for being the only party in France unashamedly in favour of liberal (indeed Thatcherite) economic reforms and a wholesale withdrawal of the state from the economy.

The National Front (*Front National*, FN) was created in 1972 by Jean-Marie Le Pen – a former paratrooper who fought in the Algerian War – who succeeded in combining very different parties of the extreme right: fundamentalist Catholics, neo-fascists and the anti-immigrant populist right. Its first electoral success came in the 1980s. Placed at a distinct disadvantage by the French electoral system – the centre right has consistently refused to form electoral alliances or agreements with the FN – the party benefited immensely from the switch to proportional representation for the 1986 legislative elections, winning 35 seats but then losing them again in 1988 when the two-ballot majority system was again in place. Excluded from the National Assembly, the FN has achieved some electoral success in second-order elections which use PR (notably European parliamentary and regional elections). Since the 1998 regional elections, the UDF has controversially relied on the support of the FN in over 10 regional councils, despite several UDF members being thrown out of their national party organisations. The National Front also won control of four south-eastern French cities with populations of more than 30 000 (Marignane, Toulon, Orange and Vitrolles). The FN is an anti-system party that boasts its anti-establishment credentials. It is opposed to any further immigration, has recommended the repatriation of non-European ethnic minorities (although Le Pen has toned down his rhetoric on this matter in recent years), and is in favour of providing special assistance for disadvantaged whites (*préférence nationale*) not available to ethnic minorities. The party also emphasises law and order and the defence of French traditions over any form of emerging French multiculturalism. It attracts votes from a cross-section of French society, from people concerned with high unemployment, crime and immigration (three issues that it links together). The party suffered a debilitating division when Bruno Mégret – its leading intellectual – and several other leading members fed up with Le Pen's leadership left to form a new party, the *Front National-Mouvement National*, subsequently relabelled the MNR (*Mouvement National Républicain*). However, many observers confused organisational division with collapse and the new party only deprived the FN of a small fraction of its votes in the 2002 elections. The electoral success of the party has relied to a great extent on Le Pen himself, who in presidential elections has repeatedly scored better than his party in national contests. Le Pen's success in the first ballot of the presidential elections in 2002 (see pp. 81–3) should not be considered a significant surge in support for the far right.

The left

The Socialist Party (*Parti Socialiste*, PS) was the largest political party in France from the 1978 to the 1993 legislative elections, in terms of membership, votes and seats in the National Assembly. It was created in 1969 by an older left-wing party dating back to the Third Republic: the SFIO (*Section Française de l'Internationale Ouvrière*). François Mitterrand took control of the party at the Epinay Congress in 1971, merged it with another left-wing party, the PSU, led by Michel Rocard, and transformed it into the mass party it is today. As party leader, then leading member, Mitterrand became the first Socialist president of the republic, a post he held from 1981 to 1995. The party has always been strongly divided into factions, distinguished by their ideological orientation, which follow particular party leaders (for example, Michel Rocard in the 1970s and 1980s, the left-wing nationalist Jean-Pierre Chevènement, and the so-called 'social liberalism' of Laurent Fabius today). Mitterrand's great skill as leader was his ability to manipulate the different factions to his political advantage. The factions have engaged in a long struggle to dominate party policy, with some party leaders determined to root the party in the centre, even pulling it in the direction of Tony Blair's New Labour, while others insist on embedding it firmly on the left. The majority of the party activists are more left-wing, and when in opposition the party is likely to swing to the left (as it did under Lionel Jospin's leadership following the 1993 defeat). Jospin demonstrated great political skill in government (1997–2002), pursuing both liberalising and interventionist economic and social reforms under the guise of his 'Modern Socialism' (see Chapter 8 on economic policy), thus maintaining the support of not only most of his party but also the diverse components of the Plural Left government. In the aftermath of the double defeat of 2002 and Jospin's resignation, a battle is set for control over the party between the so-called 'social liberal' modernisers and the left.

The French Communist Party (PCF) was, from the *Libération* until the mid-1970s, the largest political party on the French left. From the 1950s to the 1970s, the party's hard-line support of Stalin, all the policies adopted by the Soviet Union and its foreign interventions, and the party's hierarchical structure and lack of internal democracy disenchanted most of its intellectual support and that of much of its rank and file. In the 1970s the party was split between those who wanted to follow the more liberal Eurocommunism embraced by the Italian Communist Party and a stubbornly pro-Moscow leadership clique which successfully saw off attempts to cut links with Moscow. Out-manoeuvred by Mitterrand in the 1970s in electoral alliances that involved the Joint Programme, the party lost a large number of voters to the more moderate Socialist Party. In 1981 the PCF was invited by the Socialists to participate in government. This had the effect of further weakening public support for the party, which shared the blame for the government's austerity measures imposed from 1982. Communist ministers withdrew from the government in 1984 to salvage what was left of the party's reputation. The party's share of the vote stagnated at around the 10 per cent level for most of the 1980s and 1990s despite the collapse of Communist regimes in Central and Eastern Europe. Famously, in the era of Soviet *glasnost* and *perestroika*, President Mikail Gorbachev visited the old-guard leader of the PCF, Georges Marchais, in order to recommend that the French party embrace change. The PCF continued to attract the ageing hard core of France's Communist subculture and even regained some support thanks to growing disillusionment on the left with Socialist government policies. Under the leadership of Robert Hue the party has also undergone a limited liberalisation, introducing greater party democracy and recognising the importance of individual rights (property and so on) to respond to accusations of lingering Stalinism. The PCF joined the Plural Left coalition in the lead-up to the 1997 National Assembly elections and entered the government in 1997, holding important ministerial posts. The party appears to have paid a price for its 5 years in office – its scores in recent elections have reached historic lows, in particular its 4.7 per cent result in the June 2002 National Assembly elections, its worst result since the 1920s. Two small extreme-left parties continue to attract the bulk of the revolutionary hard core of the French population: the Trotskyite *Lutte Ouvrière* – whose presidential candidate, Arlette Laguiller, out-polled Robert Hue in the first ballot of the 2002 presidential elections – and the *Ligue Communiste Révolutionnaire*. Ideological bickering and mutual suspicion make unity on the extreme left unlikely in the foreseeable future.

The Greens (*Verts*) have enjoyed only recent success in French national and second-order elections, although in the 1990s they enjoyed a higher average percentage of the vote than their German comrades. The *Ecologistes* led by Brice Lalonde performed surprisingly well in the 1989 European Parliament elections when they received 10.6 per cent and eight seats, and in the 1992 regional elections together with their rival Greens (*Verts*) (led by Dominique Voynet) they won almost 14 per cent and 100 seats. Division between the *Ecologistes* and the Greens – based on ideology and leadership – greatly damaged the parties in both the 1993 National Assembly elections and 1994 European Parliament elections. Dominique Voynet succeed in reunifying most of the environmentalist vote under her leadership and took the Greens into a very successful 1997 legislative election, winning 6.8 per cent of the vote, seven seats in the National Assembly and a ministerial portfolio in the government, the first ever for a Green minister in France (becoming minister of the environment). Daniel Cöhn-Bendit – the charismatic German-Jewish student leader of the May 1968 student uprising at the Sorbonne – returned to France to lead the Green party list in an upbeat pro-European campaign for the 1999 European Parliament elections (the Maastricht Treaty enabled EU citizens to run in local and European elections in other EU member states). Threatening Voynet's leadership of the party and uniting most of the Green movement in France behind his (Antoine Waechter ran a Eurosceptic Green list), Cöhn-Bendit achieved the party's second highest score to date, winning 9.72 per cent of the vote and nine seats. The *Verts* performed less well than hoped in the June 2002 legislative elections, winning only 4.4 per cent of the vote, over 2 per cent less than their 1997 score, and losing four of seven seats, including Voynet's own.

Finally on the left, the MDC (*Mouvement des Citoyens*, relabelled *Pôle Républicain* (PR) for the 2002 presidential and legislative elections) was created by Jean-Pierre Chevènement following his 1991 departure from the Socialist government and party due to his opposition to the Gulf War (he was minister of defence at the time). From 1981, Chevènement enjoyed uneasy relations with the Socialist Party. His CERES (*Centre d'Études et de Recherches Socialistes*) faction had enjoyed a brief period as the party's leading ideological light in the late 1970s as Mitterrand positioned himself on the left to ensure the support of a majority of the rank and file and the PCF. However, following the 1981 election victories, CERES was increasingly marginalised on the left. Chevènement can be described as a Socialist Jacobin republican. He has consistently opposed further European economic integration and favours protectionist strategies over trade liberalisation. He is also a staunch defender of the republican tradition and is opposed to loss of 'sovereignty' to the European Union, including EMU, and to excessive decentralisation of powers from the French state to local government. In 2000 he resigned for the third time during his career as a government minister, opposed in principle to the recognition of a special constitutional status for Corsica on the grounds that it contradicted the principle of the 'one and indivisible republic'. Chevènement's MDC was part of the Plural Left coalition that came to power in 1997. After a strong start in the 2002 presidential campaign, as the *bête noir* maverick candidate, Chevènement performed less well than anticipated (5.3 per cent, in sixth place behind the *Lutte Ouvrière* veteran candidate, Arlette Laguiller) and even lost his Belfort seat – held since 1974 – in the June 2002 National Assembly elections. The *Pôle Républicain* failed to win any seats in the elections.

The party system

A party system can be defined as a relatively stable network of relationships between political parties that is structured by their number, size and ideological orientation. A party system is normally defined by the number of parties that are likely to form or participate in government. The UK has a two-and-a-half-party system in the sense that there are only two parties that compete for power (Labour and Tories) but the possibility exists that the Liberal Democrat Party (which wins a significant number of seats) might form a coalition with one of the two main parties. The smaller parties do not win enough seats to be able to force the two leading parties into coalition governments. France has always had a multiparty system but since the early 1980s only one party (the PS) has been in the position to form a government on its own, although it has not been able to do so since 1986 and probably will not be able to do so in the near future. (See Table 4.1 on page 78 on the development of the French party system.) Since the 1970s, the neo-Gaullist RPR and the UDF confederation have had to form coalition governments together, and the creation of the umbrella *Union pour la Majorité Présidentielle* (UPM) in the campaign for the 2002 legislative elections is unlikely to change this. Neither the RPR nor the UDF has ever won enough seats to govern alone (although the RPR's Gaullist predecessors were able to do so from 1968 to 1973). The UDF confederation consists of very diverse parties (which agree among themselves in which constituencies they run candidates under the UDF banner). The Communist Party (PCF) is by far the largest of the small parties. The Greens (*Verts*), MDC, *Chevènementistes* and left-wing Radicals

(*Radicaux de Gauche*, a small centre-left party) win a small number of seats at the national level. The centre-left government in France from 1997 to 2002 was a coalition – the Plural Left – consisting of these parties but led by the Socialists who held the large majority (over three-quarters) of the government's seats. In order to maintain the support of these parties, the PS had to give them some ministerial portfolios and a degree of influence in the overall direction of policy making.

There are four factors that affect any party system: the electoral system, distinct regional identities, political culture and traditions, and polarisation on particular issues. During most of the Fifth Republic, France has had a two-ballot system for legislative elections. In theory such a system should discriminate against smaller parties and extremist parties, and indeed some smaller parties have been consistently prevented from winning any seats or seats in numbers proportional to their votes. The National Front, although it won roughly 14.9 per cent in the 1997 legislative elections, won no seats in the National Assembly (even though it won more votes than the UDF (14.2 per cent and 108 seats!), Communists (PCF) (9.9 per cent and 38 seats) and much more than the Greens and MDC). As already noted, when the electoral system was changed to a PR list system for the 1986 legislative elections, the National Front won 35 seats. The electoral system should also in theory encourage the formation of stable majority governments consisting of only one party. However, as already noted, most French governments have not been majority governments. There have only been a couple of exceptions in the history of the Fifth Republic: the Gaullists between 1968 and 1973 (they were four seats short in the 1962 elections but governed with little difficulty, thanks to right-wing allies) and the Socialists between 1981 and 1986 (which nonetheless formed a broad coalition of the left including Communist ministers who stayed until 1984). The two-ballot majority electoral system has also encouraged alliance strategies. Mainstream right-wing parties and the major left-wing parties normally agree to alliances that involve agreements on candidates stepping down after the first ballot and encouraging vote transfers. Clearly, the impact of the electoral system on the party system has been qualified by other factors in French political life.

Distinct regional voting patterns, often linked to strong local identities, also shape the party system. The working-class areas around Paris and in the north have traditionally voted Communist. Bucking a national trend of rural voters supporting conservative parties, the rural south-west of France has voted Socialist for most of the post-war period. In the conservative Vendée (a rural *département* near Nantes) the left has long performed very badly (even by the standards of most of rural France), while the National Front has particularly strong support in Provence–Alpes–Côtes d'Azur (the south-east region including Marseille, Nice, Toulon), in part because of the large presence there of the *Pieds Noirs* – the Europeans who left Algeria *en masse* at the time of independence – and their offspring.

Political culture and political traditions (see Chapter 1) form a third factor that shapes party systems. One noteworthy feature of French political culture is that the tendency to personalise politics and factionalism in parties based on support for a leader is strong in comparison to that found in British parties. The tendency towards division is therefore greater. Many centrists left the Gaullist party in the late 1960s and early 1970s to support an intelligent young technocrat, formerly a leading Gaullist politician (Giscard d'Estaing). The MDC (left-wing republican nationalists led by former Socialist minister Jean-Pierre Chevènement) broke off from the Socialist Party in the early 1990s. Another important feature of French political culture is its well-entrenched extremist political traditions, rooted in strong intellectual movements, on both the right and the left, which has contributed to the rise and survival of the National Front, the PCF and the other far-left parties which have yet to win representation in the National Assembly but have won seats in the European Parliament and some regional assemblies where voting takes place on the basis of PR. The Radical tradition, with roots dating back to the creation of the Third Republic in the 1870s, lingers in small centre-right and centre-left parties which win seats in alliance with the UDF parties and the Socialists respectively.

As in most European countries, polarisation on a rough left–right ideological spectrum has shaped the French party system in the Fifth Republic. However, this represents a dramatic change from the Fourth Republic when the political parties were polarised on both ideology and willingness to support the existence of the Fourth Republic, which had greater political salience. Gaullists and Communists were opposed to the regime and refused to participate in governments, whereas the Socialists (at the time the SFIO) and the *Mouvement Républicain Populaire* (Christian Democrats) were in favour. Therefore, unstable coalition governments were created consisting of political parties and politicians with very different – often diametrically opposed – views on questions of redistributive justice and state ownership. Initially, during the Fifth Republic, parties polarised on support for or opposition to the constitution and institutions of the new republic – support for or opposition to President de Gaulle. This roughly corresponded to the left–right split as the Socialists and Communists both opposed the institutional arrangement of the Fifth Republic. However, de Gaulle also succeeded in attracting many left-leaning voters and his party, then called the UNR, became the first French 'catch-all party', appealing to voters from across the political spectrum – with some noteworthy exceptions – and the first to win a majority of seats in the National Assembly. After de Gaulle's resignation and death, the neo-Gaullist party transformed into more of a traditional conservative party (which even briefly came to advocate liberal economic policies in the mid-1980s) and the left–right polarisation was reinforced. The presidentialisation of electoral politics also contributed to bipolarisation. From 1974 to 1995 the second ballot in the presidential elections involved a run-off between a Socialist and right-wing (RPR or UDF) candidate. More recently, the issue of Europe has become of increasing salience to French party politics. On the right, the National Front has attracted the support of many of those who view European integration as a fundamentally unhealthy undermining of national identity. While there are divisions within all the parties, opposition to further European integration

Table 4.1 The development of the French party system

	1958	1968	1974	1981	1986	1997	2002
Number of parties in parliament	3 main parties, several smaller parties	3 main parties, several smaller parties	4 main parties, fewer other parties	4 main parties, fewer other parties	5 main parties, several smaller parties	4 main parties, with two smaller parties in government	2/3 main parties
Gaullist/ neo-Gaullist	UNR (near majority)	UDR (majority)	UDR (slightly larger coalition partner)	RPR (slightly larger opposition party)	RPR (slightly larger coalition partner)	RPR (slightly larger opposition party)	RPR (principal party on the right within UMP; failure of other Gaullist party, RPF)
Socialist (left-leaning)	Socialist party, but loss of support to smaller left-wing parties	Socialist party, but loss of support to smaller left-wing parties	Formed PS in 1969; other parties join	PS (majority)	PS largest party, yet in opposition; starting to lose support to Verts, etc.	PS largest party in coalition; lost support to MDC, Verts, etc.	PS largest single party; fewer seats won than in 1993
Centrists	Several parties	Several parties	UDF, etc.	UDF	UDF	UDF	UDF much weakened; lost numerous leading candidates to the UMP; likelihood of rebuilding
PCF	Second largest party	Weakens vs. UDR and Socialists; still 2nd party	Still second largest party; PS catching up	In late 1970s declines dramatically; weak in 1981	Loses more support	Support stabilises at 9–10%	Considerable drop in support and seats
Others					Greens win seats; lose in 1988	Greens win seats, MDC as well.	Greens and MDC lose ground (votes and seats)
Far right	Weak/divided	Weak/divided	Weak/divided	Weak/divided	Unified, 4th party	Less divided, no representation	Split between FN and MN-FN fails to damage FN significantly; No seats

encouraged Charles Pasqua – the former RPR minister who had been encouraged to leave the party following his stubborn refusal to endorse the Amsterdam Treaty – to form a Eurosceptic neo-Gaullist list for the June 1999 European Parliament elections and the Eurosceptic RPF. Attitudes to European integration also constituted a factor (although not the only one) encouraging some Chevènement supporters to leave the Socialists and form the MDC.

Rising apathy and the fragmentation of the vote

During the 1980s and 1990s, French elections were marked by growing apathy (a decline in the number of people voting) and an increasing fragmentation of the vote (an increasing percentage of votes cast for extremist or smaller mainstream parties). However, this has yet to translate into a significant fragmentation of the party system at the national level – when large parties lose seats in the National Assembly and the number of political parties winning seats in the Assembly increases. During this period, the conservative parties and PCF lost much support to the extreme-right National Front, which – for reasons already noted – is unable to win seats in the National Assembly. The Socialist Party lost many supporters in the 1980s and 1990s, principally those on the left who were disillusioned with its cautious, far from radical, policy making in government. Support transferred to the Greens, the far-left fringe parties and, in the 1990s, to Chevènement's MDC. The move to PR (multimember constituencies based upon French *départements*) for the 1986 legislative elections encouraged fragmentation in both the vote and the party system. The readoption of the two-ballot majority system did not prevent further fragmentation of the vote as the system creates possibilities for relatively small parties as long as they cooperate with the larger parties in electoral alliances. However, the fragmentation of the party system remained limited. The percentage of the vote won by the three largest mainstream parties – the UDF (confederation), RPR and Socialists – has continued to shrink since 1981. Collectively, the three parties won 77.9 per cent of the vote in the first ballot of the 1981 National Assembly elections; 65.1 per cent in 1986; 75.2 per cent in 1988; but only 57.6 per cent in 1993 and 53.4 per cent in 1997. However, this has not yet amounted to an equivalent loss of National Assembly seats: 436 (out of 491) (89 per cent) in 1981, 498 (out of 577) (86 per cent) in 1986 (535 out of 577) (93 per cent) in 1988, 530 (92 per cent) in 1993 and 514 (89 per cent) in 1997. Of course, many observers have questioned the long-term legitimacy of an electoral system that allows the two dominant parties and the UDF confederation to maintain such an impressive hold over National Assembly seats despite a shrinking percentage of the vote. It should also be stressed that the fragmentation of the vote and even – eventually – seats does not mean unstable government, as the Plural Left has shown over the past 5 years.

It is difficult to predict the future, given so many variables affecting the party system. In the short and medium term, no party seems able to form a single-party majority government. The Socialists will only eventually be able to do so if they succeed in attracting back support lost to the Greens and non-Socialist left-wing parties. However, only unique conditions have allowed in the past for the rise of a dominant single party which could form a majority government on its own on either the left or the right: the need to 'defend' de Gaulle's republic in its early years and in the early 1980s when the Socialists – not yet compromised by the challenges of government – could appeal to a broad band of public opinion fed up with the hitherto centre-right domination of the Fifth Republic. In November 2002, the UMP succeeded in transforming itself into a single umbrella party which includes the large majority of right-wing *députés*, making the new UMP the largest party of the right in the fifth Republic since the UDR in the early 1970s. Whether this umbrella party survives the next election remains to be seen. The Socialists – whose vote in the 1993, 1997 and 2002 elections held steady at approximately a quarter of the electorate – are most likely set to continue their domination of the left. The creation of the UMP is forcing the left to consider consolidation as well for electoral reasons – although ideological differences may be too significant to allow this. Despite further fragmentation of the vote, the two main parties (the UMP and PS) will maintain their domination of National Assembly seats, but only at the price of growing apathy. The National Front has established itself quite firmly in south-eastern France. However, it is unlikely that it will win more than the occasional National Assembly seat given the stigma attached to forming alliances with it. After holding steady from the mid-1980s to the mid-1990s, support for the PCF has continued to drop, as has its number of seats. While the other far-left parties have picked up some of this vote, they have yet to win seats, a development which further reinforces the dominant position of the Socialists on the left.

THE 2002 PRESIDENTIAL AND LEGISLATIVE ELECTIONS

The April/May presidential elections: 'à la recherche du clivage perdu'

Observing the 2002 presidential electoral contest between the two leading candidates – the incumbent neo-Gaullist President Jacques Chirac and the incumbent Socialist Prime Minister Lionel Jospin – one could argue that the stability of the Fifth Republic has come at a price. As the Socialist Party became the major party on the left in the 1970s and consolidated that position in the 1980s, it also gradually moderated its policies, attempting to appeal more to centrist voters. Likewise, the mainstream right, despite occasional and partial flirtations with economic liberalism – never a vote-winner in France – has maintained a spirited defence of public services and the generous French welfare state. Ideological and policy differences continued to punctuate presidential and other election campaigns throughout the 1980s and 1990s. The Socialists were drawn back to the left following their disastrous defeat in the 1993 elections and in the context of the Plural Left common platform for the 1997 legislative elections with the Communists, Greens and *Chevènementistes* (MDC). After a relatively successful 5 years in government pursuing a generally popular mix of liberalisation and interventionism, Lionel Jospin was not in a position to promise radical left-wing reforms, while President Chirac refused to pursue a more liberal economic agenda. The two-ballot electoral system also encouraged moderation in policy pronouncements, with the leading mainstream candidates pursuing the crucial wavering vote of the political centre in the second ballot. Moderation, however, undermined the distinctiveness of Chirac's and Jospin's policy programme to such an extent that 74 per cent of the electorate could not tell the difference between them (*L'Express*, 12 April 2002). There were differences, notably on the question of tax: Chirac promised more substantial cuts. However, this was not a major ideological struggle between the two leading candidates and Chirac refused to accept any corresponding cuts to government service and in fact called for increased government spending in the areas of policing and defence. The move to the centre caused considerable consternation among a French intelligentsia traditionally most happy in the realm of ideological struggle. Moreover, opinion polls over the previous years demonstrated that cohabitation had been embraced by the French electorate as an acceptable and even desirable feature of French political life, rather than an institutional morass best avoided. Both Jospin and Chirac scored high approval ratings for much of their terms in office, especially in the lead-up to the presidential elections. The 2002 campaign focused on the personal differences of the two candidates: Chirac's *bonhomie* and his *sympathique* character and Jospin's 'protestant' austerity and professorial seriousness. The one significant political issue which could have sparked some life into the electoral campaign – accusations of Chirac's long-term corrupt practices; accusations which would have ended the career of any British or American politician – was avoided by Jospin as an inappropriate matter for public debate during an electoral contest.

Le Pen's surprising first-ballot success

Perceiving the run-off between Chirac and Jospin as inevitable, and disappointed by the limited difference between the two candidates, many moderate French voters decided to abstain in the first ballot of the French presidential elections, dropping the turn-out to the lowest in the history of the Fifth Republic. A record number, on both the left and the right, opted for more extremist candidates. Much to the surprise of most French people, the National Front leader Jean-Marie Le Pen won a greater share of the vote in the first ballot (just under 17 per cent) than the Socialist candidate Lionel Jospin (16.2 per cent). Le Pen had won 14 and 15 per cent of the vote in the first round of the 1988 and 1995 presidential elections respectively and, despite the lower overall turn-out, won 4.8 million votes in 2002, over a million votes more than in 1995. Bruno Mégret, the other far-right candidate in the first ballot, polled 2.3 per cent, most of which would likely go to Le Pen in the second round. Chirac won more votes than any other candidate (19.9 per cent) but the least of any incumbent president and any front-runner since the first presidential elections of the Fifth Republic in 1963. The Christian Democrat, François Bayrou (representing the UDF), came a disappointing fourth with 6.8 per cent of the vote, followed by two left-wing candidates, Arlette Laguiller, the *Lutte Ouvrière* veteran of five presidential elections on the Trotskyite far left (5.7 per cent), and Jean-Pierre Chevènement, *Pôle Républicain*, on the republican nationalist left (a disappointing 5.2 per cent). In all, nearly a quarter of the vote (23.4 per cent) went to the three candidates of the far or populist right (including the candidate of the CPNT (*Chasse, Pêche, Nature et Traditions*/Hunting, Fishing, Nature and Traditions Party), while the five candidates on the far or nationalist left won just over 19 per cent of the vote (including Chevènement), bringing the total for the more extremist fringe – all of whom opposed further European integration and French participation in the Euro – to 42.5 per cent of the vote. Most surprising, Le Pen was the leading candidate in half the 96 French *départements*.

Arguably, Le Pen's vote was also surprising given the extent to which the French political establishment and media had attempted to demonise the National Front leader over the previous two decades. Many people voted for Le Pen precisely because he presented himself as the anti-establishment candidate – when the so-called establishment had demonstrated its inadequacy and corruption – and campaigned vigorously on law and order issues. Many voted for him despite his views on the EU and immigration and immigrants and, indeed, many also voted for him because of his views on these subjects. Le Pen's success in the first ballot also challenged preconceived ideas that relative economic success, which France had enjoyed over the previous 5 years, was enough to discourage support for extremism. It was surprising, too, because all the pollsters had been predicting a second-ballot show-down between Jospin and Chirac, which in effect discouraged many from turning out to vote in the first round. Subsequently, a law suit was introduced against the polling companies on the grounds that they misled the French voting public.

The defeated left – including the more extremist elements – closed ranks to defeat Le Pen in the second ballot, calling upon supporters to vote for Chirac, however distasteful this might be. Lionel Jospin accepted responsibility for his poor results and Le Pen's success, and resigned as the leader of the Socialist Party. The following 2 weeks were marked by anti-Le Pen demonstrations throughout France – normally dominated by the young – while Chirac refused to participate in a televised debate with his rival to avoid giving him excessive publicity. Several leading members of the French national football team declared that they would not play in the World Cup in Japan if Le Pen won, while even senior diplomats – who normally stay out of domestic politics – argued that France's reputation abroad would be for ever sullied. Chirac succeeded in presenting himself as the candidate of 'democratic' France, although it was clear that virtually all the support that rallied round him from the left and other mainstream right sources was temporary. Many Le Pen supporters shied away from airing the reasons for their support. Nonetheless, Le Pen held several well-attended rallies throughout France and took maximum advantage of the unprecedented media limelight. Impressively, violence between the two sides was largely averted.

In the second ballot, unsurprisingly, Chirac won the presidency by a large margin of 82 per cent of a relatively impressive turn-out of 84 per cent. If the first round of the elections could be described as a rejection of the French political establishment, the second demonstrated the strong attachment to the institutions of the Fifth Republic. However, and disturbingly for France, Le Pen not only increased his score thanks to Mégret's first-ballot vote; he also attracted a further half a million votes, thus bringing his total to just under 6 million, his highest to date. Le Pen announced that this vote would bring great success for the party in the June 2002 parliamentary elections. However, owing to the high threshold of the two-ballot majority system – and the continuing refusal of the mainstream right parties to form electoral alliances with the National Front – such hopes were not fulfilled.

The June 2002 legislative elections

Prior to the presidential elections, the legislative election campaign focused upon crime and tax cuts, favourite issues of the right. Despite the mobilisation created by the anti-Le Pen movement and the strong turn-out in the second ballot of the presidential elections, the abstention rate in the first ballot of the legislative elections reached 35.58 per cent (64.42 per cent voted or 26.4 million of nearly 41 million possible voters) and in the second ballot 39.71 per cent (60.29 per cent participated, casting 22.2 million votes), lower than the rates in the British general election of June 2001, and a disturbing manifestation of a Europe-wide trend. The results, however, undermined the prophets of doom who only a month earlier were predicting the strong rise of the French far right. The parties of Le Pen and Mégret won no seats between them. The UMP mirrored the success achieved by the right in several West European countries over the previous year (including Italy, Spain and Portugal). On the coat-tails of Chirac's election, the RPR-dominated UMP won 33.4 per cent of the vote in the first ballot and 355 seats in the second, the first single right-wing party grouping to achieve a majority of the seats in the National Assembly since the Gaullist UDR in the period 1968–73. Seven of the interim UMP government ministers won National Assembly seats already in the first round (winning more than 50 per cent of the votes cast).

All the parties participating in the former Plural Left government obtained a disappointing 36 per cent of the vote in the first ballot and only 178 seats in the second. The 'mainstream' right garnered a total of 43.7 per cent of the votes with particularly low scores for all the other elements of the right which had refused to join the UMP. Bayrou's UDF won 4.79 per cent (22 seats in the second ballot), which enabled the UDF to maintain its status as a party group but denied it the role of king-maker in a coalition with the UMP. The rest of the mainstream right running outside the UMP achieved disappointingly low scores in the first ballot and only 8 seats in the second. The leaders of *Démocratie Libérale* and *Mouvement pour la France* – Alain Madelin and Philippe de Villiers respectively – retained their seats. The CPNT obtained only 1.64 per cent of the vote and no seats.

Despite the poor outcome in terms of seats (141), it is important to note that the Socialist first-ballot vote (23.78 per cent) was only slightly down

Table 4.2 Results of the 2002 legislative elections

Party/party family/ leader	% of vote in 1997 legislative elections, second round (number of seats in brackets)	% of vote in 2002 legislative elections, first round	Number of seats in the National Assembly 2002–7
'Mainstream' right total	36.5 (256)	43.8	399
UMP (Raffarin)	RPR only: 15.7 (134)	33.7	369
RPF (Pasqua)*	N/A	0.4	
UDF (Bayrou)*	Including DL: 14.2 (108)	4.8	29
DL (Madélin)*		0.4	1
MPF (*Mouvement pour la France*) (de Villiers)	See other right	0.8	1
Various other right	6.6 (14)	3.7	9
CPNT (*Chasse, Pêche Nature et Traditions*) Saint-Josse		1.7	–
Extreme Right total	15.0 (1)	12.4	–
FN (Le Pen)	14.9 (1)	11.3	–
MNR (Mègret)	N/A	1.1	–
Plural Left total	44.4 (314)	36.1	178
PS (Hollande)	23.5 (241)	24.1	140
Verts (Voynet)	6.8 (7)	4.5	3
PCF (Hue)	9.9 (38)	4.8	21
PRG	1.4 (12)	1.5	7
PR (*Pôle Républicain*) (Chevènement)	MDC (*Mouvement des Citoyens*) (5)	1.2	
Other various left	2.8 (21) (including MDC's 5 seats)	1.1	6
Extreme Left total	2.5 (0)		–
LO (*Lutte Ouvrière*) (Laguiller)		1.2	–
LCR (*Ligue Communiste Révolutionnaire*)		1.3	–
Regionalist parties		0.3	1
Ecologistes		1.2	–
Various others	1.4 (1)	0.8	–

Note: *Votes for candidates of these three parties who did not run under the UMP banner.

from 1997. Still, several leading Socialist politicians were defeated, including Martine Aubry (mayor of Lille and minister of social affairs during the first half of the Jospin government), and seven ministers from the previous government, including Pierre Moscovici (former minister of European affairs), Catherine Trautmann (mayor of Strasbourg and former minister). However, for the rest of the left, the elections caused great upset. The PCF's vote plummetted to its lowest level in a national election since the Communists first ran candidates in French elections (4.9 per cent) and its seat total dropped to 21, the lowest number since the 1944 Liberation. The Greens also performed badly with 4.4 per cent of the vote, a considerable drop from 1997, and only three seats. The leaders of the PCF, Greens and *Pôle Républicain* – Robert Hue, Dominique Voynet and Jean-Pierre Chevènement respectively – were all defeated in the second ballot run-off. The extreme right (FN and MNR) suffered a relatively low vote of 12.2 per cent (FN, 11.12; MNR, 1.08), down from the 14.7 per cent won in the parliamentary elections in 1997 and considerably lower than Le Pen's score in the first and second rounds of the presidential elections. The National Front's hopes of being a spoiler on the right in the second ballot were also dashed as the party won 12.5 per cent of the total possible in far fewer constituencies than it had hoped and was consequently able to run candidates in only 36 second-ballot contests. It failed to win a single seat, coming closest in Orange, where the mayor, Jacques Bompard, with 42.3 per cent of the vote, lost to the UMP incumbent. After the shock of the first round of the presidential elections, it appears as though France returned to normal recentred and bipolar politics.

Despite the widespread relief that the French political landscape had returned to more familiar contours after the upset of the first ballot of the presidential elections, analysts warned that a great deal of political discontent remained, demonstrated by the historically high abstention rates. The large number of Le Pen voters who either abstained or voted for the UMP constituted an unpredictable 'swinging vote' that could re-emerge in upcoming elections. In the immediate aftermath of the elections, there was considerable doubt about what the swing to the right would bring. During the presidential and legislative campaign reducing tax was a popular issue, but so too was increasing public spending, especially on police and defence (Chirac and the Raffarin interim government called for the construction of a second French aircraft carrier). Following the second round of the legislative elections, the Raffarin government set out to fulfil its short-term campaign promises with new laws on police and justice matters, lowering income tax by 5 per cent and a general amnesty (for unpaid parking tickets and other minor fines), the latter being a traditional way for newly elected French presidents to thank the nation. Chirac and UMP ministers also played with the idea of delaying the 2004 goal of balancing French public spending in line with European goals, although one should be sceptical of the willingness of the new government to upset its European partners. Despite the UMP's parading the benefits of the market it was highly unlikely that the new government had any serious intention of dismantling existing social protection and the 35-hour-week policy, although the possibility of relaxing the application of the latter in some areas of the economy was mooted by Chirac and UMP politicians during the campaigns.

The new government, appointed 17 June, consisted of 14 full cabinet ministers, 11 junior ministers (*ministres délégués*) and 12 secretaries of state (*secrétaires*

Exhibit 4.1: The Raffarin government June 2002

Prime minister: Jean-Pierre Raffarin (RPR)
Minister of the interior, of internal security and local powers: Nicolas Sarkozy (RPR)
Minister of social affairs, employment and solidarity: François Fillon (RPR)
Minister of justice (Garde des Sceaux): Dominique Perben*
Minister of defence: Michèle Alliot-Marie (RPR)
Minister of youth affairs, education and research: Luc Ferry*
Minister of economics, finance and industry: Francis Mer*
Minister of public procurement, transport, housing and
    tourism and the sea: Gilles de Robien (UDF)
Minister of the environment and
    sustainable development: Roselyn Bachelot-Narquin (RPR)
Minister of health, the family and the disabled: Jean-François Mattei (DL)
Minister of agriculture, food, fishing and rural affairs: Hervé Gaymard (RPR)
Minister of culture and commmunications: Jean-Jacques Aillagon (RPR)
Minister of administration, state reform and
    local development: Jean-Paul Delevoye (RPR)
Minister of overseas territories: Brigitte Girardin*
Minister of sports: Jean-François Lamour*

* Without party label at the time of appointment.

d'état). The majority of government ministers were from the RPR (8 ministers and 8 junior ministers and secretaries of state), but a majority of more junior government posts went to those politicians from the UDF, *Démocratie Libérale* and other parties who had decided to run under the UMP label. As in the first Juppé government of June 1995, a relatively large number of women were appointed and important allies of President Chirac were given leading posts.

On the right, the outright UMP victory and the poor showing of the smaller right-wing parties made the possibility of unity stronger than at any time since de Gaulle's era. One should remain sceptical of the ability of the historically faction-prone parties of the right to overcome well-established rivalries to unite for long under a single leader. While the UMP was consolidated into a single party on the right, on the left, the elections reconfirmed the dominant position of the Socialist Party. Despite the party's defeat, its score in the first ballot (23.78 per cent) was only slightly lower than in 1997. The decline in vote for the PCF further reinforces the strong position of the Socialists. Likewise, the extreme left, whose candidates polled so well in the first ballot of the presidential election, did very poorly in the first ballot of the legislative elections. The Socialists faced an upcoming battle for the party leadership that was set to be ideologically tense. Jospin himself profited from a similar battle in the period following the defeat of the Socialists in the 1993 legislative elections, which suggests that a more left-wing candidate, better able to appeal to the majority of the party rank and file, stands a better chance of being chosen leader when the party is in opposition. At the time of writing (late 2002), of the four leading contenders for the job of party leader, François Hollande and Henri Emmanueli appeared better placed to win over their more 'Blairite' rivals, the former finance ministers Dominique Strauss-Kahn and Laurent Fabius (also a former prime minister).

Despite the criticisms by some – in particular Anglo-American – observers following the outcome of the first ballot of the presidential election and the high abstention rates in the legislative elections (due in part to voter fatigue), the French electoral system is unlikely to be changed. As discussed in the last chapter, the political system of the Fifth Republic more generally has proved remarkably durable. The change from the *septennat* to *quinquennat* has, if anything, increased the president-centred nature of both the parliamentary election campaign and the regime. With parliamentary elections to follow presidential elections, the chances of cohabitation occurring as regularly as it did during the past 20 years appear slim. After three periods of cohabitation and weak French presidents, the semi-presidential nature of the Fifth Republic has been reinforced.

The most amazing feature of the elections was the overwhelming nature of Chirac's victory. The day after the first ballot of the legislative elections, *Le Monde* claimed that 'never in [France's] political history [had] there been, to the benefit of one person, such an alignment of the planets of our system'. With a strong majority in government behind him, Chirac and his staff at the Elysée Palace were in a position to dominate government policy making for the next 5 years. This was the first time since the 1970s that the right was set to govern on its own for a full term – an abrupt turn-around from Chirac's weak position in cohabitation over the previous 5 years and the damage done to his political reputation by quite credible accusations of corruption.

JACQUES CHIRAC: A CONTROVERSIAL POLITICAL SURVIVOR

Chirac has been the leading figure on the French right ever since President Georges Pompidou annointed his 'bulldozer' – Pompidou's nickname for Chirac, who got things done – as his chosen successor. Chirac's success owed a great deal to Pompidou's patronage but also to his own political style and character. Over the years he has variously been described as impressively flexible ideologically, not very preoccupied with ideas, and a 'man of the people' with a good feeling for the mood of the French public, capable of demonstrating a nearly constant *bonhomie*. The comedy television programme *Les Guignols de l'Info* – the 'Spitting Image' imitation in France – has long portrayed Chirac as a blunderer with no fixed agenda apart from achieving power for power's sake. He also worked hard for the people of his Corrèze fiefdom, implementing a large number of generous public works to ensure their constant loyalty.

Chirac became leader of the Gaullist UDR upon the death of Pompidou in 1974 and re-established it as the RPR in 1976. He served as prime minister between 1974 and 1976 but resigned because of disagreements over economic policy with the UDF president, Giscard d'Estaing. Chirac then became the first elected mayor of Paris in 1977, a post he held until 1994. He was an active mayor, greatly improving the muncipal services of the city, famous for keeping the city clean (thanks to the green 'pooper scoopers') and promoting Paris abroad. Chirac served as prime minister again from 1986 to 1988 and, having failed to attain the post in 1988, was elected president in 1995. His 'outsider's' victory in the first ballot of the 1995 presidential elections over the leading candidate on the right, Prime Minister Edouard Balladur, demonstrated Chirac's impressive political skills as he positioned himself as the candidate to heal the social divisions of France and defend the country's generous social security system.

As mayor of Paris for 17 years, he used his office to consolidate his position in the RPR and strengthen the party. He created a very 'well-oiled' system: giving jobs to the boys and their offspring and – it has been widely claimed – using public funds from the city of Paris to create fictitious jobs and finance party debt, the restoration of his chateau in his Corrèze fiefdom and even family holidays. There have been further accusations of influence-peddling, money given directly to Chirac and his family or to the RPR. It has also been claimed that he used his influence to ensure that his chateau be classified an historic monument so that all the work undertaken on it would be tax deductible.

Rumours of corruption continued to hound Chirac following his election to the presidency in 1995, when former associates came forward to disclose the extent of illegal activities in Chirac's city hall and RPR officials were brought to trial, including the wife of Chirac's successor as mayor of Paris, Jean Tibéri, and the former treasurer of the RPR. Police investigations into the misuse of public funds during Chirac's time as mayor have, however, been hampered by numerous missing files. Investigations into his activities by journalists and magistrates have also been hindered. One journalist was briefly incarcerated, while the magistrate Eric Halphen, investigating from 1994 to 2001 into the illegal transfer by the Paris mayor's office of funds for social housing to the RPR, was repeatedly obstructed in his task by city of Paris officials, spied upon for a prolonged period and finally blocked in his efforts by Chirac himself who, claiming the president's right to immunity, refused to go on the stand to testify (see Halphen's book *Sept ans de solitude* (2002)). An effort to impeach Chirac in 2001 was blocked by the Constitutional Council on the grounds that impeachment of a president could only arise in the event of a treasonable offence.

In the lead-up to the 2002 presidential elections, the numerous accusations of corruption did not, however, become a major campaign issue upon which the other leading candidates could monopolise. Amazing though it may be for a British or American audience, French political culture does not tolerate such mud-slinging. Moreover, famous French TV journalists tend not to engage in the kind of aggressive interviewing found in the UK (*à la* Jeremy Paxman). Nonetheless, the producers of *Les Guignols de l'Info* certainly felt up to the task and branded Chirac 'Super Liar' (*Super-menteur*), dressing his puppet in a Superman costume. Less than a year before the elections, Chirac's former chauffeur, Jean-Claude Leaumont, also broke ranks, publishing an account of life on the road with Chirac, and focusing on the large number of women Chirac had sexual encounters with, as well as his – now infamous – rapidity in the act, earning him the sobriquet *trois minutes douche compris*. The loyal wife, Bernadette Chirac, wrote and published her own book, defending her husband and explaining the difficulty of being married to such a handsome, famous and powerful man whom women apparently find irresistible. In a Gallic culture still tinged which a strong dose of *machoisme*, such revelations were unlikely to hurt Chirac's chances at the polls.

Chirac's victory as the candidate to save France from the likes of Jean-Marie Le Pen sits uncomfortably with the sheer weight of evidence of corruption building up against him. Many French voters opted for Chirac out of duty but with considerable regret. Chirac now remains protected by his cloak of immunity until 2007. However, with no statute of limitations in France, there remains a good chance that the president will not enjoy a peaceful retirement.

ORGANISED INTERESTS

The claims made in the 1960s by academics Stanley Hoffmann (1963) and Michel Crozier (1964) that the individualist French were much less likely to join collective organisations than their Anglo-American and Northern European counterparts have become increasingly less true. Historically, the political activity of associations was regarded with suspicion by public opinion generally and by politicians infused with a republican ethos which saw the role of the state as upholding the 'general' interest over the sectional. The French still remain somewhat less inclined to join associations than Americans (50 per cent versus 73 per cent). However, much of this difference can be explained by low French membership in religious organisations and trade unions. Association membership in France is today at a similar level to Germany. Indeed, the number of associations created annually during the 1990s has far exceeded the number for the 1970s (with 62 987 associations established in 1997). Public opinion has become much more favourable than was previously the case, a development linked in part to increasing mistrust of the political classes and the competence of state authorities. Governments themselves – in need of advice from groups affected by public policy – have, since the start of the Fifth Republic, also sought to encourage the expansion of associational activity. The term 'association' itself refers to groups formed for the purposes of collective endeavour as defined by the 1901 law that established free association in France to be registered with the public authorities. Most associations have little political relevance – 27 per cent related to sports and 9 per cent to culture or music (Suleiman 1995). However, many seek, at least in part, to influence public policy: from gay action groups to hunting associations. Here we focus on the four families of associations representing occupational interests which have had the most significant political role during the life of the Fifth Republic: business associations, trade unions, agricultural organisations and teachers' associations.

MEDEF (*le Mouvement des Entreprises de France*) – until 1998 the CNPF (*Conseil National du Patronat Français*) or *Patronat* – is the national business association representing over 900 000 companies of varying types and size. Since the late 1960s, the organisation has been a confederation with the authority to sign agreements with the state and trade unions that are binding on its affiliates. While MEDEF is a powerful organisation, its position in relation to the state has often been undermined by the legacy of *pantouflage*. Where many senior managers of the biggest firms are former civil servants and maintain close links to the state, government can bypass the confederation and deal directly with these managers and sectoral trade associations. MEDEF's power is also somewhat undermined by several smaller semi-autonomous organisations which have arisen over the years because of the feeling that the *Patronat* was excessively biased in favour of big business: thus the *Confédération Générale des Petites et Moyennes Entreprises* (CGPME) and *Confédération Intersyndicale de Défense–Union Nationale des Artisans et Travailleurs Indépendants* (CID–UNATI). The role of MEDEF's leadership is particularly difficult: on the one hand it must work with government to retain its influence while on the other it must stand up for the interests of its membership and oppose government policy. In recent years MEDEF has played an increasing public and publicised role in its efforts to shape public policy, especially with regard to its opposition to the Jospin government's 35-hour week and support for major reforms to the social security system.

Trade unions (*syndicats*) in France are noteworthy for their strong political allegiances, divisions, poor organisation, weakness and militancy. The unions include the following:

- *Confédération Générale du Travail* (CGT): the oldest union, strong in industry and officially communist with historically strong links to the Communist Party, with an estimated membership of 700 000 in the 1990s, dominant in the *conseils de prud'hommes* (labour dispute tribunals) with 33 per cent of the votes cast in their elections, a decline on previous years
- *Confédération Française Démocratique du Travail* (CFDT): traditionally linked to the Socialist Party – although more ambiguously so over the past decade – with an estimated membership of between 500 000 and 700 000 in the 1990s; 25 per cent of the votes in elections to the *conseils de prud'hommes*
- *Force Ouvrière* (FO): the result of a split from the CGT in 1948, emphasises pragmatic collective bargaining over ideologically inspired mobilisation, estimated membership of 500 000 in the 1990s and just above 20 per cent of the votes in elections to the *conseils de prud'hommes* (an increase since the 1970s)
- *Confédération Française des Travailleurs Chrétiens* (CFTC): the nominally Christian trade union, much smaller membership than the big three and only 8 per cent of the vote in the *conseils de prud'hommes* elections
- *Confédération Générale des Cadres* (CGC): the leading union for managers with 6 per cent of the vote in the elections to the *conseils de prud'hommes*.

France is among the least unionised countries in Western Europe, with less than 8 per cent of the workforce belonging to a union – according to the unions' own problematic figures (compared to 30 per cent in the UK). Various explanations for the comparative weakness of French unions have been given over the years: the large number of small firms, the history of partisan factionalism and disunity, the absence of regulations (such as closed shop) that can make union membership compulsory in other countries. The decline in membership over the past three decades has also been steeper in France than in other European countries (down to 8 per cent from 23 per cent in 1975), which has been attributed in large part to structural changes in the economy, notably the decline in heavy industry and the rise of the service sector as the principal source of employment and the increased number of women in the workforce. The comparatively great decline in France is owing to relatively high unemployment (reaching 13 per cent in 1997), the increased insecurity of employment, the declining role of the state in the economy and its reduced interventionism in industrial conflict.

The French associations enjoying the highest profile in the rest of the world are from the agricultural sector. The *Fédération Nationale des Syndicats d'Exploitants Agricoles* (FNSEA) is the top association representing the *département* farmers' federations, sectoral producer groups and other associations, principally the FNSEA's youth branch, the *Centre Nationale des Jeunes Agriculteurs* (CNJA). As with trade unions, support for agricultural organisations has also been divided along ideological lines and other smaller organisations have Communist, Socialist and right-wing links. French farmers are infamous for their militancy: blocking roads with tractors, organising large demonstrations in towns and cities and harassing public officials. The FNSEA is also known for its close relationship with government, unique among French associations, through which it has 'co-managed' the agricultural modernisation process since the late 1950s. Thanks to the FNSEA's strength, policies have been developed at the domestic and European levels (through the Common Agricultural Policy, CAP) to make modernisation less painful to the farming population and to slow down its decline. Modernisation has also transformed France into the world's second largest exporter of agricultural produce (Keeler 1987). Although the FNSEA enjoys the support of a large percentage of French farmers (approximately 44 per cent in the early twenty-first century, which is substantially higher than it was in the 1950s), total membership has been in constant decline over the past half-century with the general drop in the farming population (from more than 20 per cent in the 1960s to slightly more than 5 per cent today). Moreover, the FNSEA enjoys the support of a smaller percentage of farmers than the major farmers' unions in Germany or Britain.

The *Fédération de l'Education Nationale* (FEN) was until the early 1990s the leading association of French teachers, with numerous semi-autonomous affiliates including notably the *Syndicat Nationale des Instituteurs* (SNI), which represents primary school teachers, and the *Syndicat Nationale d'Enseignement Supérieur* (SNES) for secondary school teachers. While FEN gradually lost its predominant position (down from 77 per cent of French education employees in the 1950s to the low 40s by the 1990s), it remained the most representative public-sector union in France (Ambler 1996). FEN suffered from partisan div-isiveness among its affiliates with a marked division over the years between itself and the SNI, both dominated by Socialists, and the SNES, dominated by Communists. In the early 1990s, divisiveness resulted in formal institutional division: the SNES and other affiliates were expelled from FEN and formed the *Fédération Syndicale Unitaire* (FSU), while FEN was restructured and renamed the *Syndicat de l'Enseignement Supérieur* (SE). The FSU has since over-taken the SE as the most supported association.

NEW SOCIAL MOVEMENTS

Over the past three decades several new social movements (NSMs) have arisen in France to promote particular agendas on specific issues – from the environment to the concerns of women, ethnic minorities and homosexuals – and shape public policy. In several cases, government has helped these move-ments by providing financial support to involved associations. Probably the most high-profile NSM has focused upon the issue of racism. Support for it has arisen in direct reaction to the rise of the National Front. Anti-racist organ-isations, most predominantly *SOS Racisme*, have organised hundreds of demonstrations throughout France over the past two decades. These demon-strations reached their peak in the late 1980s, when at least four *SOS Racisme* demonstrations attracted over 200 000 participants. Although the demon-strations of the 1990s were less well attended, anti-racist organisations still succeeded in mobilising tens of thousands against the Pasqua laws on immi-gration (Duyvendak 1995) and in favour of illegal immigrants (*les sans-papiers*) (Siméant 1998) and most recently played a major role in galvanising street protests against Jean-Marie Le Pen and the National Front between the first and second ballots of the 2002 presidential elections.

The environmental movement has been another important NSM, although considerably less successful in France than in several West European coun-tries, notably Germany. The relative lack of success can best be explained by partisan division and the near uniform support for nuclear power among French political parties. The success of the *Ecologistes* in the 1989 European Parliament elections and of the Green Party in the 1997 legislative elections and the 1999 European elections has increased the profile of the movement, while growing public concern over genetically modified foods has attracted many new members over the past half-decade. The most significant environ-mentalist organisation has been the *Fédération Française des Sociétés de la Protection de la Nature*, with ministry of environment subsidies and a member-ship of nearly 800 000 during the 1990s. More radical groups include the anti-nuclear energy group *Réseau pour un Avenir Sans Nucléaire* (RASN).

The anti-globlisation movement which has gained such a high profile in other West European countries has assumed a uniquely Gallic character in France which fuses with a long-standing anti-Americanism, particularly on the left. Many French people, of all ages, are concerned about the economic, social and cultural impact of 'globalisation' – notably, the increased exposure of the country to international market forces and global (read 'American') culture. A rather amorphous movement of defiance has arisen with sporadic well-supported protests of varying forms directed against obvious manifestations of the global economy and culture. The anti-GATT protests of 1993 in defence of French farmers had a strong element of anti-globalisation/anti-American feeling about them. Most famously, a farmer from Larzac, José Bové, has engaged in – and been arrested for – well-publicised attacks on a local McDonald's restaurant and other symbols of global culture. While few French men and women have taken a leading role in the wider international protest movement – so noticeable at European and international summits of world leaders – the progress in Internet use in France (taking off only since 1997) has made participation in the international movement easier than ever before.

With the slow economic growth of the 1990s and rising levels of unemployment for most of the decade, new NSMs arose, focusing on more materialistic concerns of particular importance to young people: education funding and unemployment. In 1999 and 2000, secondary school students engaged in street protests to demand more funding for secondary education. The *Mouvement des Chômeurs* of the winter of 1997/8 became the most active movement of its kind in Western Europe, mobilising unemployed people and their supporters from a number of different organisations to participate in street protests in major French cities, including the illegal occupation of UNEDIC (benefit) centres (Combesque 1998). This movement centred around the issue of employment as well as of access to a level of social participation denied the long-term unemployed by lack of resources. Diverse collective acts of protest have taken place over the last few years which reflect the all-too-material concerns of different social groups in addition to occupational groups.

Other French NSMs have been noteworthy for their relative lack of success and weak political position: notably those representing women and homosexuals. The French women's movement has been relatively weak compared both to other French NSMs and other West European women's movements. The *Mouvement de la Libération des Femmes* (MLF) and *Choisir* fought actively to encourage the government to push through a liberal abortion law (achieved in 1974) and create special government ministries dedicated to women's rights (as existed from 1974 to 1986 and from 1988 to 1993). More recently, the women's movement spear-headed the campaign to embrace the principle of *parité* in French elections to increase the female presence in elected assemblies at the different levels of government (see pp. 95–8). The relative lack of success of the French women's movement has been the subject of debate, with explanations focusing upon partisan divisions and cultural resistance to feminism (Mazur 1995). Gay organisations only began to mobilise successfully in France over the past 15 years with the rise of the AIDS issue (*Sida*). The arguably slow reaction of the government to the problem of AIDS in France encouraged gay organisations to improve awareness of the disease. The first anti-AIDS group, called *Vaincre le Sida*, was created in 1983, followed by *Aides*, founded in 1984 by Daniel Defert, the partner of the philosopher Michel Foucault who died of AIDS.

ANOTHER MAY '68?

Crozier famously claimed in *La Société bloquée* (1964) that for diverse sociological and psychological reasons, French society was incapable of far-reaching reform and changed only through periodic violent upheavals. May 1968 is seen as a manifestation of this thesis: inflationary wage settlements and the expansion of higher education came about only as a result of widespread demonstrations and strikes by students, workers and various other groups and the occupation of universities, factories and offices which paralysed France. While recognising the dangers of prediction in the social sciences, we would argue that despite major structural problems in the French state, economy and society more generally, another May 1968 is unlikely, at least for the next few decades. Sociologists and political scientists disagree as to the precise causes of May '68. However, most accept that it was the culmination of almost a decade of low inflation, austerity and underfunding and overcrowding in French universities, despite strong economic growth, and of ideological tensions fuelled by the exclusion of the left from power at the national level. Since May '68, France has witnessed thousands of mass demonstrations but never on the same scale and only occasionally nationwide. Major demonstrations against the GATT Blair House accord of December 1992 took place during the first half of 1993, led by agricultural organisations which sought to protect the interests of French farmers against trade liberalisation but joined by many more opposing trade liberalisation and 'Americanisation' more generally. In the spring of 1994, university students went on strike in opposition to the proposed *contrat d'insertion professionnel*, widely labelled the *Smic-Jeune* because the policy would have allowed firms to hire young people on an initial salary below the minimum wage. This policy – which the government dropped to avert widespread student protest – would certainly have helped to lower youth unemployment, then reaching record levels.

France came closest to repeating May '68 during the widespread demonstrations and strikes following the announcement of the Juppé Plan on social security reform on 15 November 1995. The proposed reforms were designed to help France cut public-sector spending sustainably, a necessity in itself – long overdue – given the constant rise in social security spending, but also a requirement to enable France to meet the convergence criteria of the Maastricht Treaty and qualify to participate in EMU. The announced reforms came, however, after 4 years of economic recession, record high interest rates and rising unemployment. Several trade unions – notably the CGT – called for a general strike against the main element of the plan: the proposed reforms reducing the role of the administrative councils in the management of social insurance funds and increasing the role of the National Assembly (thus the government), a measure which was intended to improve control over social security spending. At the same time, the *cheminots* – the train and metro conductors – went on strike against the proposed reform to their very generous pension plan to align them with others in the public sector. The urban centres of France were paralysed, while many groups – notably workers and French youth – protested in large and frequently violent demonstrations throughout France. French public opinion, while accepting the necessity of such reforms, expressed considerable sympathy for the strikers (Sofres 1996). Prime Minister Alain Juppé, after whom the plan was – perhaps unwisely – named, back-tracked on the pension reforms (and announcing these at the same time as the plan was probably his main political error), but the plan itself was kept intact and introduced gradually over the next year. Some strikes were called, but these were more limited and less debilitating to the government.

We would conclude unsurprisingly that the French propensity to demonstrate, protest and strike to protect sectional interests is great. Over the last half-decade alone, France has seen major demonstrations by NSMs and professional groups of a wide variety. While protest on behalf of sectional interests is hardly new to French society, the number, duration and size of the protests have increased, even though the capacity of the French state to address the concerns of most of those protesting has declined. However, few protests demand a dramatic transformation of French society and/or the political system. Collective protest has become a much more 'normal' part of French politics than ever before (Galland and Lemel 1998; Groux 1998), demonstrating that France is experiencing the same trend towards 'contentious politics' as all advanced democratic societies (Lafargue 1998; Meyer and Tarrow 1998), which also, arguably, demonstrates the democratic vigour of these societies (Perrineau 1994, 1998). Thus, France is less unusual in its protest culture than it perhaps once was. In the 'movement society' the NSMs 'combine disruptive and conventional activities and forms of organization, while institutional actors like interest groups and parties increasingly engage in contentious behavior' (Meyer and Tarrow 1998: 25). In France, current and future governments are unlikely to ignore the lessons of the past: principally that they must tread carefully, engage actively with both organised interests and social movements and introduce reform gradually. Juppé and his ministers engaged in widespread consultations on social security reform prior to the announcement of the Juppé Plan, but they forgot the vital element of gradualism, which – given the massive public backlash to the proposed reforms – future governments are unlikely to ignore.

REPRESENTATION ISSUES: FEWER WHITE MALES PLEASE ...

The 1999 parité reforms

The 2002 legislative elections have been historically noteworthy as the first operating under the legal obligation of *parité* established by a law adopted in May 2000, which requires each party to run an equal number of male and female candidates (give or take a 2 per cent difference) in the 577 constituencies.

The law also requires an equal number of candidates from the two sexes in elections using the PR system with party lists: municipal, regional, European and some Senate elections. The insufficient presence of women in national political life has affected all countries, but the French feminist movement is known for its relative lack of success in many realms, including the representation of women, and France has faced a particularly serious shortage. Prior to 2002, France had one of the lowest percentages of female elected politicians in the national legislature in Western Europe and one of the lowest among all liberal democracies. Between 1973 and 1993, women never held more than 8 per cent of National Assembly seats (with a lower proportion in the indirectly elected Senate and not much higher in local government assemblies). In 1999, the year the constitution was amended to incorporate the principle of *parité*, a record – but still disappointing – 10.9 per cent of National Assembly seats were held by women, 5.9 per cent of Senate seats and only 7.8 per cent of regional assembly seats. Only 8 per cent of France's mayors were women and only one regional assembly president. The publication of comparative data by the Inter-Parliamentary Union in 1991 demonstrated that France had fallen to joint eightieth place in this regard (with Liberia and Uruguay) (out of 171 single chambers or lower houses) at only just above the world average (of 10.10 per cent) and near the bottom of the EU pile, apart from Greece. When, in 1993, the percentage of women fell back to 6 per cent in the National Assembly (approaching the 5.7 per cent elected in 1945 when women were first allowed to vote and hold office) much of the French political class reacted with alarm and a process was started to introduce legal changes to increase the number of female representatives.

France has been one of the few countries to adopt special laws to increase the number of female candidates and the only one to date to adopt the legal principle of equal numbers. The decision to embark on such a major legal development, which required the modification of the French constitution, was owing in part to the very poor position of France in the world league tables for female representation. However, this alone cannot explain the decision to make such an unprecedented move, particularly in a country that has historically resisted all forms of 'affirmative action'. Lovecy (2000) argues that it is also necessary to examine three other developments: the dynamics of feminist mobilisation for new gender-based citizenship rights; the translation of such claimed rights into the arenas of party and electoral competition (especially in the presidential elections and in the competition between local political elites); and the wider resonance these claims achieved in French public opinion. The idea of using legislation to diminish the gender imbalance in representation has circulated in French politics since the 1970s and was first brought to centre stage by President Giscard d'Estaing. Attempts to introduce quotas in parties achieved only limited success. This was more politically manageable for the less important second-order PR-list elections to the regional assemblies and the European Parliament (EP). In the June 1999 EP elections, several lists ensured equal female candidates and representatives through the use of the zipper model (alternating male and female candidates).

Despite their poor presence in the National Assembly, throughout the 1980s and 1990s there was a growing number of women ministers, thanks to the placing of some particularly talented female candidates in relatively safe seats. Several women have become leading national political figures: Michèle Alliot-Marie (RPR), Simone Veil (UDF), Edith Cresson, Elisabeth Guigou, Catherine Trautmann and Martine Aubry (Socialist) and Dominique Voynet (Green) spring to mind. There was also a degree of tokenism. In the first Juppé government a record number of women were appointed – mostly junior ministers – only for several to lose their posts in a reshuffle a few months later. Edith Cresson's rather disappointing short term as prime minister (1991–2) did not establish a very positive precedent.

From an early date in the 1970s, the legislative option was considered a desirable development. Françoise Giroud, the UDF junior minister for *Condition Féminine,* introduced a law that would force municipal candidate lists to include no more than 85 per cent of either sex. This would have been adopted but for the victory of François Mitterrand, which ended the legislative programme of the right. The Socialist government subsequently reintroduced legislation requiring municipal lists to have a maximum of 75 per cent of any one gender. However, this was struck down as unconstitutional by the Constitutional Council in 1982, a ruling which contributed to the realisation that constitutional reform was necessary for affirmative action to be permissible under the law. A decade later, in 1992, a campaign was launched by several organisations advocating the constitutionalisation of the principle of *représentation paritaire* – that is, of all elective offices being filled by equal numbers of men and women – in order to renew French democracy, ushering in a new form of democratic polity, *une démocratie paritaire* (Gaspard *et al.* 1992). These organisations produced several studies on the issue, including *Association Choisir*'s major 1994 document, *Femmes: moitié de la terre, moitié du pouvoir* ('Women: half the world, half the power'). These were joined by a growing number of government and academic studies. The impressive campaign increased the popularity of the rather abstract principle of gender parity among leading politicians on both the right and the left and also across a very broad swathe of public opinion (Sofres 1998) despite the problematic application of the principle to France's two-ballot electoral system based on single-member constituencies. The poor showing for women in the 1993 elections contributed further to the momentum behind the movement.

The parliamentary debate on both the concept of *parité* and its related principle of *représentation paritaire* was long and drawn out. On 28 June 1999 the members of France's lower and upper chambers, meeting in congress at Versailles, endorsed by a very substantial majority – 745 in favour and only 43 against – a double amendment to the constitution's preamble introducing the principle. (The irony here should be noted: a country that has long scorned positive discrimination as fundamentally contrary to the principles of the equal treatment of citizens has become the first in Western Europe to embrace a limited form of such discrimination in its constitution.) Legislation introducing *parité* was adopted less than a year later. The 2002 elections to the National Assembly thus involved record numbers of female candidates although – because of the large number of women placed in constituencies where parties did not have safe seats – the actual number of women elected was a very disappointing 71, only 9 more than the out-going assembly and 12.3 per cent of the total rather than 10.7. This was hardly a victory for equal representation. Moreover, the Raffarin government remains overwhelmingly male, with only three female cabinet ministers and six female junior ministers. In National Assembly elections the application of *parité* clearly does not mean equal representation. However, the second-order elections using PR list-systems represent a much better opportunity for change, with the zipper principle applied for every candidate or at most every six candidates. The political training provided to increased numbers of women at the local level will almost certainly improve the profile of more female politicians and spill over into improved representation in the National Assembly. It remains to be seen how long this spill-over process will take.

The under-representation of French ethnic minorities: a case of 'institutional racism'?

The principles that encourage the introduction of *parité* for female represen-tation have not been applied to ethnic minorities. The large and growing eth-nic minority population in metropolitan France has little or no political representation at all levels of government. In the current National Assembly (since June 2002) there is no black or *beur* member – the long-standing single black member, Kofi Yamgnane, a Socialist from Finistère, having lost his seat in the parliamentary elections. Two junior ministers of Arab extraction, from the French Senate, were appointed to the Raffarin government, marking a high point in ethnic minority representation which serves principally to underline the seriousness of the problem.

There is no precise data on the current number of ethnic minority repre-sentatives, but, by all accounts, minorities are seriously under-represented. One study counted 67 local councillors nationwide in the 1989–95 municipal mandate (Geisser 1997). Between 1989 and 1995 the municipal councils of the *département* of Seine St-Denis, north of Paris, had only 10 ethnic minority councillors between them, although the area has one of the largest foreign-born populations (the actual population of ethnic minorities being con-siderably larger although precise figures are unavailable given France's colour-blind census). Other areas with large immigrant populations, such as Lyon, the industrial north-east (Alsace and Lorraine) and the north, had sim-ilar rates of representation. The northern industrial town of Roubaix is one of a very small number of partial exceptions: here 9 per cent of the councillors are of ethnic minority background for an estimated 35 per cent of the population. The 1995 municipal elections saw the loss of the limited gains that had been made in 1989, with the number of ethnic minority candidates dropping for all the main parties, while the situation improved little in the 2001 elections.

Ethnic minority electoral participation reached its peak in the lead-up to the 1989 municipal elections, in the wake of the *beur* movement. This was a nationwide protest movement started in 1982 by second-generation North African youths rebelling against a wave of racist violence (Jazouli 1986). It led to the creation of influential groups such as *SOS Racisme* and *France Plus* and put the issue of the political incorporation of ethnic minorities on the political agenda. However, success has been limited: more ethnic minority candidates were included on the municipal slates but only a total of 67 ethnic minority councillors were elected.

Local representation is particularly significant for ethnic minorities in that it normally precedes representation at the national level. Local mandates provide a training ground for future national office. Garbaye (2000: 3) writes that 'political incorporation is both an indicator and a factor of social incorporation in the host society. Hence, the problem of the relatively low [ethnic minority] representation in French cities is a key element to the understanding of the political processes that underpin immigrant incorporation in France' (see also Poinsot (1993) and Geisser (1997)).

How can we explain the relative absence of local political representation of ethnic minorities in French cities? Is this a matter of 'institutional racism' – roughly defined as embedded discriminatory practices in French electoral processes, parties and institutions of government? Or more simply, is this a manifestation of a generally racist society? Several specific causal factors can be evoked (Garbaye 2000). First, the large majority of first-generation immigrants lack the right to vote, leaving political participation to the relatively young and inexperienced second-generation ethnic minorities, which has greatly weakened the ethnic minority voice in electoral politics. Second, some observers (Lapeyronnie 1993) argue that insufficient time has passed since the arrival of the first significant waves of ethnic minority immigration (in the 1950s and 1960s) and the social incorporation process (in comparison to that of the UK) has further to go. Third, the socio-economic profile of the large majority of ethnic minorities – working class, less educated and more likely to be unemployed – corresponds to the groups most likely to abstain in elections. Fourth, some observers (Stora 1992) argue that cultural factors must also be considered to explain poor participation rates in elections. Democratic traditions in the countries from which the large majority of ethnic minority immigrants have come are non-existent or limited, and this has translated institutionally into tight control in France by the *Amicales*, ethnic minority associations controlled by local foreign consulates. In the case of Algerians, it has also been argued that participation in French political life is further inhibited by the war against France in the 1950s which alienated many from French institutions and provoked deep and long-standing divisions within the Algerian community in France (Stora 1992).

Garbaye (2000) offers an additional explanation focusing upon political opportunity structures (POS). He argues that 'the pattern of alliances available to ethnic minorities in French political arenas has not been conducive to the emergence of [political elites in their communities] and to their subsequent election as municipal councillors' (ibid.: 4). The lack of POS is a problem at both the national and local levels. The national debate on immigration has been constructed in such a way as to discourage the political participation of ethnic minorities at the local level. From the early days of National Front electoral success in 1983, the major political parties (Socialists included) have sought to distinguish themselves from the interests of ethnic minorities and to keep the issue of immigration out of the electoral arena despite the public's concern (Weil 1991; Schain 1988). This has contributed to the decline in the *beur* movement and has hindered other forms of mobilisation. Significantly, the Socialist Party completely dropped its earlier plans to grant voting rights for all foreigners in local elections and silenced debate on the matter.

At the local level, the rise of the National Front further reinforced the direction of debate towards immigrants as objects of policy – Are there too many? Is it possible to assimilate them and how should one go about doing so? – as opposed to citizens/consumers of policy as in Britain (Crowley 1993). As a result, the continuing tendency in French political life is to exclude immigrants and ethnic minorities more generally. Local structures have also had an impact upon ethnic minority participation. In most local government, the party controlling the local council tends to wield a great amount of control, stifling the possibility for grass-roots movements to influence party policies. Where political parties are relatively weak and there is a volatility of party alliances combined with a relatively high level of ethnic minority community and associational activity, there also tend to be more ethnic minority councillors and in more important positions. The infrequency of this political opportunity structure combined with the numerical importance of the ethnic minority population has led to the development of an ethnic minority elite in a only a handful of cities.

CONCLUSION

The disastrously low numbers of women in the 2002–7 National Assembly and the disappointing number of female members in the Raffarin government mean that the *parité* law has not spelled the end of one of the most significant political debates in France during the 1990s. The strikingly low numbers of ethnic minorities at all levels of government, however, has barely sparked any significant inter-party debate in France. Low representation remains a simmering problem, which the currently high levels of ethnic minority political apathy may work to contain, but only in the short term. The large number of immigrants granted citizenship annually and the growing ethnic minority population are bound eventually to lead to increased political weight. However, we would predict that mobilisation of a reanimated *beur* movement (or rather a wider, more inclusive equivalent) covering all ethnic minorities will almost certainly be the only way that the issue is forced onto the political agenda – over-riding the electoral concerns of the mainstream parties and the rhetoric of the National Front. Protest will maintain its crucial role in French political history, shaping political parties and political institutions alike.

5

CITIZENSHIP, NATIONALISM AND NATIONAL IDENTITY

Throughout my life, I have entertained a certain idea of France. My affective side naturally imagines France, like the princess of fairy tales or the madonna of frescos, destined for an eminent and exceptional destiny. I have, instinctively, the impression that Providence has created France either for great successes or for disastrous misfortunes. If, however, it ever happens that mediocrity marks its deeds and acts, I have the feeling that it is an absurd anomaly, imputable to the flaws of the French, not to the genius of the motherland. But also the positive side of my spirit convinces me that France is not really itself unless it is of the first rank; that only major enterprises are able to counter-balance the ferments of dissolution that its people carries within itself; that our country, being as it is, among other nations, as they are, needs, on pain of mortal danger, to set its sights high and maintain a good posture. In a word, to my mind, France cannot be France without greatness [grandeur]. (Charles de Gaulle, Mémoires de guerre, *authors' translation)*

France has an exceptional place in the development of ideas, concepts and practices related to citizenship, national identity and nationality. The very concept of citizenship, the very idea of the sovereign nation and national sovereignty, assumed the meaning they have today during the seminal period and sequence of events and processes known as the French Revolution.

THE COMPLEXITIES OF FRENCH NATIONALISM: *NATIONALISME OUVERT* AND *NATIONALISME FERMÉ*?

The word *nationaliste* (probably of British origin, from the English word 'nationalist') seems to have first appeared in French in 1798, in a text written by the Abbé Barruel, who sought to stigmatise the immorality of the Jacobin version of patriotism. According to Barruel, *'le nationalisme prit la place de*

*l'amour général … Alors, il fut permis de mépriser les étrangers, de les tromper et de
les offenser'* (Girardet 1983: 7). The word was used again on various occasions
in the nineteenth century, but did not gain anything like universal popular
usage – in fact, it was ignored by most dictionaries of the time. It was during
the last decade of the nineteenth century that the adjective *nationaliste* (as
well as the noun *nationalisme*) started to designate a political tendency perceived as appertaining to the right or even the extreme right. Its introduction
in this more concrete sense is usually attributed to an article ('La querelle des
nationalistes et des cosmopolites') by Maurice Barrès in *Le Figaro* of 4 July
1892 (Girardet 1983: 8).

It cannot be over-stressed, however, that the term *nationalisme* is ambivalent. In the first place, it is used to refer to the 'nationalism' of peoples which
aspire to the creation of a sovereign nation-state of their own – in other
words, *nationalisme* is used to designate the movement of 'nationalities'
which aspired to liberate themselves from the yoke of multiethnic empires
(Habsburg, Russian, Ottoman) in nineteenth-century Europe and which
culminated in the creation of a number of new nation-states in the aftermath
of the First World War. The term *nationalisme* is used with the same meaning
in connection with the various twentieth-century liberation movements in
the non-European colonies which revolted against the colonising powers
(including France) in successive waves after the Second World War.

Yet, in the second place, the same term is used (especially from the
Dreyfus Affair onwards) to characterise the various doctrines which, within
a constituted and sovereign state (in our case, France), subordinate everything else to the exclusive interests of the nation-state, its power, grandeur or
prestige. To use Raoul Girardet's words, in this latter sense, associated in
France with the influence of Maurice Barrès and then Charles Maurras,
'nationalism will designate a system of thought essentially based on the affirm-
ation of the primacy, in the political order, of the defence of "national" values
and "national" interests'. Thus, 'in the political realm and in the context of an
already historically constituted nation-state, nationalism can also be defined
as *the prioritary solicitude to preserve the independence, to maintain the integrity
of the sovereignty and to affirm the greatness of that nation-state*. In the moral
realm it seems to amount to *the exaltation of national sentiment'* (Girardet
1983: 8–9, authors' translation). In the case of France (but also in other cases)
discussions of nationalism are additionally complicated by the need to
be aware of the fact that whoever studies nationalism should not always
take the statements or self-descriptions of the actors studied (politicians,
political thinkers, writers) at face value. Thus, we need to remember that
besides the *nationalisme des nationalistes*, the nationalism of those politicians,
thinkers or writers who expressly and explicitly claimed to be nationalists,
one needs also to study similar manifestations which amount to nationalism
on the part of actors who did not necessarily define themselves as nationalists. In other words, besides the nationalism of the declared nationalists, the
study of nationalism has to include the diffuse nationalism of those political
and cultural agents or movements who did not claim or accept the label

'nationalist' (often referring to themselves as 'patriots' instead) but whose comportment, statements and beliefs were such that they have to be classified as nationalist according to the definition given above (see Girardet 1983: 9–11).

Given all this, one could be justified in assuming that, having been a clearly recognisable and sovereign state long before the nineteenth century (the century when the wave of national liberation movements broke out), France is bound to have had experience of the second kind of nationalism identified above – the nationalism that emerges within an already existing nation-state and puts the nation, its 'national' values and its presumed interests and greatness above anything else. However, things are more complicated than that. In some very important senses, France is also the country that gave birth to the other kind of nationalism identified earlier, that which arises out of the aspiration of a group of people who see themselves as a 'nation' or 'nationality' to constitute a state of their own. This is due to the decisive influence – directly or indirectly – of the French Revolution on the rest of Europe and the world beyond.

'REPUBLICAN NATIONALISM'

It was in revolutionary France, among the French soldiers fighting the enemies of the Revolution, that the cry *Vive la nation!* replaced the *Vive le Roi!* of previous centuries. Besides the obvious patriotic dimension of the desire to expel the foreign armies from French soil, the exclamation *Vive la nation!* had also, at the same time, the implication that it affirmed the liberty and the equality of the – newly – sovereign people. To the Europe of dynasties it opposed the Europe of nations. Popular sovereignty (the sovereignty of the people within a given state) was combined or confounded with national sovereignty (the freedom of each nation to have its own sovereign state, freedom from foreign rule or yoke). In a Europe (the Europe of the 'old regime') where, up to then, political allegiances and state borders were decided by the vicissitudes of the military conquests of monarchs and by their intermarriages, the French Revolution brought the newfangled notion that political allegiances were a matter of will and choice, that the sovereign in each nation was not the monarch but rather the 'nation', and that membership in the nation was a matter of the will of the members. Theoretically, at least, the nation was now itself the result of the 'general will', a *volonté générale*. And, as the *Déclaration des droits de l'homme et du citoyen* put it explicitly: '*Le principe de toute souveraineté réside essentiellement dans la nation. Nul corps, nul individu ne peut exercer d'autorité qui n'en émane expressément*' (Winock 1990: 12–13).

Now, because it was born out of the ideas and aspirations brought to the fore by the French Revolution, the movement of nationalities (which grew gradually in the early nineteenth century and reached its climax with the European revolutions of 1848–9) at first confounded the principle of nationalities (the nationalist aspiration demanding a separate state of its own for each national group) with the democratic principle (the principle that the people should be sovereign in each state and should elect and be able to eject their governments). This was due both to the common origins of the two principles in the cauldron of the French Revolution and to the fact that the two principles had common enemies at that time (the multiethnic empires of Europe, which were opposing both the national aspirations of the various national groups subject to them and the democratic demands of their most advanced political activists and parties).

One of the results of this merger of national and democratic aspirations was that the most ardent of French patriots or nationalists had no difficulty in identifying the national prestige and *grandeur* of their own nation, France, with the cause of 'democracy', 'the Revolution', 'progress' or 'civilization'. All these things, it seemed to them, were of universal value to all nations, and France was best suited to promote them in the world, to the benefit of the whole of mankind, thanks to its civilising genius and its primacy in the realm of advanced political ideas, proved or exemplified by the French Revolution and its beneficial effects on mankind. Thus, the most striking characteristic of French nationalism for almost a century after the outbreak of the French Revolution had been its universalist pretensions: the conviction of French nationalists and patriots that by promoting the greatness, power and prestige of France they were advancing the cause of humanity as a whole. France being in their eyes the beacon of liberty, democracy and civilisation for the whole of mankind, what was good for France was good for humanity. There is no end to the list of French thinkers, historians and poets who thus combined ardent republican political affiliations at home with a strongly nationalistic frame of mind, all the while believing that their nationalism was compatible with the well-being of other nations and the whole of mankind. The most illustrious and most vociferous among them was republican historian Jules Michelet. In works like *Le Peuple* or various histories of France or of the French Revolution, Michelet sang the greatness of the French nation and its unique contribution to universal human well-being.

This kind of nationalism, republican nationalism, was far from incompatible with other nations' nationalisms and aspirations, in the eyes of its exponents. Very simply, France was the first, the best, the most advanced nation, and it had the right and the duty to aid as well as lead the rest of the world to their own salvation (national and democratic). As Michelet (for whom France was a 'religion') put it, '*Le Dieu des nations a parlé par la France*' (Winock 1990: 4). This missionary conception of French nationalism had been given its specific impetus during the wars of the French Revolution, when French patriots were all too happy to conquer other countries, one by one, and subject them to either French rule or rule by France's *protégés*, all the while being convinced that they were simply 'liberating' these countries from their autocratic rulers by subjecting them to the beneficial rule of the *grande nation*.

Given these revolutionary origins, it is not at all surprising that French republican nationalism in the nineteenth century was rabidly militaristic and completely alien to pacifism. It had itself been born in the battlefields of the first French Revolution, fed by the belief in the superiority of revolutionary ideas and ways of rule, and by the glory associated with the military exploits of the Revolution and its generals. (One of the latter, Napoléon Bonaparte, was to bring French pride in France's military achievements and prowess to its peak between 1796 and 1814, first as a general, then as the first consul, and finally as the emperor.) One of the most vociferous advocates of war in the early 1830s, in the first months and years of the July Monarchy, was Armand Carrel, chief editor of the daily *Le National*. What is most revealing is that Carrel, a staunch liberal who had initially supported wholeheartedly the new 'bourgeois' monarchy under Louis Philippe that was installed in France following the revolution of July 1830, passed gradually to the ranks of the republican opposition, primarily because of his intense frustration at the July Monarchy's 'peace at any price' foreign policy, which he, along with many men of his generation (he was 30 in 1830), born to Napoleonic glories and conquests, regarded as pusillanimous and dishonourable for France. Characteristically, Carrel combined this militant and militarist nationalism with a great concern for the fate of oppressed nationalities (like the Poles) in whose aid he believed France should act militarily.

Later in the nineteenth century, during the Franco-Prussian War, following the defeat of the armies led by Emperor Napoléon III at Sédan (1870), some of the republicans who took office as a provisional government insisted on pursuing the war against the Prussians/Germans at all costs. The most imposing figure of that period was Léon Gambetta. The founders of the new republican regime that emerged slowly in the course of the 1870s out of the ruins of the defeated Second Empire, the Third Republic (including Gambetta himself and later Jules Ferry), accomplished what is still regarded as one of the most successful enterprises in nationalist-patriotic indoctrination in modern history. Besides military defeat itself (traumatic enough for a nation that had come to see itself again as the most powerful in Continental Europe during the second Bonaparte's reign), what had wounded French pride profoundly had been the annexation by the newly established German Empire of two hitherto French provinces, Alsace and (parts of) Lorraine. Amid various debates and theories as to what had been the main causes of France's humiliating defeat at the hands of Bismarck's German soldiers, the new rulers of France initiated a sustained long-term programme of patriotic education of the young generations of Frenchmen using, first and foremost, the educational system. History, geography, morals and civics were all taught in French schools from the perspective of building good patriots ready to sacrifice their lives, if necessary, for the fatherland (including for the liberation of the *provinces perdues*, Alsace and Lorraine). Historians such as Lavisse proved equal to the task by writing intensely nationalistic school textbooks for the French youth. Among other things, this schooling was aimed at promoting the use of the French language everywhere in the country at the expense of the (still widely used) dialects or *patois* (an endeavour already begun by the French Revolution under the instructions of the Abbé

Grégoire). Military drills and 'manly' sports were amply promoted and practised in order to prepare the young for the demands of the inevitable war that would one day need to be fought if the lost provinces were to be recovered and French pride restored. Along with the school system, military conscription was completing the task of turning 'peasants into Frenchmen', to use historian Eugen Weber's felicitous expression (Weber 1979).

'NATIONALISM OF THE RIGHT'

However, this 'republican nationalism' – often referred to also as 'nationalism of the left' (*nationalisme de gauche*) – was not the only manifestation of nationalism to emerge in France. Historians disagree as to the exact turning point, but it seems clear that by the mid-1880s there had emerged another kind of nationalism, a right-wing or conservative nationalism (*nationalisme conservateur*) alongside the republican left's version. This nationalism shifted the centre of attention from the fixation with revenge (*revanche*) abroad (against the Germans who had mutilated France by annexing Alsace and Lorraine) to the redressing of the country's internal order. For the adherents of this 'conservative' nationalism, it was the parliamentary regime itself that constituted the main enemy, the major threat to the French nation. This became the main target of one of conservative nationalism's most ardent early adherents, Paul Déroulède, founder of the *Ligue des patriotes*.

The development that gave concrete expression to the new tendency in French nationalism was the *boulangist* movement, named after General Boulanger. Its meteoric electoral rise between 1886 and 1889 was only matched by its equally rapid collapse after its peak in 1889. The vagueness of Boulanger's message (he was promising *Dissolution, Révision, Constituante* – dissolution of the existing National Assembly, revision of the constitution, and a new Constituent Assembly to draft a new constitution) helped his party to become popular with all sorts of people, from the extreme left to the extreme right (including some precursors of fascism). Within that movement, a new nationalism emerged, whose main tenets were the need for a change of regime, the installation of personal power, of a leader directly representing the national will, without the intermediary of parliament. The common enemy of these nationalists was the parliamentary republic, characterised, as they saw it, by its incessant squabbling, to the detriment of the nation, and the nation's unity and its power.

An even more decisive historical moment that contributed to the consolidation of this new 'conservative' or right-wing nationalism (or *nationalisme integral*, according to some scholars) and led it to extremes was the Dreyfus Affair. Paul Déroulède's *Ligue des patriotes* found its true vocation in mobilising former republicans (even people coming from the former extreme left) in the nationalist and *anti-dreyfusard* cause. Déroulède and his *Ligue* were implacably hostile to what they called *la comédie parlementaire*, without wishing for a dictatorship, however. What they envisioned was a popular, plebiscitary republic, whose head of state would be free from the 'oppressive tutelage of the two chambers' [of Parliament] and would rather be the people's true and direct representative. Anti-Semitism was another element of the nationalism of the right that emerged during the Dreyfus Affair. Besides the diffuse anti-Semitism that characterised the thought and statements of more or less all the major exponents of this nationalism, there were, at the time, some explicitly and primarily anti-Semitic newspapers, *ligues* and other organisations. As Michel Winock has put it: 'Serving as a substitute for the external enemy, the Jew is called upon by the anti-Semites' mythology to figure, within the country, as the necessary enemy against whom it becomes easier to achieve national cohesion' (Winock 1990: 19, authors' translation).

The *boulangist* turmoil and then the Dreyfus Affair also became the battlegrounds through which the two major intellectual fathers of this nationalism of the right emerged. The first was Maurice Barrès, a novelist from Lorraine, author of famous *romans* (like *Les Déracinés* or *Colette Baudoche*) and of various essays and journals (such as his *Cahiers*). Barrès was not a systematic or logically rigorous thinker and far from a system-maker. What he offered to nationalism, instead, was his poetic art, his sense of metaphor and artistic evocation (Winock 1990). His anti-intellectualism and his attempt to base his nationalism on the cult of *la Terre et les Morts* and on extolling the roots of the nation proved extremely effective.

This romantic turn of Barrès's work contrasted sharply with the doctrinaire positivism of the other main nationalist thinker of the period, Charles Maurras. Deeply influenced by the Comtean positivism that had permeated French intellectual life in the previous decades, Maurras had a profound impact on French nationalism by endowing it with a theoretical rigour that it lacked before him. His turn of mind was classicist, his models of civilisation were firmly in the Mediterranean, ancient Athens and then Rome, succeeded in the modern era by Latin France (Sutton 1982). It was the Dreyfus Affair that brought Maurras to the forefront of nationalist debate and politics. He saw in the affair a foreign conspiracy aimed at destroying the two pillars of the French national community: the Army and the Church. His frame of mind being firmly embedded in the anti-revolutionary tradition of French Catholic reactionary conservatism (a tradition that goes back to the fulminations against the French Revolution of Joseph de Maistre), Maurras was deeply pessimistic about human nature. As a result, he saw social coexistence and cohesion as possible only through the strictly delineated framework of institutions such as the family, the Catholic Church, the unitary state. His solution to the political problem of France was unequivocal: the restoration of the monarchy. Besides the new-found theoretical rigour of his logical constructions, what makes Maurras very significant for the history of French nationalism is the fact that he also created a school, as it were, of followers and founded various organisations that offered the nationalism he advocated an institutional backing which allowed it to flourish in the following years and decades. Most important among these was the *Ligue d'action française* (1905).

THE *UNION* SACRÉE AND THE MERGER OF THE TWO NATIONALISMS

In the early years of the twentieth century opposition between the two quite different currents of French nationalism subsided, and a degree of merger took place as a result of international events. This development started from 1905 onwards as a result of German moves which were perceived as direct provocations against France and as omens of imminent war. (Things worsened still further after 1911 and the Agadir crisis.) As a result of this heightened sense of external threat, republicans and conservatives, left and right, gradually converged in a nationalist amalgam that culminated in the so-called *Union sacrée* of August 1914, when almost all French parties and factions joined forces in welcoming the Great War (including some, like most of the Socialists, who had up to then been staunchly in support of pacifism). As Michel Winock (1990) has remarked, a good example of this convergence is the case of Charles Péguy. Having started as a militant *Dreyfusard*, a secularist republican and a Socialist, Péguy, between 1905 and 1914, moved increasingly to a position of hostility to Jean Jaurès's pacifist Socialists, and to a renewal of his Catholic faith. It is not that Péguy suddenly became a nationalist; this he had always been. Rather, it is that his republican nationalism came to be more and more at odds with the pacifist obsession of the leaders of the Socialist Party and closer to the themes dear to all nationalists: the desire for *revanche*, military *grandeur* and preparedness. It was not Péguy, but the climate and the times that had changed, and with them the emphases and manifestations of nationalist attachment. Pacifist attitudes became characteristic of minorities only. In 1913 Raymond Poincaré, a republican of the moderate right, and a staunch nationalist, was elected President of the republic. In August of the same year a law was passed which increased military service to 3 years. The cult of the nation, of military prowess, of 'manly' sports, of discipline and order, came to represent the tendencies of a new generation, as shown by various publications of the time. It should be stressed, however, that this diffuse nationalism that was alive in France during the years preceding the First World War was not simply a conversion of the country to the so-called nationalism of the right. It was also the old republican nationalism that was revived alongside the more conservative nationalism that had emerged since the *boulangist* episode.

The Socialists, whose pacifist leader, Jean Jaurès, was assassinated on 31 July 1914, and who had earlier 'declared war on war', in the end joined in the vast patriotic rally, the *Union sacrée*, as did the *syndicalistes* of the CGT trade union, earlier implacably hostile to the prospect of a war. This patriotic unity was strong enough to last until 1918, the end of the war, despite the unprecedented destruction and suffering witnessed during the conflict. By the summer of 1914, even those who were staunch pacifists had come to declare that they would defend the French soil if necessary, because by defending France against militarist and aggressive Germany they felt they would be defending the 'Revolution' and its legacy, for the benefit of the whole of mankind. The old republican nationalism, identifying France and its destiny with the universal interests of humanity, was still potent.

After the end of the Great War, the nationalist ardour subsided gradually – inevitably, given that France was among the victors of the war, had recovered its lost provinces of Alsace and Lorraine, and had its revenge against Germany. For some years after the war nationalist attitudes lingered on in terms of the treatment of defeated Germany, with most French people and their politicians insisting that Germany should pay fully for the destruction caused by the war, despite the belief of the American and British allies that leniency should be shown if the newly established democratic regime imposed on Germany by the victorious allies (the so-called Weimar Republic) were to have any chance of taking root. The French government did not hesitate to occupy the Ruhr in 1923 in order to pressurise Germany to comply with its treaty obligations. However, from the mid-1920s onwards, French policy shifted towards ideals of collective security and pacifism, particularly due to the policy of Foreign Minister Aristide Briand and his attempts at Franco-German understanding and friendship. The international situation deteriorated dramatically in the 1930s, with aggressive regimes having the upper hand in Japan, Italy and Germany (Hitler's Nazis), up until the declaration of war in 1939. During these difficult years the prevailing mood in France, which had now no open wounds or grievances, was one of pacifism at almost any price. The cataclysmic dimensions of the destruction brought about by the Great War of 1914–18 had led to a profound urge for peace, *Plus jamais ça!* being the overwhelming cry of most French people. However, what was striking as well, during the 1930s (and at an increasing rate as the decade proceeded), was the extent to which anti-Semitism was on the ascendant. Extreme-right organisations and *ligues* were increasingly targeting the 'internal enemy' again, be it the Jews, the Socialists (whose leader and 'Popular Front' prime minister in 1936, Léon Blum, happened to be Jewish as well), the Communists or the freemasons.

RÉVOLUTION NATIONALE, RESISTANCE AND DE GAULLE'S NATIONALISM

When the Second World War did come, the mood of the vast majority of the French was very different from that at the outbreak of the First World War. The result was France's collapse and complete capitulation within weeks of the invasion, the occupation of the northern half of the country by the Germans and the creation of Marshal Philippe Pétain's collaborationist Vichy regime in control of the south. The Vichy regime returned to the logic of anti-Dreyfusard nationalism: the priority was to deal with the internal enemies, the republican regime itself (even the very name *république* was abolished, and France became '*L'État français*' instead), the parliamentary system and the Jews. Anti-republicanism, anti-parliamentarianism and anti-Semitism were the driving forces behind the Vichy regime's self-proclaimed *Révolution nationale*. Although most of the French conservative nationalists who manned the Vichy regime had been raised with nationalist hatred against Germany, they now preferred to collaborate with Hitler's regime and gain for France what they hoped would be a privileged position in the Nazis' 'New Europe' than to contemplate the possibility of the victory of the *anglo-saxons*, the plutocratic liberals whom they hated more than anyone else.

However, Pétain, the collaborationists and the simple collaborators were not the only French agents active during the crucial years between 1940 and 1944. As soon as France fell, Charles de Gaulle escaped immediately to London, whence he made his famous BBC radio appeal to the French nation in June 1940. An officer and a thinker of Catholic conservative background, by no means xenophobic or anti-Semitic, he urged France to say *Non* and organised the 'Free French' in order to resist German occupation and the Vichy regime. First from London, and then moving in various fronts in North Africa, until he finally landed in France and managed to have Paris liberated by his French fighters rather than by *les anglo-saxons*, de Gaulle saved what was paramount in his eyes, the 'honour' of France. According to his version, France was not represented by the treacherous Vichy regime, but by himself and his Free French. Throughout the war in a difficult if mutually respectful relationship with the British prime minister, Winston Churchill, and in almost open hostility with the American president, Franklin D. Roosevelt, who considered him no more than an aspiring military dictator, de Gaulle managed against all the odds to survive and achieve what must have seemed a wild dream during the first stages of the war: the liberation of Paris by French soldiers under a French general. As a result of his efforts and perseverance, France, a country that had been defeated painfully rapidly and then collaborated with the Germans, came to be treated after the war as one of the victorious allies, and was even one of the five great powers that were given a permanent seat in the Security Council of the newly established United Nations.

As one of the students of de Gaulle's ideas has put it, the general's nationalism was 'a synthetic nationalism, an amalgam of nationalisms that incorporates in one synthesis all the ages and all the forms of French nationalism' (Touchard 1978: 299, authors' translation). Jeanne d'Arc and Marianne were harmoniously combined in de Gaulle's vision of a perennial France, and if one wanted to single out the most important influence on his thought on nationhood it would probably have to be Péguy. There was no xenophobia and no anti-Semitism in de Gaulle's nationalism, which distinguishes it sharply from that of Maurras, for instance. And one should never forget that de Gaulle's intellectual formation had been decisively affected by his Catholicism (within which the teachings of the Universal Church left no room for xenophobia).

As Winock notes, despite de Gaulle's own ardent nationalism, the defining moments of 1940–4 and of 1958 found him standing implacably opposed to other nationalists (the Vichyites and collaborators in the first case, the adherents of *Algérie française* in the second case (Winock 1990: 34–5; 416–35)). It is characteristic in this respect that the leader of the extreme-right National Front, Jean-Marie Le Pen, still today, after all these years, misses no opportunity to fulminate against de Gaulle for accepting Algerian independence.

Whether a distinction can be made between simple patriotism and nationalism is debatable (see Varouxakis 2001), but most analysts would agree that General de Gaulle was a nationalist. It is the exact content of his nationalism that is interesting. De Gaulle pursued a deliberate policy aiming at *grandeur*, and tried to elevate France to the position of a Third Force between the United States and the Soviet Union during his presidency (1958–69), in the midst of the Cold War between the western and eastern blocs. By presiding over decolonisation, de Gaulle enabled France to claim again to be the champion of national liberation movements. (Thus, during a visit to Canada, he was able to shout *Vive le Québec libre* from the balcony of the Montreal city hall!) It is not that he was unaware of the limits of France's actual power. Rather, though conscious of his country's weakness in comparison to the USA and the USSR, he was also aware of the imaginative needs of his compatriots. He knew that it had become part of French self-perception and French national identity, at least since the French Revolution, to see France as playing a major and unique role in the world drama, promoting causes seen as good for the world as a whole. De Gaulle was painfully conscious of the profound truth contained in Napoléon Bonaparte's statement: '*Je n'agis que sur les imaginations de la nation; lorsque ce moyen me manquera, je ne serai plus rien*' ('I only act on the nation's imagination. When I lack this, I will be nothing'). According to de Gaulle, Napoléon had many flaws, but he had made his compatriots 'dream'. Similarly, de Gaulle made no secret of his hope, 'in Chateaubriand's phrase, "to lead them [the French] there by means of dreams"' (Cerny 1980: 80). For a significant period of time, he was remarkably successful in this attempt. No matter what they might have thought of the general and his policies in the domestic domain, the vast majority of the French seem to have regained in the 1960s a degree of national self-confidence French people had not felt for a long time (some argue not since the time of the first Napoléon, or even since the time of Louis XIV). This, in a country as profoundly humiliated as France had been during the Second World War, was a most remarkable achievement.

What distinguishes de Gaulle's nationalism from that of his nationalist opponents in 1940–44 and in 1958 is perhaps best captured by Michel Winock's (1990) distinction between a *nationalisme ouvert* and a *nationalisme fermé*. The distinction applies to the whole of modern French history since the French Revolution, and the two forms appear either separately or, quite often, combined in the same movements or even in the thought, politics and writings of the self-same personalities, in different proportions depending on the circumstances and the historical conjuncture. On the one hand, there has been a *nationalisme ouvert*: 'that of a nation, permeated by a civilising mission [*une mission civilisatrice*], admiring itself for its virtues and its heroes, readily forgetting its flaws, yet generous, hospitable, showing solidarity towards other nations on their way to their own formation, defender of the oppressed, raising the flag of liberty and of independence for all the peoples of the world' (Winock 1990: 37, authors' translation). On the other hand,

> another nationalism (that of '*la France aux Français*') resurfaces periodically, at times of great crises: economic crisis, crisis of institutions, intellectual and moral crisis ... boulangism, Dreyfus affair, crisis of the 1930s, decolonisation, economic depression, [French] history reverberates with these periods and these dramatic events during which an exclusive nationalism [*un nationalisme fermé*] presents its successive avatars as remedies. A closed nationalism [*un nationalisme clos*], frightened [*apeuré*], exclusive [*exclusif*], defining the nation by the elimination of intruders: Jews, immigrants, revolutionaries; a collective paranoia, fed by the obsessions of decadence and conspiracy theories. A focalisation on the French essence, each time reinvented in accordance with the respective fashions and the scientific discoveries of the time, which lead to giving varying degrees of weight to the Gauloise influence or the Germanic influence, the contribution of the North and that of the Mediterranean, the song of the bards and the verses of the troubadours. This nationalism ... is a treasure to be protected against all those – innumerable – who covet it. (Winock 1990: 38, authors' translation)

According to Winock, one 'can read in the successive expressions of this obsessive nationalism the resistances to the successive manifestations of modernity: the fear of liberty, the fear of urban civilization, the fear of the encounter with the Other in all its forms' (1990: 38, authors' translation). Winock, who introduced this distinction, is however adamant that these two versions of French nationalism are not always neatly distinguishable; they are often mingled together, or at any rate coincide at the same time in different quarters. 'Since the morning of [the battle of] Valmy, French nationalism has not ceased to convey the best and the worst.' The difference is far from insignificant. No matter how removed from historical realities and accuracy the 'open nationalist' version might be in most cases, its pious and self-flattering imaginings did at least impel the French to aim at serving humanity as a whole, to excel in things that were serviceable to mankind, to seek the admiration of the rest of the world. To put it simply, the desire to shine in the eyes of foreigners, no matter how childish it might seem, does tend to promote an attitude towards the rest of the world which is generous and cosmopolitan. On the other hand, the 'closed' version of nationalism tends to promote national selfishness, exclusiveness, narrowness, defensiveness. Both are nationalisms, but they produce quite different results and international comportments.

De Gaulle's nationalism was, as Winock correctly argues, a version of *nationalisme ouvert*. The general tried (successfully, to an astonishing extent) to inspire in his compatriots a desire to shine in the eyes of the world, to be seen as great, as a beacon of light, civilisation, liberty. There was a lot of vacuous boasting involved, but his was not an aggressive or vicious nationalism. He aimed to fight against what he saw as the fissiparous elements in the French national character, the tendency of his compatriots to quarrel and be divided, and to promote national unity instead. He believed strongly that the best way of achieving this was by cultivating *grandeur*, and in this he was far from alone. Political thinkers and analysts of all persuasions during the nineteenth and twentieth centuries were convinced of the peculiar inclination of the French to desire *grandeur*. This is how Alexis de Tocqueville (a member of the French Chamber of Deputies at the time) put it in the early 1840s:

> One cannot let a nation … like ours … take up easily the habit of sacrificing what it believes to be its grandeur to its repose, great matters to petty ones; … it is not healthy to allow such a nation to believe that its place in the world is smaller, that it has fallen from the level on which its ancestors had put it, but that it must console itself by making railroads and by making prosper in the bosom of its peace, under whatever conditions this peace is obtained, the well-being of each private individual. It is necessary that those who march at the head of such a nation should always keep a proud attitude, if they do not wish to allow the level of national mores to fall very low. [For the context in which de Tocqueville wrote these lines see: Varouxakis (2002: 140–6).]

In this as well as in many other statements, de Tocqueville (arguably the sharpest observer of France in the nineteenth century) came quite close to anticipating directly what de Gaulle (arguably one of the sharpest observers of France in the twentieth century) was to think and say.

However, in some important respects, perhaps suggested by the comparison with de Tocqueville, de Gaulle's 'idea of France' was tuned to the past more than to the future. He was a man of the late nineteenth century in his intellectual formation, and the explicitness with which he sought *grandeur* for France has not, since his resignation in 1969, been repeated or imitated by other French presidents. Perhaps François Mitterrand (president between 1981 and 1995) came closest to adapting some of de Gaulle's themes to changed times in his attempt to gain greatness and influence for France through closer European integration and a hegemonic role for France in the European Community (EC)/European Union (EU).

What also emerged in the late twentieth century was a renewed version of the *nationalisme fermé* Winock has identified, in the shape of Le Pen's *Front National* (FN), a significant political force since the early 1980s. There are factors which have given Le Pen scope for such an initiative. In a sense, France has been in a prolonged economic crisis since the oil crisis in the mid-1970s. Increased European integration, while seen by many as enhancing France's assets, has also been dreaded by others as a threat against the very Frenchness of France. This fear was aggravated by German reunification in the early 1990s, which many French believed would dramatically change the balance of power within the EC/EU in favour of Germany, at the expense of France. The collapse of the Soviet Union and of the eastern bloc, and the consequent emergence of the United States of America as the indisputable *hyperpuissance* (cf. Vedrine 2001) have exacerbated traditional French distrust of the US (and the *anglo-saxons* more generally) and envy and resentment at American predominance. So-called 'globalisation' has become the new bugbear for many people in France, who usually see it as a euphemism for 'Americanisation' and – equally dreaded by most of them – 'liberalisation'. Some of these fears may be under-standable, but there is no gainsaying that among some people – including politicians across the political spectrum, and intellectuals of the left in partic-ular, often referred to as *souverainistes* (see Lacroix 2000) – this negative atti-tude towards whatever is seen as com-ing from abroad, from *l'étranger*, be it the EU, economic liberalisation, Americanisation or globalisation, does on occasion seem paranoid. In some quarters, *nationalisme fermé* has re-emerged under new guises, as testified by Le Pen's success in the first round of the 2002 presidential elections. If the 82 per cent vote for incumbent President Chirac in the second ballot, despite his relative unpopularity, shows that the majority of the French have not fallen for Le Pen's *nationalisme fermé* for the moment, the politicians of the mainstream (or 'republican') right who were elected in June 2002 to govern France for 5 years are well aware that there is no room for complacency. Unless they are seen to be solving some of the most pressing problems that fed Le Pen's relative electoral success, the tide might turn against the whole political establishment and its shibboleths next time. As has been the case so many times in modern French history, *nationalisme fermé* coex-ists with *nationalisme ouvert*.

CITIZENSHIP, NATIONALITY AND MULTICULTURALISM

France today is a curious paradox in terms of its attitude towards immigra-tion, nationhood and multiculturalism. It is a society of immigrants which nonetheless is not and does not see itself as a pluralist society (Jennings 2000: 575). Multiculturalism (the theory and practice of recognising the existence of different cultural, religious or ethnic groups within a country and granting them specific *group* rights designed to accommodate their specific needs and sensitivities) has met with vigorous resistance in France, at least in compari-son to some English-speaking countries (the USA, the UK and Australia).

To Anglo-American eyes, French attitudes towards multiculturalist demands often appear prickly or simply racist. Why are the French unable to accept that cultural pluralism is a good and enriching thing, and celebrate rather than fear the cultural, religious and ethnic diversity that constitutes the reality of their country, as many British and Americans do? What is wrong with admitting into the body of French citizenry 'hyphenated' forms (French-Muslim, French-Arab, French-Caribbean, French-Italian, French-Breton, French-Corsican) like the 'hyphenated' identities that are common in the United States? There is a lot of complacent self-congratulation among the British and American commentators who criticise France on this count, but also a lot of genuine frustration at what is seen as yet another 'French excep-tion' that is not particularly commendable. It has to be remembered that there is a deeper reason for French reluctance to accept multiculturalism: a more general reluctance to accept diversity in the public domain, an insis-tence on the *indivisible* character of the public realm. It is not accidental that Article 2 of the constitution of the Fifth French Republic reads: 'France is a

Republic, indivisible, secular, democratic and social.' Those who draft new constitutions wish to enshrine those principles that they feel need to be defended and may be threatened.

As one of France's most eminent intellectuals and academics today, Pierre Rosanvallon, has argued, French political culture is 'illiberal' because it is characterised by a 'monist vision of the social and the political'. 'According to the English vision, liberty is born from plurality because it [plurality] prevents any one power from prevailing over the other powers'; while, 'according to the French vision, liberty is born out of the generality. It is the capacity of the generality to absorb all particulars which is the true condition of liberty' (Rosanvallon 2001; authors' translation). It is in the same context that the role of the *État rationalisateur* is stressed (Rosanvallon 2001). (Let us remind ourselves that, according to de Gaulle, 'France exists thanks to the state alone'.) The desperate pursuit of unity and the cult of the generality, as opposed to the selfish and fissiparous action of 'factions', corporations and organised groups and interests, goes back to at least Jean-Jacques Rousseau, whose influence on the thinking of some of the most important actors in the French Revolution can hardly be overestimated. Through concrete laws, the revolutionaries made sure that no groups or corporations of any kind could claim any rights or privileges collectively. The French Revolution proclaimed the rights of men and citizens *as individuals*, and emphatically rejected groups' rights. There was nothing between free and equal individuals and the state. No matter how many things may have changed, this perception of the social permeates French attitudes and French political culture still today, which is one very important reason why there is so much resistance to multiculturalism and to the recognition of the rights of groups *as groups* (religious, feminist, ethnic and so on). It is in a similar logic that the French govenment refused stubbornly for a long time in the 1990s to sign and subscribe to European conventions for the protection of regional languages. While French politicians and many French intellectuals clamour in favour of linguistic diversity when the issue is the predominance of the English language in the world (meaning, of course, that French has to be protected against the inroads of English as a means of preserving diversity), they are vociferously opposed to any encouragement of linguistic diversity within France (which would promote regional languages or dialects spoken in various parts of France). Again, the idea is that the unity of the republic is not negotiable at any level (cf. Laborde 2001).

There are other factors that account for French resistance to multiculturalism. For a very long period in French history (particularly during the Third Republic) the issue of group rights was associated with the religious question. The Catholic Church was seen as a fractious group which threatened the very nature of the republic, whose secularism it did not want to recognise. With the victory of the secularists, those who insisted that the republic was *laïque*, the fate of groups claiming special rights within France was sealed. This is of great importance for an understanding of contemporary disputes. What makes multiculturalism as contentious as it is in France is the fact that the minority communities that are claiming special rights and recognition are often religiously defined communities. Islam in particular, the second greatest religion among French citizens after Catholicism, causes much fear among the enemies of multiculturalism in France. After having fought many battles against giving any special rights (particularly in the educational field) to the Catholic Church, French republicans find it difficult to accept that the republic could cede special rights to a religious community (Islam) without fatally impairing its very nature. Very simply, *laïcité* and republicanism have come to be seen as synonymous. This is one reason why the notorious *affaire des foulards* (affair of the headscarfs) in 1989 became so contentious (see also Chapter 1). According to those who supported the expulsion of girls wearing Islamic headscarfs to school, religious insignia like the headscarf should be left at home. Allowing pupils to wear them would compromise the secular and neutral character of the republican school. More generally, many among those who rejected the wearing of headscarfs by Muslim girls insisted (and still insist) that the French Republic has a duty to protect its individual members (in this case, Muslim girls) from the oppressive group practices and obligations imposed on them by their respective cultural or religious communities. Thus, paradoxically for those who do not share their logic, many French republicans want to ban the wearing of headscarfs or other signs of religious affiliation *in the name of liberty*: the liberty of the individuals to be just individuals, equal in the eyes of the secular republic, which does not recognise any distinctions of race, ethnic or cultural origins, religion or class. It is in the name of freedom and universality, defended by the French Republic, that the demands for special recognition of cultural, religious or ethnic groups are rejected.

The issue of the unitary and indivisible nature of the French Republic acquired new dimensions and urgency when former Socialist prime minister Lionel Jospin attempted, in the late 1990s, to devolve to Corsica a degree of constitutional autonomy (see Chapter 3). The high-profile minister of the interior, Jean-Pierre Chevènement, resigned from the government in protest against the move. Since then Chevènement has tried (through his *Mouvement des Citoyens* and then in the 2002 elections the ill-fated *Pole Républicain*) to become the major representative of the *souverainiste* tendency in French politics. The vehemence of the debate showed once more how contentious the issue is and how strong the opposition to any threat to the unitary and indivisible nature of the French state is. As has been the case since the French revolutionaries adopted Rousseau's denunciation of particularism in favour of the general (Rousseau's famous concept of the 'general will' was enunciated in this context), no special status and rights are recognised for groups smaller than the nation of free and equal individuals as a whole. As noted in Chapter 4, the adoption of the principle of *parité* in a 1999 constitutional amendment was an important exception to this tradition.

Yet is not the nation itself a form of particularism *vis-à-vis* the universal? Yes, but this is not how it has been seen in French self-perceptions and national mythology. As we saw earlier in this chapter, France is seen as representing the universal; France is in the vanguard of civilisation; it is the country of the rights of man, of 'liberty, equality and fraternity'. Being a French patriot is not regarded as particularist but rather as fully compatible with being a universalist cosmopolitan, solicitous of the interests of the whole of mankind.

It is in this spirit that one needs to understand manifestations of French opinion like the 1995 annual report of the *Haut Conseil à l'intégration*, which denounces 'the dangers of communitarianism'. The report accepts 'community' only in the form of 'a common sense of belonging, consented to or accepted, without judicial or institutional consequences' but by no means in the form of 'an organised and institutionalised grouping of part of the population according to ethnic or religious criteria, recognised by the public authorities' (Jennings 2000: 583). According to the 1997 report of the *Haut Conseil*, France 'has always refused to recognise collective rights that are specific to groups or minorities. It is to each man and each woman that it has granted full rights in order to allow him or her individually to take a place in French society' (Jennings 2000: 583).

Jeremy Jennings identifies four basic policy principles within this republican philosophy of integration:

1 The integration of immigrants must be in accord with the secularism of the state: the latter respects religions, philosophies and beliefs but gives them no special support.
2 It is individuals rather than groups that integrate and at no time can or ought the action of integration to contribute towards the constitution of structured communities.
3 Integration presupposes rights and duties: an immigrant must respect French law as it is: in return, the law naturally respects their culture and traditions.
4 Immigrants and the French must be treated equally, without developing the sentiment that immigrants are better treated than French people who are their neighbours. As such, integration is not designed in order to favour immigrants but for the benefit of all and their collective cohesion. (Jennings 2000: 583)

IMMIGRATION

France has the longest history of immigration in Europe and was the only country to have experienced significant inward migration prior to the Second World War. Today, over one in six people (10 million) are either themselves immigrants or have at least one immigrant parent or grandparent (Weil 2001: 211). At the same time, this country of immigrants has given substantial electoral gains to a party that is explicitly anti-immigration, the *Front National*. Almost one in five French people are sufficiently sympathetic to M. Le Pen's anti-immigration message to go and vote for him. Although he has softened parts of his discourse in order to gain wider acceptance, Le Pen has been identified with his early proposal to deport *all* non-European immigrants to their countries of origin.

There is a persistently recurring view of a French conception of nationhood, of a French way of defining a nation, in turn determining immigration policy and the criteria as to who becomes a citizen, which is equally consistently juxtaposed to a so-called 'German' conception of nationhood, seen as its exact opposite (Brubaker 1992). During the French Revolution a quasi-universal *droit du sol* was in place for some time, combined with the wish to grant French nationality to foreign friends of the Revolution. The *droit du sol* was reintroduced during the second half of the nineteenth century in order to force the children of foreign immigrants to discharge their military duties (in *départements* with high concentrations of foreign immigrants – particularly Belgians and Italians), not least because their exemption from military service provoked strong resentment; indigenous young Frenchmen complained that, during their absence on military service, exempt foreigners were taking 'our places, our jobs, our fiancées' (Weil 2002). As Patrick Weil has recently shown, it was to address this problem, rather than out of any 'republican' or egalitarian ideological magnanimity, that it was stipulated during the Third Republic that children born in France of immigrant parents would be granted French citizenship as soon as they should become of age, as well as that the grandchildren of immigrants would be granted French nationality automatically on birth. In other words, the granting of French nationality was based on enforced socialisation into French life of the immigrant children concerned, rather than on any voluntary criterion, any expression of the will on their part to become French citizens, as later republican mythology would have one believe. (It may not be accidental then that it was Patrick Weil who wrote the report commissioned by Socialist prime minister Lionel Jospin in 1998, which challenged the notion of *manifestation de volonté* that had been introduced to the Pasqua nationality law by the conservative Balladur government in 1993.)

After the carnage of the Great War of 1914–18, the law of nationality was influenced decisively by demographic considerations. In 1927, by reducing to 3 years the time it was necessary for foreigners to have resided in France before they were eligible for naturalisation, the Third Republic attempted to deal with France's serious demographic problem (particularly by comparison to ever-dreaded Germany) by literally creating new French nationals out of foreign immigrants (mainly from European countries – Italy, Poland, Spain).

Today, France grants its nationality to around 100 000 people every year. According to the 1999 census there were 3 260 000 foreign residents in France. Among them, 17 per cent were Portuguese, 15.4 per cent Moroccans, 14.6 per cent Algerians, 6.4 per cent Turks, 6.2 per cent Italians, 5 per cent Spanish, 4.7 per cent Tunisians and around 7 per cent nationals of various Sub-Saharan African countries. Besides other historical factors, the diversity in the descent of these immigrants reflects the fact that the legislation that shaped France's immigration policies after the end of the Second World War (promulgated on 2 November 1945) 'organised an egalitarian, individualist and progressive system of issuing permits without ethnic criteria for selection'

(Weil 2001: 213). Not that the idea of ethnic or racial criteria and quotas had not been discussed. Patrick Weil has shown that a 'racial' approach was given serious consideration in France during the interwar period, which would have made the level of 'assimilability' of different ethnic groups the criterion for granting permits to enter France (such a policy was being implemented in the USA at that time). Thus, the Vichy regime's racial (particularly anti-Semitic) policies were not as complete an aberration as subsequent national mythology would have one believe. In fact, according to Weil, even General de Gaulle considered implementing a system of selection based on crtiteria of assimilability of various ethnic groups after the Liberation. In the end, however, such ideas were abandoned, as 'some key civil servants in the French Council of state opposed the project, arguing that any legislation based on the explicit mention of national criteria as a basis for the selection of immigrants would too closely resemble racist Nazi ideology' (Weil 2001: 213; cf. Weil 1995; Weil 2002). Thus, the 'progressive' legislation that was adopted in 1945, and which still permeates the framework of immigration policies today, encouraged immigration of workers, but also of their families (unlike, for instance, German post-war legislation, which regarded the so-called 'guest-workers' as bound to return to their families in their countries of origin). This legislative framework was later complemented by a special protective status for refugees (which was subsequently guaranteed by the international Geneva Convention (1951)). The 1945 immigration legislation was meant to facilitate the entry into France of any worker (industrial or agricultural) able to present a promise of employment or a contract with an employer within France. However, the fact that the official legislation did not apply racial or ethnic considerations to immigration does not mean that such considerations did not influence French policy at all after the Second World War. The *Office National d'Immigration*, a government agency, did have ways in practice of favouring recruitment from some countries rather than others – for example, preference was given to Italians over Turks (Weil 2001: 213). Because it was feared that there were too many Algerians entering France, encouragement was given to the immigration of Italians, Spanish and Portuguese, then Yugoslavian and even Moroccan and Tunisian workers.

Between 1974 and 1984 the economic crisis led to a more explicit battle. Centrist president Valéry Giscard d'Estaing attempted between 1978 and 1980 a forced repatriation of the majority of legal North African immigrants, especially Algerians (Weil 1995). A strong reaction from the left-wing parties, from the trade unions, but also from the neo-Gaullist RPR, combined with the reaction of the Council of State (*Conseil d'État*) – France's top administrative court – led to the failure of the attempt. The *Conseil d'État* took a decision rejecting President Giscard d'Estaing's plan on the grounds of its incompatibility with French republican values and principles enshrined in the constitution, as well as considerations of the potential of such a policy to tarnish France's image abroad. Socialist president François Mitterrand's first government followed policies completely different from those of Giscard, in the first years of its rule, 1981 to 1983. However, in 1983 a new factor emerged on the political horizon that was to change the French political landscape for good, transforming immigration into a major issue of contention in party politics: Le Pen's *Front National* enjoyed it first successes in local elections.

During the 1980s, although the total numbers of foreigners residing in France fell slightly, there was greater concentration of immigrants (both legal and illegal immigrants tending to live together) in certain areas, which coincided with continuously rising unemployment. This led to more and more resentment of immigrants among some segments of the population, but also to considerable mistrust of politicians, who kept asserting that immigration was falling or had disappeared, and an ever-growing perception that the state was not effective.

It was in order to combat such perceptions that the 'Pasqua laws' (named after Charles Pasqua, minister of the interior in Edouard Balladur's centre-right government of 1993–5), were passed. These laws led to a significant decrease in the number of legal immigrants, but had the effect of increasing the numbers of those residing in the country illegally (Weil 2001: 218). In 1997 the 'Debré law' (named after Jean Louis Debré, interior minister in Alain Juppé's government (1995–7)) reinforced the same line of policy. Following the election of the Plural Left government in June 1997, Jospin sought to introduce meaningful changes to France's immigration and citizenship policies. He commissioned the political scientist Patrick Weil to write a report with recommendations for reform. The Weil Report (July 1997), according to its author himself:

> proposed to develop a strategy of action according to a consensus among the various groups and individuals affected by the issue: a seemingly paradoxical convergence between those dedicated to advancing the rights of immigrants and those representing law enforcement officials. ... [Thus, as] a result of this co-ordination between various groups with direct 'stakes' in immigration, the 1998 law, largely based on the 1997 Weil Report, achieved a number of important goals regarded as beneficial both to immigrants and to the body polit[ic]. Thus the 1998 law not only promulgated a moderate liberalisation of procedures for family reunification and for granting asylum and refugee status, but also, for the first time in recent years, began to encourage the immigration of qualified workers, including students and researchers. Indeed, the promises of 'ending immigration' or 'zero immigration' had never been realistic and the new law recognises the basic fact that immigration remains, and must remain, legally authorised for certain categories of persons, including immigrant families who are legal residents of France, political refugees, EU nationals and spouses of French nationals. (Weil 2001: 219–20)

There may or may not be some degree of self-congratulation in Patrick Weil's recent statement that 'the new legislation is already having a significant effect' (Weil 2001: 220), but if Le Pen's score in April–May 2002 as well as the socialists' abysmally bad showings in both the presidential elections of 21 April and the legislative elections of June 2002 are anything to go by, their policies have not been perceived as particularly effective by the voters.

'INTEGRATION' OF IMMIGRANTS

France has traditionally been seen (and has seen itself) as a country which did not make any distinctions of race, religion or ethnic origin among its citizens, but rather absorbed them all in a French 'melting-pot' and gave them equal rights as individuals irrespective of where they came from. The term traditionally used for this process was 'assimilation'. However, when, in the years 1974–84 (following an end to the immigration of new workers), a debate started as to the fate of those foreigners already residing permanently in France, the negative aspects of the concept 'assimilation' were highlighted. The term was seen as implying the idea of a unilateral adaptation of immigrants to the laws and customs of France and of the French. It was regarded as entailing the notion of the superiority of French culture and the need for the elimination of the immigrants' own identity and culture.

During these debates, the term 'insertion' appeared increasingly preferable. For the supporters of immigrants and for the political left, 'insertion' meant installation into French society while retaining the right to refuse assimilation and to defend and preserve original collective identities. Initially, those on the right or extreme right who wished to have non-European immigrants deported were in favour of the concept of 'insertion', as it meant that immigrants would remain different and alien from French society and thus their wished-for deportation would be easier. After President Giscard's deportation policies failed, from around 1983–4 onwards, Le Pen used a different strategy, which in turn changed the attitude of his opponents. Le Pen started to apply the right to retain collective cultural differences (*droit à la différence*) to the French themselves, arguing that they also had a right to be different from the non-European immigrants and that this implied a right to deport foreigners.

In response to this, Le Pen's opponents, politicians as well as anti-racist organisations, started campaigning for what they now called the 'integration' of foreign residents in France, which meant their right to equality, to stay in France and become French. Although the use of 'integration' is far from unambiguous, depending on who uses it, the concept has been defined in the following terms:

> a goal to model society according to a secular tradition is matched by the abandonment of the traditional assumption of France's superiority compared to other cultures. In short, the adaptation of the migrants is no longer a self-evidently one-way process but becomes interactive. The immigrants' presence and their right to preserve in private – individually and collectively – their own culture will transform French society. One notable example is that French society has to adapt itself to the right of millions of Muslims to practise their religion. (Weil 2001: 223)

6

INTELLECTUAL LIFE

From the point of view of the English-speaking world, France is a country of intellectuals *par excellence*. We tend to have a certain fixed idea of the French intellectual: chain-smoking (preferably *Gauloises* without filter) in Parisian cafés (in which other capital does one find cafés named *Les philosophes* or *Bar littéraire*, the one across the road from the other? Not in Britain in any case); 'ever-talking, ever-gesticulating' (as Thomas Carlyle put it in the nineteenth century), coming up with a generalised theory on anything from politics through art to his (or her) complicated sexual practices; teaching at a *grande école* or some other higher-education institution; being politically committed, usually a communist, inveighing against capitalism, imperialism and, of course, the Americans, or more often *les anglo-saxons* in general. It has been said of the Parisian intellectual that he (or she) can think of three reasons to sign a petition or to commit suicide every morning before breakfast; that you ask a Parisian intellectual a simple question and they come up with a thesis. It has also been said of many of them that they have precious little to say which is either new or makes any sense, but that they have an amazing talent and eloquence in saying it. As with all stereotypes, there is a lot of truth in most of this, as well as a lot of jaundiced or ignorant prejudice, or simply failure to catch up with developments in the last two decades. In direct proportion to the degree to which French intellectuals take themselves very seriously, the majority of their stiffer British counterparts (who call themselves anything but 'intellectuals') refuse to take them seriously, denounce what they see as their pretentiousness, or write them off as charlatans. Perhaps, though, some of these British cannot help envying the relative importance and consideration enjoyed by their French counterparts.

In any case, the notion that intellect was particularly valued in France (especially in contrast to England) is an old one. Some nineteenth-century British thinkers and writers invoked France repeatedly in this respect in order to shame their compatriots out of their 'philistinism', their exclusive devotion to practical and material ends and to the struggle to 'get on' in the world. Equally widespread already in the nineteenth century was the stereotype of the French as possessing a genius for generalisation and abstraction, as opposed to the empirical *anglo-saxons* (see Varouxakis 2002). In other words, France was seen as the country of ideas. Not the least of the reasons for this perception (which was shared by the French themselves) had been the phenomenon of the eighteenth-century *philosophes* or men (and a few women) of letters, the personnel of the French Enlightenment, the *Lumières*. In books, articles, entries in the extremely influential *Encyclopédie*, and, not least, in frequent discussions in the various *salons*, the *philosophes* developed a model of the man of letters who popularises philosophy and science, and engages in debates about all sorts of issues. The most emblematic figure in this role, the epitome of the whole French Enlightenment in many respects, was Voltaire. He concentrated in his person and activity some of the most important features that came to be associated with the *Lumières*. He used the power of his pen to criticise, caricature and sap the foundations of all sorts of abuses and absurdities in the society in which he lived. His long and uphill campaign (eventually successful) to rehabilitate the reputation of a man who had been wrongly accused, known as the Calas case, became the first famous campaign conducted by a man of letters to achieve a political end in the name of abstract and universal values such as justice and toleration of difference. Overall, the influence of the *philosophes* in eighteenth-century France, most notably Rousseau and Voltaire, was such that many historians and thinkers, from the early nineteenth century until today, have attributed to it the very eruption of the French Revolution in 1789 and the subsequent turn of events during the whole revolutionary period. Others dispute this thesis, but its mere existence goes a long way to show how important these men of letters were perceived as having been in France.

After the French Revolution and the Napoleonic era, in the nineteenth century, the figure of the *philosophe* came to be replaced by that of the *savant*, who tended to be more specialised in his expertise, be it history or science. The public esteem which derived from their specific expertise allowed the *savants* to pronounce on issues beyond their technical competence. But the actual figure of what is today called the *intellectuel* emerged in the specific context of a historical episode in late-1890s France, the notorious Dreyfus Affair.

THE EMERGENCE AND ROLES OF THE *INTELLECTUELS*

Although it was first used in isolation by Saint-Simon as early as in 1821, the word *intellectuel* as a description of a distinct category of people appeared in the 1890s and became current from January 1898, when Emile Zola published in *L'Aurore* his famous open letter to the President of the French Republic, entitled *J'accuse*. An Alsatian army officer of Jewish descent, Captain Alfred Dreyfus, had been accused and, in 1894, convicted of spying for the Germans. However, the evidence was very slim, and later revelations indicated clearly that it had been fabricated by people within the French army. The intervention of a great number of famous writers, philosophers, journalists and artists (including, besides Zola, Anatole France, André Gide,

Marcel Proust, Charles Péguy and many others), demanding a retrial of Dreyfus, put the affair in the spotlight and provoked a protracted struggle between two bitterly divided camps, the *Dreyfusards* and the *anti-Dreyfusards* (those who argued that the honour of the French army and the French nation mattered more than the issue of individual rights and justice). Initially the term *intellectuels* was used ironically to describe writers and artists who had sided with Dreyfus, but soon it was also used to describe writers, philosophers, artists (and so on) who opposed Dreyfus – Maurice Barrès figuring prominently among them – and eventually it came to apply to a whole new category of people within French society.

Zola's famous intervention, entitled by him *Lettre à Monsieur Félix Faure président de la République*, was published on 13 January 1898 under the title chosen by the chief editor of *L'Aurore*, Georges Clemenceau (later to become a prime minister): *J'accuse*. The following day *L'Aurore* also published a petition calling for a retrial of Captain Dreyfus, signed by hundreds of university professors, literary figures and artists. This petition came to be known afterwards as the manifesto of the intellectuals, and it became a model of how intellectuals could participate in political debates, which was to be followed very extensively in twentieth-century France. Time and again, intellectuals would sign petitions or open letters as a means of participating in the country's politics, and thus they acquired an influence out of all proportion to their numbers. The feature that should be borne in mind is that the Dreyfus Affair established a pattern of individuals exploiting reputations founded on literary, academic or artistic distinction in order to pronounce on matters outside their recognised expertise (Charle 1990). This is why in the petitions their names have usually been followed by their status and qualifications. Intellectuals in France learned from the Dreyfus Affair how to convert their moral authority and intellectual capital into *action* in the name of a judicial or humanitarian cause.

The next major battle that divided French intellectuals into two camps (most of them the very same people who had been the protagonists during the Dreyfus Affair) came with the advent of the 'Great War', the First World War of 1914–18. There were those (the majority) who, whatever their political affiliations, joined the adherents of 'integral patriotism' in a patriotic fervour against what they saw as German militarism and barbarity. Intellectuals such as Charles Péguy lost their lives after volunteering for active service at the front. Others opted for pacifism, even at the price of being accused as traitors.

In the years after the First World War and following the Bolshevik Revolution in Russia in 1917, a new factor emerged on the political scene. As the Communist Party of the newly established Soviet Union, under Lenin's leadership, demanded to be blindly followed by the forces loyal to Marxism all over the world in the interests of international revolution, a split took place (in 1920) in France. On the one hand, there were those who decided to follow the lead of Moscow, and left the Socialist Party to form the new *Parti Communiste Français* (PCF); on the other hand there were those who refused to accept the call of Lenin and remained loyal to the Socialist Party, then called SFIO. Intellectuals of the left were inevitably divided on this issue, and the presence of the *Parti Communiste* and its special relation of servility to Moscow would prove an extremely important factor for the politics of twentieth-century France in general, and for the role and fate of intellectuals in particular. A group of quite idiosyncratic intellectuals around André Breton, the *surréalistes*, followed the pacifist trend of the time as well as the *Parti Communiste* (which Breton joined in 1927, only to be expelled in 1933 for being too intractable and libertarian).

Another major figure in the intellectual life of the time, André Gide (one of the *Dreyfusards* of 1898), was also very impressed and excited by the Bolshevik Revolution in Russia. However, a stay in the Soviet Union made him see things very differently, and his book *Retour de l'URSS* (1936) was one of the first powerful warnings French intellectuals had of the stern realities of life in the Soviet Union, which was quite different from the idealised utopia of their armchair speculations. The warning was not heeded, and French intellectuals were to pay a price for this after the Second World War. Instead, Gide was denounced as an incompetent judge of the Soviet project or as a traitor to the cause.

The interwar period of the 1920s and 1930s was more generally marked, on the one hand, by the rise of fascism, encouraged by the example of Mussolini's successes in neighbouring Italy, and the threat this posed to the democratic French Third Republic, and, on the other hand, by the growing support for communism. On the right, Charles Maurras's *Action Française* had made great strides. Intellectuals of the left responded to the growing threat posed by right-wing fascism by creating, in the 1930s, the *Comité de Vigilance des Intellectuels Antifascistes*. Things became conspicuously polarised between left and right following first the failed *coup d'état* of 6 February 1934 and then the victory of the Popular Front government in 1936, headed by Socialist leader Léon Blum. The Spanish Civil War also provided another battle-line between left and right at the same period. The approach of the Second World War increased the sense of urgency of intellectual involvement, but the catastrophe could not be prevented by intellectuals, and France found herself humiliatingly defeated within weeks after the German invasion in the summer of 1940.

The entrancement of many in the French intellectual left with communism and similar manifestations of ideological involvement on the part of intellectuals on the right during the 1920s led to one of the most powerful theoretical articulations of what the role of the intellectuals should be. Julien Benda (*Dreyfusard* in the 1890s), having had enough of ideologically committed and partisan intellectuals, wrote in 1927 *La Trahison des clercs* (The Treason of the Intellectuals). There he castigated the attitude of those intellectuals of both left and right who were engaging in partisan combats to the detriment of what he saw as their duty to serve the interests of truth and justice. (Given that Benda is remembered today particularly on account of this work, it is ironic that he himself became an active fellow-traveller, a *compagnon de route*, of the Communist Party after 1944.) From about 1890 onwards, Benda argued, the intellectuals, the *clercs*, had compromised their universalist duty in order to serve the particular interests of race, nationality, class, ideology, and so on. Instead of pursuing concrete results and advantages, intellectuals should remain detached from society, capable of judging it in terms of abstract principles. This view was challenged already before the Second World War by Paul Nizan in his book *Les Chiens de garde* (The Watchdogs). Nizan was the first to articulate the doctrine of 'commitment' of intellectuals (which was to become predominant after the war thanks to its reformulation by Jean-Paul Sartre). According to Nizan, detachment from the everyday realities of society was not an option. An intellectual who decided to stand back and not participate, who wished not to take a position, was deluding himself, because, very simply, refusing to make a choice was itself a choice, not taking a definite political position was itself a political position. It was all very well for Benda to ask the intellectual to serve the eternal values of truth and justice, but this amounted to a refusal to talk of 'war, colonialism, the speed-up of industry, love, the varieties of death, unemployment, politics ... all the things that occupy the minds of the planet's inhabitants' – it was an attempt 'to obscure the miseries of contemporary reality' (Jennings 1993: 71). The intellectual had to choose between being for the oppressed or being for the oppressors; he should form 'the closest possible ties with the class that is the bearer of revolution' and 'denounce all the conditions which prevent men from being human'. In other words, the intellectual should become a 'technician of revolutionary philosophy' (Jennings 1993: 71).

1945–68: THE *INTELLECTUEL ENGAGÉ* AND THE *COMPAGNON DE ROUTE*

The notion of intellectual commitment, of the *intellectuel engagé*, was elaborated to great effect immediately after the Liberation by Jean-Paul Sartre. In the very first issue of *Les Temps modernes*, the review he launched and which became central to the intellectual life of the period, Sartre characteristically declared that nineteenth-century writers Flaubert and Goncourt had been responsible for the bloody repression of the Paris Commune in 1871 by the then French government (headed by Adolphe Thiers) because they had failed to write anything that would have prevented it from happening (interestingly, Sartre himself has been accused of having kept almost completely silent during the German occupation of France which had just ended, but that is apparently another story). The message was clear: the intellectual had to be *engagé*, committed; he was obliged 'to commit himself in every one of the conflicts of our time'. Sartre himself became one of the so-called *compagnons de route* (fellow-travellers) of the *Parti Communiste*, intellectuals closely associated with the PCF (though at the same time deeply distrusted by the party apparatus). It was not until 1968 that Sartre broke with and denounced the PCF.

The degree to which so many French intellectuals, theoretically independent-minded, sophisticated writers, subjected themselves to the highly regimented discipline required by the Stalinist French Communist Party is an extremely interesting phenomenon of post-Second-World-War French life. A beginning of an explanation was given by one of those intellectuals long after he had abandoned the party, historian François Furet, in his *Le Passé d'une illusion: essai sur l'idée communiste au XXe siècle* (1995). In the prevailing atmosphere of post-war France, the *Parti Communiste* had an enormously increased moral stature and prestige owing to several factors: its leading role in the Resistance after 1941 (in sharp contrast to the discrediting of the right due to the collaboration of many of its leading figures with the Germans or their involvement with the collaborationist Vichy regime of Marshal Pétain); the increased prestige of the Soviet Union due to its major contribution to the defeat of Hitler; the legacy of the 1930s, when left-wing intellectuals had rallied to the defence of the Popular Front coalition against the attacks of the extreme right and fascists; and, not least, a very French trend, anti-Americanism (the *Parti Communiste* and its press were the most vociferous critics of what they denounced as the *Coca-Colonisation de la France*, ever-increasing American cultural penetration of France in the wake of, as well as by means of the Marshall Plan). French intellectuals who traditionally saw the United States as a cultural desert now apparently intent on imposing its shallow mass-culture on the rest of the world were attracted by the Communists' anti-American message. Given also that the Cold War between the two superpowers set in from 1947 onwards, and that the USA was in the grip of its most conservative elements for the best part of a couple of decades, the Communist message denouncing the Americans as imperialists was quite plausible for the majority of French intellectuals, who chose not to see the flaws or crimes of the second superpower of the time, the Soviet Union. They remained blind, most of them, until 1974. In a controversial book denouncing the attitudes of the majority of French intellectuals during these crucial post-war years, British-born historian Tony Judt has dissected the attitudes and political culture that led to this outcome. In *Past Imperfect: French Intellectuals 1944–56* (1992), Judt castigates what he sees as the collective myopia of French intellectuals before the cruel and liberty-destroying practices of the Soviet regime under Joseph Stalin. (Needless to say, Sartre, his partner Simone de Beauvoir and their circle are among Judt's major targets.)

Sartre was seen as the guru of French intellectuals, the very incarnation of the post-war French thinker and writer – an image he himself had carefully orchestrated. His role even seems to have gained him a degree of impunity. It is said that, when it was proposed to arrest him for his encouragement of mutiny in the French army during the Algerian war of independence, General de Gaulle, President of the Republic, retorted, 'We cannot imprison Voltaire' (*'On n'embastille pas Voltaire'*) – implying that, like Voltaire in the eighteenth century, Sartre was performing the role of conscience of society, of the critical intellectual. Sartre's notoriety and paradigmatic status were not due simply to his political commitment. They were also built on his bohemian lifestyle and his idiosyncratic relationship with fellow-writer Simone de Beauvoir (1908–86). In order to make a feminist statement de Beauvoir refused to marry Sartre, but she lived with him until his death, although they seem to have had an open relationship, having agreed to experiment with sexual encounters with other men and women. (Some biographers charge them with hypocrisy and with having cruelly exploited some of their lovers.) Also, in a show of nonconformism, Sartre refused in 1964 to accept the Nobel Prize. In the late 1950s and early 1960s he supported the Algerian nationalists who were fighting for independence from France and was one of those who signed the *manifeste des 121*. In 1961 Sartre wrote a famous preface to Frantz Fanon's *Les Damnés de la terre*, in which he justified the liberating violence of the colonised, in this case the violence used by the Algerian FLN (Drake 2002: 124).

THE DOMINANCE OF MARXISM, EXISTENTIALO-MARXISM AND SOVIETOPHILIA

The dominant intellectual trend between 1944 and 1974 was a commitment to Marxism of one sort (or interpretation) or another. Under Sartre's influence Marxism was combined with existentialism to produce *existentialo-marxisme*, which remained the order of the day until the late 1960s. Moreover, in the years 1944 to 1956 most of the intellectuals of the left were united in their admiration for the Soviet Union and Communism. Sartre's article 'Les communistes et la paix' in 1952 was a fully-fledged *plaidoyer* for the *Parti Communiste*. In 1960 Sartre, then at the summit of his glory, was faced with the challenge of a debate with Louis Althusser (1918–90), who was to become the major guru of Marxism and interpreter of Marx in France in the 1960s, particularly through his seminars at the *École Normale Supérieure* in Rue Ulm.

To come back to the 1950s, few things can show the hegemony of pro-Soviet Marxists in the intellectual climate of this period better than the experience of fugitive intellectuals from Eastern and Central Europe escaping Communism and seeking refuge in Paris. Polish dissident poet and writer Czeslaw Milosz, for example, had escaped Communist rule in his native country and sought refuge in Paris. Milosz painted an extremely powerful picture of the grim realities of life in the so-called 'people's democracies' of Central and Eastern Europe in a classic book published in 1951, *La Pensée captive* (The Captive Mind). To his great and painful disappointment, the book was received with extreme coldness by the people he wanted to convince and influence in the country where he was living, French intellectuals, who, due to their love affair with Communism and the Soviet Union, tended in those years to regard anyone who criticised the Soviet system as little better than reactionaries or even 'fascists'. As he has recounted in later interviews, it was this hostile climate that led him to leave France and move to the United States.

THE NEW FAD: *TIERSMONDISME*

The faith of the majority of French left-wing intellectuals in Communism and the Soviet Union was shaken by events that started in the year 1956, the *année inoubliable* for some French Communists. First, there came Soviet leader Nikita Khrushchev's revelations (in a report to the 20th Congress of the Communist Party of the Soviet Union, in February 1956) about Stalin's practices and crimes (Stalin had died 3 years earlier). Then the Soviet tanks invaded Hungary, in November 1956, and brutally repressed the revolt in Budapest. Following these developments, intellectuals of the left started turning away from Communism and the Soviet Union without, however, abandoning or questioning their commitment to Marxism as a philosophy and analytical orthodoxy. Instead, they turned *en masse* to *tiersmondisme*, lending their admiring support to all sorts of revolutionary movements or regimes in the non-European so-called Third World (mainly anti-colonialist movements and/or Communist regimes). First it was Algeria, then Fidel Castro's Cuba, then Mao's China, Vietnam, Cambodia, and, for some, the Palestinian movement. (Prominent among the intellectuals concerned were of course Sartre and Simone de Beauvoir, who made a high-profile visit to Cuba in 1960.)

According to Tony Judt (1992) the eruption of the Algerian revolt for independence from France, and then the rest of the anti-colonial movements in the non-European world, offered the French intellectuals who had blindly supported the Soviet Union up to 1956 a face-saving way out of the potential embarrassment of having to account for their Sovietophilia and 'Stalinolatry' once the Soviet regime's unpalatable aspects had become difficult to deny. Very simply, according to Judt, they abandoned Communism and philo-Sovietism by moving on to their new *tiersmondiste* enthusiasms, without facing up to their support for the Soviet Union and without any serious reflection or debate as to the whole experience. This was not to come until the mid-1970s, following the publication in 1974 of a French translation of *The Gulag Archipelago (L'Archipel du Goulag)* by distinguished Soviet dissenter Alexander Solzhenitsyn, which exposed the crimes committed in Soviet labour camps and related oppression and further weakened the appeal of Marxism. The final blow to the ideology came with the collapse of the Communist regimes of Central and Eastern Europe and the Soviet Union itself between 1989 and 1991.

DISSENTING VOICES

Not that there were no dissenting voices at all, but they were either in the minority or completely isolated. Some, however, were too distinguished to go unnoticed, and their work has come to be appreciated as among the best things French thought and literature have produced in the twentieth century.

The names of Camus and Aron must be singled out in this connection. Albert Camus (1913–60) was born in Algiers to a French working-class family. His thought was formed away from the Parisian elite institutions, having studied philosophy at the University of Algiers and then worked as a journalist there. By the time of his premature death in a car accident in January 1960 he had become one of the most distinguished French writers of the twentieth century, the author of some very powerful novels, essays and theatre plays. His reputation was to grow enormously after his death, both in France and abroad.

Camus came to France during the Occupation and was actively involved in the Resistance (from September 1943 he was chief editor of the clandestine newspaper *Combat*). After the Liberation he opposed the retribution against those accused of having collaborated with the Germans or the Vichy regime and insisted on the importance of pardon. He opposed the philo-communist and pro-Stalin stance of the majority of French intellectuals and tried to pro-mote, instead, a social-democratic vision of the left, combining concern for the oppressed and weak with a commitment to the preservation of liberty. First with *Ni victimes ni bourreaux* (1946) and then particularly with *L'Homme révolté* (1951), Camus condemned Stalinist communism, as well as all sorts of totalitarianism, distinguished between legitimate revolt and its revolution-ary perversion, and pronounced himself in favour of social democracy and trade-union action. With the publication of *L'Homme révolté* Camus became a major target of Communist criticism and fell out with his erstwhile friend of sorts, Sartre, who had by then turned more and more into a panegyrist of the virtues of the communist system. Besides their differences on the issue of communism and Stalinism, as well as their completely different moral tem-pers, Camus and Sartre took opposite sides on the issue of the intellectual's commitment. Camus rejected Sartre's demand that the intellectual be *engagé* and pleaded instead for the artist's political independence. As he put it char-acteristically once, 'in 1957 Racine would be apologising for having written *Bérénice* instead of fighting for the defence of the Edict of Nantes' (an allusion apparently to Sartre's indictment against Flaubert and Goncourt in the first issue of *Les Temps modernes* which we referred to earlier).

But this does not mean that Camus had no political concerns or involve-ment: far from that. What it means is that he opted for more serious, measured, discreet and responsible ways of getting involved in the struggles of his times than Sartre's sensationalist (and often irresponsible) gestures. Few instances show this more than the way in which Camus reacted to the Algerian War in the late 1950s. Unlike Sartre and the other Parisian intellectuals who pronounced vociferously on the subject, Camus was directly and painfully involved, being himself a French Algerian, one of the community known as the *pieds noirs*, who had to leave Algeria and move to France after independence was granted to Algeria's Arab majority in 1962. Camus condemned both the terrorism of the Algerian nationalists of the FLN and the brutal repres-sion by the French army in Algeria. He was painfully prescient of the miseries that were to befall all Algerians, Arab and French, if independence were to be granted the way it eventually happened, and he fought discreetly – and, in the end, unsuccessfully – for a negotiated solution that would have allowed both communities to live side by side in Algeria. Once he realised his preferred solution had no chance, he remained silent and preferred to keep his humanitarian interventions out of the public domain.

In his grasp of the miseries that were to be faced by Algerians, in his very early condemnation of Stalinist communism and his distinction between two different kinds of left, as well as in many other issues, Camus showed a wisdom and foresight that isolated him from the prevailing temper and views of the times. To use a phrase of his own, he had the misfortune of having been right too early. It may be a consolation, though, that posterity has come to see him as 'the noble witness of a rather ignoble age' (Julliard and Winock, 1996), a man of principle, measured responsibility, moral integrity and intellectual consistency, at a time when these things were most unfashionable and guaranteed to make him unpopular.

Similar things can be said for the other great dissenting voice of post-war French intelligentsia, Raymond Aron (1905–83). Though far less isolated than Camus and much more involved with intellectual and political circles, Aron was in the minority throughout most of his life. Unlike Camus, however, Aron lived long enough to see himself not only vindicated but almost revered in the last years of his life, when even his severest former critics came to appreciate the validity of the sceptical liberalism that had characterised his stance for several decades. Aron did not accept Sartre's notion of the *intellectuel engagé*. Instead, he developed his own, more modest and more pragmatic notion of the role of the intellectual (see Exhibit 6.1 on p. 139). According to Aron, the intellectual should be a 'committed observer' (*spectateur engagé*). Aron believed that in most cases the dilemmas faced by intellectuals were much more complicated and nuanced than in the Dreyfus Affair, where the choices were, in his opinion, clear and straightforward. Therefore, Aron wanted the intellectual to display modesty, moderation and moral clarity about what was involved in each case (Jennings 1997: 75). Instead of being carried away by the search for moral absolutes and the ideal society, Aron asked intellectuals to *think politically*, to reflect on the ambiguities of each situation, the difficult choices and decisions those in power were facing, and to come up with pragmatic answers to the concrete questions posed (Jennings 1997).

According to one of Aron's associates, Jean-Claude Casanova (editor of the review *Commentaire*, founded by Aron in 1978), this attitude was the result of an episode that happened in the early 1930s when Aron, who was studying in Germany (1930–33), took advantage of a sojourn in France to give a talk on the situation in Germany. At the end of the talk, a minister asked him what should be done, what he as a minister should do, according to his analysis. Casanova says that Aron was unable to reply. As a result of that experience he promised himself never again to offer a political analysis from which a possible, feasible policy did not follow. Thus, already before he submitted his doctoral thesis (*Introduction à la philosophie de l'histoire*) in 1938, Aron had decided to put himself in the place of the person with responsibility, the minister or prime minister, every time he made a political judgement. In *L'Opium des intellectuels* (1955) Aron vigorously challenged the kind of engagement undertaken in the name of an ideal society or of Marxism. He amplified still further on his notion of the 'committed spectator' in *Le Spectateur engagé*, a series of interviews published in 1981.

Aron's loneliness should not be overestimated. It is not that he was a completely isolated figure writing only for posterity. He was involved in the Resistance with de Gaulle's Free French in London, and, after the Liberation, he was for a brief period quite involved with the Gaullist movement, the RPF (1947–51), through his membership of the movement's *Comité d'études*. In those years he was writing a lot in the reviews *Preuves* and, between 1949 and 1953, *Liberté de l'esprit* (which he co-founded with André Malraux and Claude Mauriac), both of them anti-communist. But then, as Tony Judt has remarked, it is quite characteristic that among the writers who wrote for these two reviews in the early 1950s there was 'a disproportionate presence of foreigners' (Judt 1992: 243). Aron was not alone, but he was in the minority among French intellectuals. So great was the attractive force of Marxism in those days, that a slogan current among intellectuals asserted that it was 'better to be wrong with Sartre, than right with Aron' – *'avoir tort avec Sartre plutôt qu'avoir raison avec Aron'* (Renaut 1999: 23). However that might be, Aron was indisputably the most important of the people trying in those years to keep alive serious political thought on liberal democracy. Among the majority of intellectuals, however, liberal democracy – seen as the legitimising gloss of bourgeois capitalism and the American way of life – was deeply despised, as was any serious reflection on its evolution. After the sea change in the political and intellectual climate in France from 1974 onwards, Aron became more and more respected and influential. In 1978 he founded the review *Commentaire*, which still exists today, as a forum of serious and informed discussion on political issues.

Besides Camus, Aron and his few mainly Gaullist associates, there were only a few dissenting voices to the communist pro-Soviet orthodoxy that dominated French intellectual life in the late 1940s and the 1950s. Maurice Merleau-Ponty (1908–61), initially a close associate of Sartre and *Les Temps modernes*, distanced himself increasingly, after the Korean War, from the communism he had initially espoused. The final break came with the publication of his *Aventures de la dialectique*, in 1955, where he attacked Sartre's *ultra-bolchevisme*. But more important was the vigorous and sustained criticism of the bureaucratic totalitarianism of Soviet communism on the part of a small group of dissident Trotskyites called *Socialisme ou Barbarie*, founded in 1948 by Cornelius Castoriadis and Claude Lefort – who also founded a review of the same name in 1949. Theirs was an anarcho-syndicalist perspective and they sought to recruit workers and to offer 'manual and intellectual workers' the tools of analysis that would lead to revolution. The review and the group continued to be active until 1965, driven mainly by Castoriadis. When the major revolts of May 1968 took place, many said that *Socialisme ou Barbarie* was one of the principal precursors of the movement.

New challenges: Foucault and the 'specific intellectual'

In the 1970s, the model of the intellectual as projected by Sartre received a new challenge from the philosopher Michel Foucault (1926–84), professor of the history of systems of thought at the *Collège de France*. Foucault rejected the pretensions to mastery of truth and justice inherent in the role of the universal intellectual, proposing instead the model of the 'specific intellectual'. According to Foucault, the intellectual could not pretend to act as the 'moral legislator' of the world, giving lessons to others and moulding their political will. Instead, the intellectual's role was 'to make visible the mechanisms of repressive power which operate in a hidden manner', by providing 'the instruments of analysis' drawn from his/her own work 'within specific sectors' (Jennings 1997: 75-6). Thus, intellectuals should function not as 'universal prophets' but rather as 'specialists'. Foucault himself exemplified the model he was proposing with his own activity. Through a series of historical studies in which he tried to expose the ways in which power operates through all sorts of institutions, from mental hospitals and clinics to prisons, he hoped to offer 'the instruments of analysis' – the *outils* – with which people would be enabled to recognise the mechanisms of repressive power which operated in a hidden manner. In his extensive public and political activism Foucault got involved in causes aimed at 'giving those without a voice the possibility of being heard' (Jennings 1997: 76). In this spirit he helped set up the *Groupe d'information sur les prisons* in 1971, he participated actively in the then emerging homosexual movement in France, helped Bernard Kouchner establish the *Médecins Sans Frontières*, supported the Polish Solidarity movement, and, more controversially in the end, gave enthusiastic backing to the Iranian revolution. When Foucault died of AIDS in a Parisian hospital, in June 1984, he left an original and voluminous body of work that had already made him world famous and had contributed significantly to new ways of looking at things.

Bourdieu: *l'intellectuel dominant?*

Pierre Bourdieu (1930–2002) was France's leading sociologist of the late twentieth century and likely the most famous French sociologist of all time. His attitude towards intellectuals shifted remarkably during his academic career. He started by offering, in the 1970s, a powerful and strongly critical sociological unmasking of the intellectuals, their roles and interests. He defined intellectuals as the 'possessors of cultural capital': 'they represent a dominated fraction within the dominant class and many of the positions they adopt, in politics for example, arise from the ambiguity of their position as the dominated amongst the dominant' (Sand 1993: 53). Bourdieu was clearly critical of intellectuals' pretensions to speak on political and other matters by virtue of the authority they had acquired in another field: 'It occurs only too frequently', he observed, 'that intellectuals make use of the competence (in a quasi-judicial sense of the term) that society recognises in them in order to speak with authority about things well beyond the limits of their technical competence, especially in the area of politics' (Sand 1993: 54). However, from the mid-1980s and even more in the 1990s, Bourdieu had become in the eyes of many the aspirant successor to Sartre as the dominant intellectual surrounded by a group of adherents and poised against the powers that be. Moreover, he had come increasingly to argue for the need for intellectuals to establish and preserve their autonomy in relation to all authority, as well as for the need 'to keep the most autonomous cultural producers from the temptation of the ivory tower by creating appropriate institutions to enable them to intervene collectively in politics under their own specific authority' (Sand 1993: 55). Thus, during the 1990s, Bourdieu developed a theory of the importance for intellectuals to organise themselves and stick together in order to fight for independence from the control of technocrats and economic interests and freedom from the incursions of journalists and publicists. He called for an 'international of intellectuals' and in 1993 he participated in the creation of the *Parlement International des Écrivains*. According to Bourdieu, institutions like this would allow intellectuals to be a 'critical countervailing power', able to resist the pressures of other powers, thus serving the interests of the universal.

It was particularly from the time of the fall of the first Communist regimes in Central and Eastern Europe in 1989 that Bourdieu moved steadily towards the role of an intellectual who intervened in public life on political issues and invited others to join him – to such an extent, in fact, that he was called (in an article in *Le Nouvel Observateur* of 25 June–1 July 1998: 109) *'maître agitateur depuis le mouvement de décembre 1995'* – referring to Bourdieu's public support and encouragement of strikers who were protesting, in late 1995, against the changes in the social security system proposed by the government of Alain Juppé. Bourdieu was one of the intellectuals who signed petitions supporting the strikers (while other intellectuals signed petitions in favour of the government's proposed measures and their acceptance by one of the trade unions, the *Confédération Française Democratique du Travail*, CFDT). To give an idea of the extent to which Bourdieu was perceived until his death, in early 2002, as playing – or, at any rate, pursuing – the role of the leading intellectual of France, suffice it to say that the *Magazine Littéraire* dedicated a special issue to the topic: *Pierre Bourdieu: L'intellectuel dominant?* (no. 369, October 1998); and that a scholar who had previously written books exposing the flaws and irresponsibility of Sartre's political interventions, Jeannine Verdès-Leroux, published in 1998 a book entitled *Le Savant et la politique: Essai sur le terrorisme sociologique de Pierre Bourdieu*. Verdès-Leroux is far from alone in accusing Bourdieu of being hypersensitive to anything approaching criticism of his theories, of having steadily built a school and a coterie around himself and his work (the so-called *Bourdieusiens*), and of having tolerated no other attitude than veneration of his work and pronouncements. It has also been remarked that Bourdieu had, at the same time, his own review, his own collection in a publishing house and his own research centre. He was awarded (in 1993) the gold medal of the CNRS (*Centre National de la Recherche Scientifique*), the highest distinction in the field of research in France, for the first time awarded to a sociologist; and he was the only sociologist in the extremely prestigious *Collège de France* (where he had a chair from 1981 until his death).

Bourdieu proclaimed repeatedly that it is not enough for sociology to reveal the structures of society and the representations individuals have of those structures; it also has to act on these representations in order to change the world. As he put it, sociology is *une science qui dérange*, a science that disturbs, makes trouble, unsettles. It was in the 1990s particularly that Bourdieu formulated a concrete role for intellectuals and their importance in public life and actively intervened in several causes. This had not always been the case, as we saw. As he told the Swiss paper *Le Temps* (28 March 1998), 'I myself was a victim of that moralism of neutrality, of the non-implication of the academic researcher. ... As if one could speak of the social world without getting involved in politics [*faire de la politique*]! One could say that a sociologist gets more involved in politics the more he thinks he does not.' As far as his own political activism was concerned, Bourdieu had assumed during the 1990s the role of the leading resistant to what he called *l'invasion néolibérale*. He was (and still is) the main inspiration and intellectual reference of those (many, in France) who attack what they call *la pensée unique*, the emerging consensus in French policy-making circles with regard to economic orthodoxy, including sound financial policies and European economic and monetary integration. (This tendency to struggle against *la pensée unique* and globalisation is mainly represented in the serious press by the monthly *Le Monde diplomatique*, which, continuing its tradition as one of the main pillars of *tiersmondisme*, has not ceased to denounce *l'impérialisme américain*.)

LES ANNÉES DÉBAT AND THE DECLARATION OF WAR ON SARTRE'S CONCEPTION OF THE INTELLECTUAL

Finally, there is another approach to the role of the intellectual – quite fashionable at the moment in France – which was made explicit with the publication, in 1980, of a new review called *Le Débat*, founded and edited by historian Pierre Nora and political philosopher Marcel Gauchet (each edition sells between 8000 and 15 000 copies depending on the topics discussed). In the first issue (which, fate had it, appeared on the very day of Sartre's death in 1980) Nora made clear his wish to make of *Le Débat* '*le contre-pied des* Temps modernes *et de la philosophie de l'engagement*' (*Les Temps modernes* being, of course, Sartre's review, and *la philosophie de l'engagement* being Sartre's theory of the committed intellectual). As Nora himself has put it in a recent interview (*Le Nouvel Observateur*, 25 June–1 July 2002: 112), his editorial for the first issue was in fact '*une profession de foi anti-engagement, au sens sartrien du mot'* ('a profession of faith against engagement, in the Sartrian sense of the word'). The editors of *Les Temps modernes*, despondent at the death of their *maître à penser*, saw it as a declaration of war. Nora announced then that the editors of the new review wished to propose 'a form of intervention by intellectuals in social life which is radically different from that practised until now'. The intellectual should no longer play the role of the prophet or hero, but rather was to be *un éclaireur compétent*. He should stop having pretensions to speak in the name of those whose voices could not be heard, and he should not presume to preach. Instead, he should use his 'critical capacities' and his 'judgement' in order to enlighten and to inform.

It should be noted that the timing of the launching of *Le Débat* (1980) was not accidental. Three years earlier, in 1977, Paul Thibaud launched a new series of *Esprit* (Emmanuel Mounier's old review) and declared, prophetically, that *'le temps des revues est revenu'*. The year after, in 1978, Raymond Aron founded *Commentaire*, which was destined to play an important role in French intellectual life. It was in this context that Nora and Gauchet established their new review in 1980 (see Exhibit 6.2 on p. 140). As Nora was to say two decades later of those years: 'There was a renewal of the intellectual landscape. We had entered into the period of post-Marxism, but also post-structuralism and post-Freudism. ... And ... I felt the change in the intellectual atmosphere that was developing, which has been called by some the epoque of *Débat'* (*Le Nouvel Observateur*, 25 June–1 July 2002: 112; authors' translation). A new controversy over the proper role of 'intellectuals' and their relationship to the 'experts' and the social scientists started in November 2002 (Lindenberg 2002) – see more in Exhibit 1.2 (p. 23).

MÉDIOCRATIE AND THE *INTELLECTUEL MÉDIATIQUE*

It has often been complained that intellectual life in France has been too influenced by its *médiatisation* (see Exhibit 6.3 on p. 140). The intellectual most associated with the formulation of this criticism is Régis Debray (born in 1940), the main detractor of the *intellectuel médiatique*. In works like *Le Pouvoir intellectuel en France* (1979) and *Le Scribe* (1980), Debray has argued that the history of twentieth-century French intellectuals can be divided into three periods: first, the university cycle (1880–1930), dominated by the archetypal figure of the academic; second, the publishing cycle (1920–60), dominated by the writer in the literary review (Debray's favourite cycle); and, third, the media cycle (from 1968 onwards), dominated by the figure of the television personality. Of this last period Debray has written: 'An Americanised intelligentsia in a Europeanised France puts the emphasis on smiles, good teeth, nice hair and the adolescent stupidity known as petulance' (Jennings 1993: 7).

The archetypal television intellectual in the last two decades in France has undoubtedly been Bernard-Henri Lévy (born in 1948). Self-proclaimed *'intellectuel du troisième type'* and leader of the so-called *'Nouveaux Philosophes'*, Bernard-Henri Lévy has been the quintessential *intellectuel médiatique*.

Charming, charismatic, photogenic, he is ubiquitous in the press and on television, and also has his own review, *La Règle du jeu* (since 1990). From the late 1970s onwards he has attained notoriety with a number of book-length essays taking advantage of (or shaping) the new ideological fashions, castigating communist totalitarianism and *la barbarie socialiste*, as well as the *maîtres à penser* of his generation, praising the prescience of Aron and Camus, and attacking anti-Semitism in French society. No matter what one thinks of these causes, most of his critics agree that he wrote on them in a shallow and vacuous way, more designed to attract notoriety and controversy than intent on serious analysis. His latest *cause célèbre* in the 1990s was his campaign against ethnic cleansing in the former Yugoslavia or, as many of his critics saw it (including Régis Debray, who was to cause a lot of controversy by supporting the Serbs against NATO in 1999), the 'demonisation' of the Serbs. He even came very close to presenting himself in the European elections of 1994 under a list headed by himself and fellow 'new philosopher' André Glucksmann, under the name *L'Europe commence à Sarajevo*, which meant to place Bosnia at the heart of the campaign (see more in Drake 2002: 187–95).

THE INSTITUTIONAL AND GEOGRAPHICAL FRAMEWORK OF INTELLECTUAL LIFE: *REVUES, ÉCOLES,* PUBLISHING AND THE PARISIAN *RIVE GAUCHE*

One of the defining characteristics of French intellectual and cultural life is the astonishing concentration of the people and institutions that make it what it is in a small geographical area on the left Bank (*Rive Gauche*) of the River Seine in Paris. It is there that the higher-education institutions which produce such a large proportion of the French intellectual elite are located, as well as the headquarters of the major publishing houses and of the reviews and periodicals that dominate French intellectual and cultural life. Extensions of these institutions exist in the no less important institutions of the cafés of that area, where conversations, debates or deals are continued informally and more congenially. The *École Normale Supérieure* on the Rue d'Ulm has had an influence on French intellectual life that can hardly be overestimated. From the *normaliens* that animated the *Dreyfusard* cause in the 1890s, through students such as Sartre and Aron who studied there together, to Louis Althusser's role in shaping a whole generation of French philosophers in its premises, this *école* has been at the very centre of French intellectual life. Of ever-increasing importance since the 1970s has been the *École des Hautes Études en Sciences Sociales* (EHESS) – presided over between 1977 and 1985 by the extremely influential historian François Furet. Also highly prestigious and influential is the *Fondation Nationale des Sciences Politiques*, better known as *Sciences-po*.

What this geographical centralisation means is that an astonishing number of higher-education teachers in provincial universities do not live where those universities are located, but prefer to live in Paris, where everything happens and everybody is to be found, and to go to their universities only for a couple of days a week to teach. These are the so-called *turbo-profs*, a phenomenon made easier by the existence and constant expansion of France's high-speed trains, the TGV.

The concentration is not only geographical, however. French intellectual life is also characterised by the phenomenon of the so-called *cumulards*. As politicians have been allowed to accumulate multiple elected functions – being, for example, at the same time, ministers and mayors, or members of the national assembly as well as members of the European Parliament – in a similar fashion many French intellectuals have tended to assume multiple functions as university professors, series editors in publishing houses with enormous power over what and who is to be published, chief editors of reviews (each of the major intellectuals tends to have his own *revue*, and most of them operate on the basis of a clique), as well as, some of them, television personalities. This has led to the phenomenon of the so-called *intellocrates* constituting a kind of intellectual establishment which operates in a rigorously hierarchical and clientelistic way.

Exhibit 6.1: Aron and Sartre

Raymond Aron (1905–83) and Jean-Paul Sartre (1905–80) were – besides having been coeval, fellow-students at the prestigious *École Normale Supérieure* on the Rue d'Ulm, as well as friends in their youth – the two leading opposing poles of post-war French intellectual life. As far as their respective views on the role of intellectuals are concerned, Sartre came immediately after the Second World War to advocate as well as practise and incarnate the notion of the committed intellectual, the *intellectuel engagé*, getting involved in all the political issues of his time, pronouncing on them, militantly participating in political struggles in favour of what he saw as the side of progress. Aron, on the other hand, had a much more measured and modest perception of the role of the intellectual, that of the committed spectator, the *spectateur engagé*. As far as their respective political and ideological stances and commitments are concerned, Sartre came to be more or less identified with Marxism and with support for the Soviet Union (which he visited in the 1950s, and praised amply on his return). Aron, on the other hand, was the most serious defender of a sceptical liberalism. No wonder, therefore, that these two old *Normaliens* (Aron always referred to Sartre as *mon petit camarade*) fell out for more than 30 years. However, their shared commitment to humanitarian causes brought them together in a spectacular symbolic move in 1979 (on the initiative of André Glucksmann, one of the so-called *nouveaux philosophes*). Following the victory of the Communist north in the bitter and protracted Vietnam War and the forceful imposition of Communist rule onto the whole of the Vietnam peninsula, many south Vietnamese found themselves stranded in boats, trying to flee. These were the famous 'boat people'. Aron and Sartre went together to the Elysée Palace to petition the President of the Republic (Valéry Giscard d'Estaing, whose candidature Aron had publicly endorsed in 1974) to help the boat people and admit many into France.

Exhibit 6.2: The 'silence of the intellectuals'

In 1983, while the Fifth Republic's first Socialist government was going through a very difficult phase, government spokesman Max Gallo (himself a writer) denounced what he called 'the silence of the intellectuals'. Where, Gallo asked, 'are the Gide, Malraux, Alain and Langevin of today?' This sparked off a protracted debate in the pages of *Le Monde* on the subject of the perceived failure of left-wing intellectuals to defend Mitterrand's Socialist government – which most of them had greeted enthusiastically when it was elected 2 years earlier, in May 1981. It is a debate that, in a sense, continues, as there is a general perception that the role of intellectuals has changed dramatically in the past 20 years or so.

Exhibit 6.3: *Apostrophes*

Apostrophes, presented by Bernard Pivot between 1975 and 1990, was the most famous of French television's literary and cultural programmes. A successor programme, *Bouillon de Culture*, also presented by Pivot, ended in the summer of 2001. At a time when French intellectual life had entered the media epoch, being seen on television and having your book discussed did count and affected sales very considerably. *Apostrophes* was enormously popular and constituted an institution in French intellectual life (*l'effet Pivot*). On occasion, Pivot would interrogate *tête à tête* some real *monstres sacrés* of the intellectual world, from Alexander Solzhenitsyn to Marguerite Yourcenar.

7

EDUCATION, YOUTH AND POPULAR CULTURE

The aim of this chapter is to give our university-aged readers a brief introduction to the issues – political, social and cultural – affecting their age group in France at the start of the twenty-first century. The chapter begins with an overview of the French education system, the egalitarian principles upon which it is founded, but also the inadequate attainment of these principles and the elitism of the *grandes écoles*. We proceed with an overview of the major social, economic and political concerns foremost in the minds of French youth today. We then conclude with a sampling of some of the most exciting developments in French popular culture and, in particular, the trends in an increasingly dynamic and inventive youth culture that owes a great deal to relatively recent immigrants to France, their children and grandchildren – notably the development of the rap and raï musical forms, the rise of the *Yamakasi* phenomenon and a few words will be said on film.

THE FRENCH EDUCATION SYSTEM

Since the early years of the Third Republic in the 1870s, the aim of the French public education system has been to provide free and secular education, equal access and thus opportunities for social mobility for those from less advantaged backgrounds. The extent to which the system has achieved this last objective has been questioned by many. While elitism exists in primary and early secondary education principally as a result of 'postcode segregation' – and, as we shall see below, because of the continued existence of private schools – at the *lycée* and post-secondary level elitism is a pronounced feature of the system, despite various efforts by French governments to widen access and improve rates of academic success.

Schooling in France is compulsory from 6 to 15/16 years of age. Primary schools (*primaires*) teach children aged from 6 to 11; junior high school (*collèges*), 11 to 15; and the non-mandatory senior high school (*lycées*), 16–17.

After *collège* the less academically gifted or inclined often go on to apprenticeship training centres (*centres de formation de l'apprentissage*). There are two kinds of *lycées*: the general and technological, which each offer 3-year courses leading to the general and technological *baccalauréat*s; and the professional, which prepare students for the professional *baccalauréat* and provide courses leading to a range of vocational qualifications. At all levels, the national ministry for education lays down the curriculum and little divergence is allowed, although some options (foreign languages, and so on) are permitted. Since the 1980s, provisions have been made to cater for groups with special learning difficulties: the 'slow learners' are taught in small groups in the *classes de perfectionnement* attached to some elementary schools; the non-francophone children of recent immigrants can benefit from beginners' classes – *classes d'initiation* (CLIN) – offered by special centres (*Centre d'Études pour la Formation et l'Information sur la Scolarisation des Enfants de Migrants* or CEFISEM). In the mid-1990s, a major reform of the *collège*s was undertaken with the aim of establishing a more flexible curriculum – one more responsive to individual needs – and providing appropriate extra teaching support for pupils in difficulty, in order to keep pupils in the mainstream of the system as long as possible.

The successful completion of junior high school is marked by a diploma (the *brevet des collège*s). Able and willing pupils continue with 3 further years at a general and technological high school (*lycée général et technologique*) which leads towards a broad-based diploma, the *baccalauréat*. The wide-ranging curriculum is supposed to provide a good general education but also enable successful candidates to embark upon more specialised higher education. The *lycée professionnel* offers a 2-year course to students seeking practical qualifications – the *Certificat d'Aptitude Professionnelle* (CAP) or the *Brevet d'Études Professionnelle* (BEP) – which will allow direct entry to the job market or the option of attempting to gain a more specialist *baccalauréat professionanel* and then entering the job market or taking a reconversion course, to attempt the technological *baccalauréat*. Those with the professional *baccalauréat* can then follow courses in higher education, especially in advanced technical departments (*sections de techniciens supérieurs*).

Student numbers in the *lycées* have increased dramatically since the 1960s: from 800 000 in 1960 to more than 2.3 million in 1995 (63 per cent of the age group achieved the diploma). This was meant to transform a system designed to provide a general education for the elite to one meeting the needs of much larger numbers of students. One major change in the 1990s was the introduction of a new *lycée* curriculum (completed in 1995) with the aim of introducing all three strands within the same institution and decreasing the relative disfavour with which the non-generalist strands (especially the 'professional' strand) were viewed. At the same time, some *lycées* continue to play host to the *sections de techniciens supérieurs* (STS) and the *classes préparatoires aux grandes écoles* (CPGE). The former provide 2-year courses leading to an advanced technical diploma in a range of options, sometimes linked to the needs of local industry and designed to produce qualified supervisors and middle managers. The latter prepare candidates for the competitive entry examinations organised by the *grandes écoles*. Since the 1989 Education Act, all schools are required to produce an institutional plan showing how the sum total of their activities – curricular and extracurricular – combine to make up the school's distinctive contribution to achieving the aims and objectives laid down nationally. Such a plan, if sufficiently impressive, may attract additional funding.

CATHOLIC SCHOOLS: THE LINGERING PRIVATE/PUBLIC DIVIDE

During the 1990s, private schools educated almost a fifth of French schoolchildren. Most (92 per cent) of these schools are Catholic, the vast majority having a contractual relationship with the state, which provides them with state funding. During the nineteenth century the French state sought to take control of education in the face of stubborn opposition from the Church, which considered teaching as one of its basic missions. With the establishment of the Third Republic in the 1870s, the state sought to expand the provision of free secular education, further challenging the role of the Church. However, Catholic education was preserved by two acts of parliament from the nineteenth century which remain in force today: the Guizot law (1833, for primary education) and the Falloux law (1850, for secondary education).

Laws of the Fifth Republic (the Debré law of 1959 and the Guermeur law of 1977) established the current relationship between the state and private education. Private institutions can choose between independence outside the state system, with income derived from fees, complete integration or association by contract, the last being chosen by the overwhelming majority of such institutions. Under these contracts, the state assumes responsibility for staff salaries and teaching materials and controls staff appointments, curricula and the building of new schools. Since the decentralisation reforms of the 1980s, the different levels of local government make a contribution to overheads and running costs. Contracting institutions must guarantee equal opportunity of access for all, irrespective of race or religion.

Despite the establishment of these relations, antagonism remains deepseated, however, and periodically resurfaces (Corbett and Moon 1996). Private schools on average achieve better results in exams than the state system and better access to the big state *lycées* which offer the most successful preparatory programmes for the *grandes écoles*. In 1982–4 the Socialist government unsuccessfully attempted to implement President Mitterrand's election promise to make education 'a unified, secular public service'. The battle-lines were familiar. The proponents of secularism, led by the *Comité National d'Action Laïque* (CNAL), restated their opposition to the perpetuation of the 'dual' provision fostered by the current system of contracts; the defenders of 'freedom of choice', with the *Comité National de l'Enseignement*

Catholique (CNEC) to the forefront, opposed any suggestion of integration or assimilation into the state system. Mass demonstrations were arranged by both camps, while those in favour of the maintenance of private schools involved more people than any previous demonstration in the history of the Fifth Republic. Fearing the loss of support from many middle-class voters, the Socialist government withdrew the proposed legislation.

UNIVERSITIES

Universities have the dual role of research and teaching the vast majority of students who proceed to post-secondary education. All holders of the *baccalauréat* (or an equivalent qualification) have the right to entry and pay only minimal registration fees, as free state provision extends to higher education. Government policy and increasing demand have meant that universities have had to expand dramatically in size and number since the 1960s. By the mid-1990s they were struggling to cope, with over 1.5 million registered students, a number which has remained stable since and is set to drop only slightly – due to demographic factors – by the middle of the first decade of the twenty-first century. Since funding and staffing have failed to keep pace with such increases, considerable strains have been imposed on the system, and a constant series of reforms has been tried in an endeavour to alleviate them. For its part, the student body has consistently been active and vocal in its denunciation of inadequate study conditions and state neglect. The most famous – and radical – of these protests came in May 1968 and resulted in significant reforms to the institutional structure of higher education which remain largely in place today. Attempts to introduce selection – as in 1987 (the Devaquet laws) – were blocked by widespread student protest.

The *loi d'orientation sur l'enseignement supérieur* (Higher Education Reform Act) passed in 1968 created 70 new multidisciplinary higher-education institutions, with greater autonomy (especially financial and administrative) and governed by bodies which guaranteed a voice to all categories of staff and students, divided into self-administering *Unités d'Enseignment et de Recherche* (UER). The aim was to break down traditional academic barriers and overcome vested interests. Degree programmes were organised into three successive tiers (cycles), of which the first two lasted for 2 years; the third was more open-ended.

- Tier one: a broadly based introduction to an area of study and to working methods leading to the award of the *Diplome d'Études Universitaires Générales* (DEUG).
- Tier two: more specialised study leading to a first degree (*licence*) after one year and a master's (*maîtrise*) – including some initiation into research methods – after a second year.
- Tier three: high specialisation (the DEA, *Diplôme d'Études Approfondies*) and doctoral research.

Universities were given a degree of control over the design of their curricula, but the state imposed guidelines to protect the national character of the awards. The 1984 Savary Act relabelled the UER as UFR (*Unités de Formation et de Recherche*) with an emphasis on career preparation, and in 1992 the units were replaced by what were considered to be more broadly based modules.

The system allows for diversity; since being granted autonomy, some universities have used their new-found freedom to delay or even to avoid applying the various reforms dictated by government. However, through its 4-year contracts with universities, the state (the Ministry of National Education) maintains an important role: it sanctions all diplomas, provides the majority of the universities' budgets, controls staff appointments and pays salaries as all permanent teachers have the status of civil servant. A state employee, the *Recteur d'Académie*, acts as chancellor of the universities within his or her administrative district.

Successive French governments have sought to tackle two dominant issues: the high failure rate – especially in the first cycle; approximately 40 per cent of university entrants leave without obtaining the DEUG – and the relevance of studies to the evolving job market. With entry selection politically unacceptable, universities have been encouraged to improve counselling for students and opportunities to change courses. There have also been attempts to create new, more vocationally oriented, technical programmes of study to provide for students who may not manage very successfully in prolonged and rather abstract study. These include special advanced post-*baccalauréat* technical education at the *lycées* (STSs) and 2-year courses in the *Instituts Universitaires de Technologie* leading to a *Diplôme Universitaire de Technologie*. Professional programmes have also been created at the second-and third-cycle levels (for example, the diploma of *ingénieur maître* awarded by the *Instituts Universitaires Professionnalisés* established in 1991). However, these are often highly selective programmes, excluding the weaker students who have little choice but to enter non-selective, traditional abstract studies if they want to remain at university. With successive French governments seeking to increase the percentage of students obtaining the *baccalauréat*, the resulting rise in demand for university places has progressively increased. The serious problems of the university system thus seem destined to continue, especially given the efforts of governments to cut public-spending deficits.

GRANDES ÉCOLES: LA CRÈME DE LA CRÈME

French higher education is unique in Western Europe in that most of the best students do not go to university. They are creamed off by the *grandes écoles* – over 150 small, selective, largely independent institutions, covering diverse subject areas, which train most of the business, academic, administrative and political elite of the country. A 1993 survey revealed that, in the leading 200 French companies, 73 per cent of the top executives were alumni of the *grandes écoles* while 50 per cent came from two of the most prestigious schools: *École*

Polytechnique or the ENA. The oldest of the schools date to the eighteenth and nineteenth centuries (the engineering school, the *École des Ponts et Chaussées*, was founded in 1747), while many are more recent creations. One of the most famous – *École Nationale d'Administration* (ENA) (examined in Chapter 3) – dates only to 1945. The schools can be generally classified into four main groups. The four *Écoles Normales Supérieures* train top-level academics and teachers and academic administrators. ENA and nine *Instituts d'Études Politiques* train their students for careers in government administration or related fields. Several *grandes écoles* (*L'École des Hautes Études Commerciales* (HEC) and the *Écoles Supérieures de Commerce*) are business schools which train financial consultants, business executives and accountants. The engineering schools (*École Nationale Supérieure des Mines, des Télécommunications, des Ponts et Chaussées*, and so on) educate technical experts and senior managers for industry and the public services.

Some of the *écoles* are funded by the state, providing salaries to students who are obliged to enter state employment upon graduation (notably, ENA, *École Polytechnique* and the four *Écoles Normales Supérieures*). Others are funded by public commercial bodies (notably the chambers of commerce) or by private groups and may charge fees. All the *grandes écoles* are highly selective and, despite expanding student numbers in most, relatively small. Entry on the basis of competitive examination requires special preparation, usually in the *Classes Préparatoires aux Grandes Ecoles* (CPGE) – which are themselves selective – provided for in the big *lycées*. The CPGE involve at least 2 years of intensive study in the humanities, economics or science. ENA hopefuls almost always attend one of the *Prep ENA* courses on offer at the *Instituts d'Études Politiques* and it is the students from the Paris Prep ENA who are the most successful. In effect, ambitious French students must truly become *bêtes à concours* ('exam animals').

The *grandes écoles* are professionally oriented and professionals in the field assist in programme design and are often involved in the teaching. Many programmes include obligatory practical placements (*stages*). The jobs that graduates enter and their salary determine in part the value of a school's diploma while the precise job and salary will be determined by the students' overall ranking, which can make for a very competitive environment in some schools. The schools also promote a strong sense of loyalty amongst alumni in order to reinforce the prestige of the institution. The *grandes écoles* have been criticised a great deal over the years for their elitism, their social composition – which reflects a strong upper-middle-class bias – and the extent to which their graduates dominate the senior posts in both the public and private sectors and create a self-perpetuating elite.

WHAT ARE THE SOCIAL ATTITUDES OF FRENCH YOUTH TODAY?

The term 'youth culture' is a difficult one to pin down and some sociologists have challenged the idea of a culture that is specific to young people.

The term usually refers to the leisure practices or, more generally, the references, icons and values seen to be specific to the 12–25 age group. The extended period of education in the context of high youth unemployment levels has helped to reinforce a distinct subculture in French society. As in other western societies, youth culture in France is closely associated with leisure technologies and audio-visual media, and is largely influenced by the United States: from McDonald's (Macdo) and other fast food, to baseball caps, to rap. Numerous surveys, covering varying age groups, provide some evidence of common activities and tastes, starting unsurprisingly with a widespread enjoyment of pop music (in 1997, 90 per cent of 15–19 year olds said they preferred some form of pop), followed by trips to the cinema, the fairground and clubs (discos) as the most popular activities (87, 69 and 56 per cent respectively went to these venues at least once in 1997). However, while these statistics are well above the national average, the tastes of French youth are significantly differentiated by social background, gender and educational attainment.

In addition to these tastes in leisure activities, which may or may not distinguish French youth as a particular social class, their more general preoccupations should be considered. In November 1999 a survey of 15–24 year olds demonstrated that unemployment and violence worried them above all other concerns.[1] They believed that money played too great a role in society, that France was excessively corrupt and unequal and that opportunities for upward social mobility did not meet their expectations. However, the large majority of French youth today clearly do not dream of revolution. Seventy per cent do not want to modify the essential aspects of French society.[2] At the same time, 70 per cent of French youth felt quite good in French society (*assez bien*), while 20 per cent felt 'very good' (*très bien*), with a positive total of 90 per cent. However, there remain serious problems: 75 per cent thought that French society did not offer 'many possibilities' for upward social mobility for a young person from a 'modest' or poor family. The large majority also believed that life in France today was more difficult than it had been for their parents.

Most young people challenged the idea that they enjoyed strong *intra*-generational solidarity. Fifty-nine per cent thought that the forces dividing them – notably social differences and, in particular, employment – were stronger than the forces that brought them together. Unemployment was considered the most serious problem of their generation, which reflects the reality that, despite the relatively strong economic growth from 1998 to 2001, French youth unemployment remains one of the highest in the European Union and affects disproportionately ethnic minorities living in the poor suburbs of urban centres (*banlieues*). Where one lives was the second most

---

1 Poll undertaken by Sofrès for the *Fédération Syndicale Unitaire*, FSU, the principal federation for education, 5–10 November 1999. See *Le Monde*, 21–22 November 1999.
2 Ten per cent want to leave French society in its current state and 60 per cent seek reform on several points but without touching on the essential, while 24 per cent want substantial reform and 6 per cent radical change.

important factor contributing to social division (*fracture sociale*), considered more important – perhaps naïvely – than social origin and level of education. French youth were also very preoccupied with violence. When asked to describe their generation in a word, they were most likely to choose 'dynamic', but immediately followed this with 'violent' (above 'realistic' and 'solidaristic'). Violence was cited as the second worst problem with which they were confronted, after unemployment but before drugs, the lack of money, AIDS, alcohol, access to housing and loneliness. The younger the person, the more violence worried them: 56 per cent of 21–24 year olds saw it as a serious problem, while 69 per cent of the 15–17 year olds shared this view. Nonetheless, violence was not considered the most serious defect of society. Above it was 'money', which French youth felt was of excessive importance in the country. Furthermore, they identified and criticised widespread dishonesty and corruption.

In terms of what French youth considered most important to their lives, 'family' topped the list, well above other considerations, followed by friendship, work and love. Family was considered more important to girls than to boys (85 versus 79 per cent found it very important) and more by younger people than older (85 per cent of the 15–17 year olds versus 80 per cent of the 21–24 age group). On the question of employment, a majority of young people felt that it was more important to have a stable job (59 per cent) than an enjoyable or interesting one (53 and 50 per cent respectively), reflecting the reality of job scarcity. Girls were more inclined than boys to value enjoyment and interest at work above salary. Girls were also much more likely (79 per cent) to believe that French society does not offer many possibilities for social mobility. Fifty-five per cent of French youth questioned think that the principal difficulty of their finding a job was employers' lack of confidence in their ability. Sixty-two per cent felt ready to make important sacrifices in their personal lives in order to succeed in their professional lives.

Not surprisingly, the level of political involvement among French youth was very low. Among 10 factors that could motivate them to become engaged in politics, the struggle against a political party that appeared dangerous was the highest. Although the National Front was not explicitly mentioned, this response ties in with the fact that French youth led and dominated demonstrations throughout the country against Le Pen in 2002. However, in 1999 only 57 per cent of French youth were ready to become part of a specific movement against the extreme right and only 2 per cent then belonged to such an organisation. As for other motivations for political action, the 'struggle against social injustice' was far ahead of 'protest against a foreign war', which perhaps explains the relatively limited mobilisation by French youth (including those of Arab extraction) against George Bush's 'War on Terror' and the Israeli occupation of the territories of Palestinian Authority in April–May 2002. As for 'militating in a *lycée* or university political organisation', 68 per cent refused. French youth appear more inclined to participate in an association than a political party: 76 per cent envisaged that they could join an 'association to defend the rights of young people' but only 1 per cent actually belonged to such a group in 1999.

On education, 91 per cent of university and *lycée* students questioned believed that their studies helped them to 'learn many useful things' (*d'apprendre beaucoup de choses*); 82 per cent appreciated the level of 'general culture' provided by their education, while 75 per cent believed that this would enable them to enter into their chosen career. Those studying for the general *baccalauréat* believed this less (only 65 per cent). A surprising (!) 90 per cent of French youth said that they thought their studies were 'interesting', while only 35 per cent of those studying for the general *baccalauréat* shared this sentiment. Eighty-five per cent of students were able to choose their preferred area of study. Also surprising is the limited criticism of school or university, though it seems that the government's efforts to make the education system more vocationally oriented and improve students' preparation for the 'real world' appear – in the eyes of most *lycée* and university students – to be inadequate. As for students at the *lycées*, most girls saw themselves becoming teachers, educationalists, or involved in some form of childcare, whereas boys thought first and foremost of a career in commerce, wished to take up a trade or dreamt of becoming professional sports stars.

Mobility is another important aspect of the lives of the average French youth and with increased mobility, communication by means of mobile phones has spread rapidly over the past half-decade. Those in the 15–24 age group are the greatest users of mobile phones, which permit a group of friends to maintain close contact (this tribe being a second family). The behaviour of French youth is very much determined (as ever) by the customs and habits of their friends: their choice of clothing, their preferred music and their manner of speaking. Clearly, French 'youth' is not one and uniform. In the realm of musical tastes, two major groups developed during the 1990s, preferring either rap (54 per cent) or techno (43 per cent). Techno music was preferred by people from a wealthier background, whereas rap was originally the means of expression of the youth from the suburbs – poorer and more likely to come from an ethnic minority – that also eventually became the music of the middle classes. This growing cultural influence of the *banlieues* among middle-class youths has gone well beyond just music: the suburbs have come to set the standard for the development of cool language and clothing (baggy trousers, sporting kit and basketball shoes, Nike and Adidas preferred). The use of cannabis and the consumption of tobacco and alcohol have become widespread. The use of heroin has declined but the consumption of synthetic drugs, including ecstasy, has become more widespread, as elsewhere in Western Europe. While music is their greatest preoccupation (playing, listening to and dancing to), cinema and television – most of it American – ranks high as well: two-thirds of the 15–24 age group saw the film *Titanic* significantly more than any single French film. However, on television, a French comedy series, *Hartley cœurs à vif*, ranks at the same level as *Friends* and *Beverly Hills 2000*. Reading is far less popular. Nonetheless, a substantial number of young people do still read regularly: 33.7 per cent of

15 year olds interviewed and 30 per cent of 18 year olds 'read a book over the past weekend'.

RECENT DEVELOPMENTS IN FRENCH POP CULTURE

Rock and pop

Long derided, French rock and pop suffered from a low status both abroad and in France until the 1980s. French rock was epitomised – pathetically – by Johnny Halliday. For good reasons, the French consistently listened to more *anglo-saxon* rock and pop than their own. However, from the 1980s, groups like *Indochine, Starshooter, Marquis de Sade, Les Négresses Vertes* and *Telephone* have demonstrated the virtues of French rock and pop and have even found international recognition. Nonetheless, American and British artists continue to attract the biggest crowds at concerts and, as in so many areas of cultural life, the French state has intervened over the years to promote French rock and pop music. In 1984 the *Zenith* at Porte de Bagnolet in Paris was launched, the first of several government-subsidised venues for rock and pop concerts. The Socialist minister of culture for most of the 1980s was the popular Jack Lang, whose zeal for promoting French pop even led to the temporary creation of a *Chargé de mission pour le rock et les variétés* (a rock and pop official representative) attached to the minister's office.

France's ethnic minority communities have made a contribution to French rock and pop that far exceeds their numerical presence in French society. Bands from the *banlieues* chose music as a form of protest against a society that excluded them, their life of deprivation, unemployment and delinquency, but also as a means of integration. They have developed new musical hybrids of diverse forms from different cultures (of jazz, rock, funk, reggae and raï) which have completely transformed the French musical scene over the past two decades. In the 1980s *Carte de Séjour* – a band from the Lyon *banlieue* Rilleux-le-Pape – was a noteworthy forerunner of this hybridisation and helped pave the way for other bands, including *Les Négresses Vertes* and *Mano Negra*. Here we focus upon two musical developments that have sprung from the *banlieues*: *raï* and rap.

Raï and *beur* music

Raï is a musical form, blending North African Arab and western forms (using more traditional western instruments and new technologies) that began in North Africa in the 1960s and 1970s (notably the Maghreb – Algeria, Morocco and Tunisia) and took off in the mid-1980s with major festivals in Oran and Algiers. *Raï* musicians, such as the Algerian (Kabyle) Idir and Djamel Allam, enjoyed successful tours in France. *Raï* began to take off in France in the mid-1980s with Cheb Khaled and Cheb Mami and the landmark *raï* festival which took place in Bobigny in 1986. It spoke above all to the rapidly growing *beur* population in France, the children and grandchildren of North African immigrants, but has also expanded its audience to other French people as well. Home-grown *raï* artists also came of age in the late 1980s, including Karim Kacel, who sang of the troubled life of the *banlieues*. Its proponents claim that *raï*, like rap, represents the need to express feelings of frustration (*malaise*) but through powerful music rather than violence and hatred (see the website of a fan at http://filoumektoub.free.fr/maghreb/rai/rai1/rai1.htm). While in Algeria it has become the expression of freedom, against both the military regime and the Islamic fundamentalists (*les barbus*), in France itself *raï* has assumed importance as a form of expression against racial discrimination and the contradictory pressures of integration that face the *beurs*. By the early 1990s, *beur* music was blossoming in France with groups emerging from the *banlieues* throughout the country: the *Zebda* offered a mixture of rock, funk and *chaâbi* (a North African form) and Big Brother Hakim, a drummer moved by *chaâbi*, American soul, reggae and jazz rock (who later turned to rap).

Rap

Like *raï*, rap has foreign sources – African American hip-hop and acid jazz – but has been transplanted into French culture by disadvantaged ethnic minority communities, both black and *beur*. While its origins mark rap as musical protest against the injustice of urban society, its French variant has developed a more amusing fun and pun dimension. Rap first appeared in France in the early 1980s and soon became an important element of the dance scene. However, it only hit the mainstream pop airwaves in 1993 when IAM's *Je danse le Mia* became a great success. The leading rap artist of the 1990s has been MC Solaar, who combines American and French musical influences and writes lyrics focusing on more mainstream themes beyond the *banlieues*. *Raï* and rap have also engaged in an appealing dialogue during the past decade. *Raï* musician Big Brother Hakim created the group *Jungle Gala* in 1993, which immediately became one of the most original voices in French rap, while *Alliance Ethnic*, another *beur* band, also developed a less harsh form of rap (*Simple et Funky*, 1995) which placed emphasis on the joy of making *beur* music.

YAMAKASI: THE NEW 'RELIGION' OF THE *BANLIEUES*

Yamakasi has become the latest cultural/sporting sensation to hit France. The name comes from the Congolese language Lingala, the word *Yamàmi* meaning 'man strong in body and mind'. *Yamakasi* is a highly dangerous activity engaged in principally by young men – mostly from ethnic minorities, mostly from the *banlieues* and mostly in their early 20s – jumping between buildings with deliberate and very concentrated control. *Yamakasi* did not actually begin in the deprived suburban council estates. It was started in the mid-1980s in Lisses, near Evry, south of Paris, by David Belle, the son of a

French veteran from the Vietnam War and then fireman in Paris. *Yamakasi* attracted a small group in Evry and, following media coverage, the numbers increased considerably. While some were tempted into commercialising their activity, others believed firmly that its principles (the *parkour*) were corrupted by money-making and publicity. (See http://filoumektoub1.free.fr/humeurs/yamakasi.) The stuff of urban legends during the 1990s, this radical new 'sport', or as the *Yamaks* would have it, 'way of life', became increasingly familiar to the French public. In April 2001 Luc Besson released his film *Yamakasi*, giving it an even greater profile (see http://www.yamakasi.com/).

Yamakasi involves the *parkour* (discipline): a strong spirit that commands the body and makes it accomplish amazing physical feats. This is the art of moving oneself in space and time using the elements of the urban environment. It involves numerous special movements, some of which have evocatively symbolic labels: to climb, leap, jump, 'be a cat, a spider or a monkey' according to the dangers of the moment, and even 'a bird'. One of the specific kinds of jump is called 'high voltage'. The *Yamaks*, light and agile, jump between buildings, scantily clad, without protection, grabbing onto the sides of edifices, jumping from roofs, falling from bridges or from staircases. The required qualities for the *parkour* are both mental (internal control of fear, of feelings and reflexes; calm; sang-froid; team spirit) and physical (agility; *souplesse*; a high level of fitness; good health). When perfect synthesis between mental and physical qualities has been achieved, when mind and body are in perfect equilibrium, it is possible to accede to the highest degree of the *parkour*. Emphasis is placed on the gradual development of one's skills, and on demonstrating perseverance, gradually pushing oneself further. The body must be kept pure with clean air, healthy food and drink (water, milk and fruit juice only), and needs two things but never in excess: rest and action. The mental preparation for *Yamakasi* jumps is crucial. The objective is always to land on one's feet and never to have an accident. Team spirit is a crucial element: the *Yamak* is never alone. The partner helps in the mental preparation to overcome fear. This link with the other is indispensable: shared challenge, friendship and honesty.

As a social phenomenon, *Yamakasi* is predominantly practised by the ethnic minority youth of the *banlieues*. It represents a way of avoiding the hazards of ghetto life – drugs, delinquency, and so on – and of achieving a feeling of self-confidence in the context of the relative poverty and deprivation of the estates. *Yamakasi* is based on the philosophy that man evolves according to his environment. To practise *Yamakasi* is to gain strength from others in the group. The group evolves together, providing a sense of competition but also support. *Yamakasi* is the constant questioning of oneself, evolution and progress without end, the perpetual stretching of physical and mental potential. The aim and motive are not to impress others: 'one is alone against the jump'. A major purpose of *Yamakasi* is also to challenge the rules society has laid down, as reflected in the buildings and passages created by urban architects: to make one's own path, to create one's own destiny, not what society has thrown at one.

The *parkour* teaches that the routes are many outside of the established paths and that everyone can find his own path. Thus the more one develops a spirit of *parkour*, the more one asks how society should be rethought.

On a more commercial note, the *Yamakasi* phenomenon was turned into a box-office hit in France, with the film *Yamakasi* directed by Ariel Zeïtoun and written in part and produced by Luc Besson (released in April 2001). The *Yamaks* are portrayed as modern-day Robin Hood characters fighting the constraining forces of French society. Many *Yamakasi* purists rejected the film. Although it showed the beneficial physical and psychological side of the sport, it was criticised as creating a false impression, having exaggerated the jumping ability of *Yamaks*. The authorities and police also criticised the film for transforming the *Yamaks* into modern-day heroes and encouraging others to join what many consider to be an excessively dangerous practice. During filming, the police sought to prevent the participation of three of the *Yamaks* who had criminal records. The film was also challenged by many for its critical portrayal of public-service elements of white French society: doctors, hospitals, politicians, police.

FILM

Cinema is a tremendously important element of French culture (see Mazdon 2000b) – generously subsidised by the French state through tariffs imposed on foreign (mostly American) films. Much of French cinema has the status of an art form worthy of intellectual attention and study at secondary and post-secondary level. At the start of the twenty-first century French films attract a decreasing share of the French market (currently below 30 per cent) but have maintained an impressive variety and quality and remain much admired abroad. A generalised development has been the move to so-called 'postmodern' or 'middle-brow' films which have attempted to erode the distinction between 'popular' and 'high' culture – furthered by the actors Gérard Depardieu and Daniel Auteil, who shift regularly between the two.

One significant trend since the mid-1980s is the expensive, designer, romanticised movie of the so-called *Forum des Halles* genre. Directors in this vein include Carax (of *Les Amants du Pont-Neuf* fame), Besson and Beineix. Another trend is the 'heritage films' directed by the likes of Rappeneau, Berri and Chéreau (*La Reine Margot*). More populist films have been directed by Jean-Marie Poiré: the immensely successful *Les Visiteurs* (1993) and *Les Anges gardiens* (1995). An important recent development – reminiscent of the social realism of the 1970s' *Nouvelle Vague* film movements but also of Spike Lee – is *beur* cinema and the *cinéma de banlieue*. Produced on a low budget and engaging with France's social problems, this cinema is attracting a wider audience – *La Haine* (1995), directed by Matthieu Kassovitz, being a noteworthy example. Hollywood continues to have great influence on French film-making, but the reverse is also true (Mazdon 2000a): Quentin Tarantino notably proclaimed the influence of Godard's *Band à Part* on *Pulp Fiction*. At the start of the twenty-first century, one of Hollywood's most popular directors is the very anti-establishment Frenchman Luc Besson (*Le Grand Bleu* (1988), *Nikita* (1990), *Léon* (1995) and *The Fifth Element* (1997)). Controversial films, such as *Romance* (Breillat, 2000) and *Baise-moi* (Despentes and Trinh Thi 2000), show that French cinema still has the capacity to shock the world.

8

FRENCH ECONOMIC AND SOCIAL POLICY IN AN ERA OF GROWING EUROPEAN AND INTERNATIONAL CONSTRAINTS

This chapter examines attempts by French governments to modernise the domestic economy and the welfare state while maintaining public support, in the context of the tightening constraints of the Single European Market (SEM), the European Monetary System (EMS), the single-currency (euro-) zone and increased exposure to the international economy. France entered the twenty-first century with an impressively robust economy, record trade surpluses and rapidly dropping unemployment figures. This promising economic situation boosted the popularity of European Monetary Union (EMU) – as demonstrated in opinion polls – which started on 1 January 1999. France was reaping the rewards of a long period of domestic adjustment that started in the late 1970s and was reinforced by the success in avoiding devaluation of the franc from 1987 onwards. The country enjoyed a strong trade surplus from the mid-1990s which continued into the new millennium despite the strong rise in domestic consumption. A substantial fall in German and French short-term interest rates between 1995 and early 1997 (the period immediately before the start of the EMU project) and during the first half of 1999 gave a much-needed push to domestic consumption and investment.

The substantial decline of the euro in relation to the dollar and the yen also suited French preferences. Throughout the 1990s French governments argued that European currencies were overvalued in relation to the dollar. In a November 1996 article in the French weekly *L'Express*, former president Giscard d'Estaing, one of France's leading proponents of EMU, called for a unilateral devaluation of the franc in the Exchange Rate Mechanism (ERM) (the margins of allowed fluctuation) of the EMS. Giscard justified this by the overvaluation of European currencies in relation to the dollar and the German refusal to lower interest rates to allow a devaluation of the deutschmark. In the campaign for the 1997 parliamentary elections, the Plural Left coalition called for a lower exchange rate with the dollar and the yen as one of its four conditions for continuing with EMU. French calls for European politicians to avoid expressing views in favour of a weak euro – notably the German chancellor, Gerhard Schröder – should *not* be seen as a reflection of the Jospin government's preoccupation with the slide of the European currency. The gradual rise in European interest rates from November 1999 also suited French economic interests. Growth was strong in 1999 and 2000, while the economy had spare capacity with potential for further growth well into 2000. A tighter but still accommodating monetary stance favoured French requirements. Germany, which was at an earlier stage in the cycle, preferred the lower rates. Reflecting the monetary power motives that drove French policy on EMU, the rate rise was seen as a manifestation of Germany's reduced influence in EMU – widely commented on in the French press – compared with its previous predominance in the ERM.

Some French politicians and top civil servants supported the creation of the EMS, SEM and EMU as *self-imposed* constraints to reinforce domestic economic restructuring and help France cope with increased international competition. President Valéry Giscard d'Estaing embraced the EMS in 1979 in order to reinforce domestic efforts to 'modernise' the state and economy, keep public spending under control and reduce inflation despite widespread reluctance in the French population and political circles. This reluctance stemmed from worries about increased exposure to European and global competition, European competition rules, and the comparatively heavy reliance on foreign capital to finance both public-sector debt and private-sector equity capital (Alphandéry 2000; Boissonnat 1998). Likewise, President François Mitterrand's March 1983 decision to keep the franc in the ERM was the symbolic moment of a policy shift to end socialist reflation, embrace open competition in the European Community (EC as the European Union was then called), and conform – at least to a certain extent – to the German economic standard. The French pursuit of EMU demonstrated the desire to ensure the continuation of reform while simultaneously loosening external constraints by sharing monetary power with the Germans. The tightness of these constraints was blamed for the excessive decline in French economic output and the growth of French unemployment, particularly in the period following German reunification.

This chapter examines the impact of these constraints (European and international) upon the development of French state identity (by which we mean the role of the state in the economy and the development of French economic and social policies). This identity has gone through considerable changes over the past two decades because of financial market liberalisation, budget reform (including reform of the social security budget and the structures controlling this budget), increasing labour-market flexibility and privatisation. EMU has required central bank independence, sought by few French policy-makers, opposed by many, and directly contrary to the French republican tradition. EMU involved modification of the role of the powerful Treasury division of the Ministry of Finance and the change in the manner in which the government presented its economic policy, notably through the establishment of medium-term stabilisation plans in coordination with its European partners to fulfil the terms of the 1997 Stability and Growth Pact. The Plural Left government of Lionel Jospin placed considerable emphasis on counter-balancing both the power of the European Central Bank (ECB) in the euro-zone by strengthening a European 'economic government', and the 'sound' money bias of EMU by reinforcing European social and employment policies.

This chapter is divided into two parts. In the first part we examine the discursive/ideological structure underpinning and shaping the impact of European and international constraints on French state structures, policy regimes and policies, and French strategic responses to these constraints. This discursive structure is shaped principally by a conservative liberalism – in the ascendant owing to economic constraints reinforced by monetary integration – and a rearguard interventionism. In the second part we show how substantive state reforms and the strategic behaviour of French policy-makers reflect the dialectic between these two ideologies, and how these factors together have contributed to reshaping French state identity. Conservative liberals dominant in the financial administrative elite have manipulated the European and international constraints to justify the adoption of policies which have resulted in stabilisation and major reforms to the welfare state to bring public spending more firmly under government control. The European and international constraints sat uneasily with a strong interventionist legacy, but EMU increased possibilities for improved EU-level coordination in economic and employment policies – 'economic government' – in whose development the Jospin government was in the vanguard. As will be demonstrated in Chapter 9, the decision to embrace EMU has also reflected, and been presented in terms of, the traditional assertiveness of the French state in the European and international arenas, backed by widespread popular approval (Howarth 2001).

Following a brief overview of the organisation of the French welfare state, the chapter ends with a section examining the economic policy-making elite in the French administration, the financial inspectors (*inspecteurs des finances*).

THE ECONOMIC IDEOLOGY BEHIND FRENCH STATE STRATEGIES

Reinforcing the conservative liberal agenda

Conservative liberalism has been the dominant economic ideology in the Treasury division of the Ministry of Finance, the Bank of France and the Financial Inspectorate, the *grand corps* of the French financial elite. However, the influence of this ideology has always been limited by its fragmentation and weakness in French party politics (Dyson *et al.* 1994: 35; Hazareesingh 1994). The creation of the EMS in 1979 corresponded to the hitherto rare predominance of conservative liberalism in government under Giscard d'Estaing as president and Raymond Barre as prime minister. This ideology was inspired more by the German model of low inflationary economic growth than Anglo-American liberalism (Dyson 1994; McNamara 1998).

Conservative liberals uphold the self-adjusting nature of market mechanisms and reject state-led reflation. They seek exchange-rate stability, low inflation, balanced budgets and current-account surpluses. Devaluation was long opposed as a fundamental threat to a social order based on savings and monetary stability. Conservative liberals embraced the EMS and EMU as useful means to import German 'sound' money policies and budget and wage discipline. They respect technical experience and expertise in economic policy and the maintenance of a measure of autonomy from political interference in the formulation and implementation of economic policy – which serves the interests of the Treasury and the Bank of France.

The EMS helped to reinforce the influence of the Treasury and the Bank of France in relation to governments. EMU helped to further reinforce conservative liberalism through the convergence criteria and the transfer of monetary policy to technocratic control in the Bank of France and the ECB. Members of the Treasury were very reluctant to embrace independent central banking as a necessary step to reinforce their economic preferences. However, the convergence criteria and the Stability and Growth Pact reinforced Treasury influence over the domestic reform agenda.

Core conservative liberal economic ideas formed the bedrock of 'competitive disinflation', the major French macroeconomic policy from the mid-1980s (Fitoussi 1992; 1995). The value of 'sound' money was linked to the idea that the weakening competitive position of French exports was due to structural problems that could not be resolved through competitive devaluations. Following Mitterrand's March 1983 decision to prioritise a stable franc in the ERM, intellectual and political support for this policy gradually solidified, labelled by critics *la pensée unique*. At the intellectual level, the extensive influence of the state in economic research, through the studies produced in the Treasury, the forecasting division of the Ministry of Finance, and the National Institute of Statistics and Economic Studies (INSEE), facilitated the rapid extension of these ideas into the academic economic community and their dominance. The ideological shift to 'competitive disinflation' was reinforced by modernisation and liberalisation of the French financial markets in the mid-1980s, including the creation of the MATIF (the French futures market), as part of the drive to reform the 'overdraft' economy (Mamou 1987; Loriaux 1991). The aim of opening access to foreign capital to finance French debt was to control inflation and lower interest rates. This increased reliance on foreign capital made both attractive rates and a strong currency more necessary than previously.

In a French political class traditionally little concerned with inflation as an economic problem, 'competitive disinflation' helped to increase the acceptability of 'sound' money policies and the EMS constraint. The demands of French governments for a more balanced convergence suggest that their principal worry was not inflation *per se* but the inflation differential and trade imbalance with France's major trading partners. The label 'competitive disinflation' is thus revealing: disinflation was required principally to improve France's competitive position *vis-à-vis* Germany. The distinction is important because it demonstrates the shallowness of anti-inflationary sentiment in French political circles beyond the small conservative liberal hardcore around Barre and Giscard and the Socialist modernisers, notably Jacques Delors and Pierre Bérégovoy. Moreover, this distinction introduces a different angle on the economic logic behind French support for the EMS constraint. The purpose of this constraint as far as many leading French politicians were concerned was to reduce the level of French inflation not as an objective in itself but in order to improve France's competitive position. The greatly improved competitiveness of French companies in the 1990s and record trade surpluses from 1994 helped to legitimise a policy that was otherwise blamed for lost economic output and high unemployment.

The continued weakness of French neo-liberalism

Neo-liberalism has been weak in the Treasury, Bank of France, and French academic and political circles, and of relatively limited direct influence in shaping French economic and social policy. Likewise, France was largely immune to Anglo-American economic arguments criticising EMU for not being an optimal currency zone (Rosa 1998). Neo-liberalism was most influential in the context of financial market liberalisation started by Bérégovoy in 1984. This process was encouraged both by EMS membership – the search for non-inflationary sources of finance – and by continued EMS membership – increasing the need for monetary stability and raising French interest rates to attract foreign capital.

Neo-liberalism enjoyed a brief period of influence in the neo-Gaullist RPR of Jacques Chirac in the mid-1980s, although this rhetoric was rejected after 1988 for electoral reasons. Overt neo-liberalism played only a limited role in the public debate on the EMS and EMU. Most frequently it has been invoked with a negative connotation by those on the left and the right opposing EMU as a neo-liberal device to reinforce the effects of globalisation and undermine the French social model.

The lingering *dirigiste* bias

Dirigisme as a manifestation of *étatisme* reflects a strong mistrust of market mechanisms, the economic utility of which is nonetheless accepted. The market is seen as being too severe for society and as failing to use the country's resources in an optimal manner. *Dirigisme* insists on the need for active state intervention in the economy, labelled *volontarisme*, in order to protect citizens. Since the Second World War French *dirigisme* has found intellectual sustenance in Keynesianism, which advocates that the market plays a central role in the economy but, as the market is unable to guarantee full employment, the state must intervene in order to create demand and stimulate the economy. This should be juxtaposed with economic liberalism, which upholds the law of the market, of supply and demand and the invisible hand (the enrichment of society through the enrichment of each person). Liberals generally believe that the intervention of the state in the economy leads to its poor operation and to non-optimal use of the country's resources. In France, a liberal tradition and a *dirigiste* tradition have coexisted since the eighteenth century. The liberal tradition is the older (from the sixteenth century), and was dominant from the nineteenth century until the 1930s. The Keynesian revolution took root as a reaction to the economic depression of the 1930s and the devastation of the war. Keynesianism dominated French economic thinking, in the administration, political sphere and academia, until well into the 1990s. In the immediate post-war period the state extended its control over large sectors of the economy. State control was further expanded in the late 1970s (when the steel sector was nationalised) and under the Socialists in 1981. *Dirigisme* required the creation of an economic and financial administrative elite to manage the economy, trained principally at the *École Nationale d'Administration* (ENA) and *École Polytechnique* (frequently referred to by the sobriquet 'X') (see the section on financial inspectors at the end of this chapter).

Dirigisme has influenced a wide spectrum of French political and public opinion to different degrees, notably the Gaullist/neo-Gaullist parties on the right, the Socialist Party on the left, in addition to the elite technical corps of the French state, which had limited influence over monetary policy. *Dirigiste*s tend to prefer the conservative liberal goals of a strong currency, monetary stability and a trade surplus, although normally for different reasons. But these goals are secondary to state-led economic growth. *Dirigiste*s also seek to place constraints on the operation of international financial markets and speculative capital. Jospin continued to call for the imposition of an international tax on speculative capital movements – the so-called Tobin tax – right up to the 1997 legislative elections.

Several forces have brought about the gradual decline of French *dirigisme* since its heyday in the 1950s and 1960s. We have seen the rise of liberal ideas since the 1970s (and especially since the 1980s) due to increased American influence in the global economy, the freeing of trade at both the European and international levels, European rules restricting state subsidies and ownership, the influx of less expensive products from outside Europe (where labour is generally cheaper, taxes lower and labour markets more flexible), and the rapid development of the economies of the Pacific Rim. Also of great importance has been rising French debt, and in particular company debt, and the inability of French governments to stem the rise of unemployment since the oil crisis of the 1970s. It was increasingly believed that the state was too big to be an effective manager in all sectors of a complex economy. In an increasingly competitive environment, French companies have had to be more effective and more flexible. The Socialist governments of the 1980s and early 1990s may have refused to accept privatisation, but they increasingly forced public-sector companies to sink or swim on their own.

Paradoxically, the decline in *dirigiste* strategies has worked to the disadvantage of the French Treasury, which had profited immensely from post-war *dirigisme* and the extension of the public sphere. The decline of *dirigisme* reflected the rise of the Treasury's ideological bias of conservative liberalism, while greatly weakening the influence of the Treasury itself. Nonetheless, the capacity of the French state, led by the Treasury, to persist in a policy of avoiding ERM parity realignments for 12 years from 1987 to the start of EMU, despite the considerable economic and political difficulties in doing so, reflects an important strength of the *dirigiste* tradition. In the 1980s and 1990s both the neo-Gaullists and the Socialists rejected many elements of *dirigisme*.

At the same time, electoral constraints – the public sanctioning of perceived excessive liberalism – forced most parties of both the mainstream left and right to continue to emphasise state-led action. Much of the electorate continues to expect interventionist state responses. Rising French unemployment has increased pressure on governments to allow the public sector to assume some of the burden and for the state to pursue activist programmes to encourage employment and training. Active state responses to the challenges of 'modernisation', particularly in social and employment policies, and the political difficulties of managing the privatisation of the public services, demonstrate the institutionally embedded ideas that make French responses to European and international constraints unique. The administrative elite and much of the political elite is trained to *diriger*. Even conservative liberals like Edouard Balladur, Edmond Alphandéry and Alain Juppé have made a spirited defence of French public services against European competition rules. Liberalisation has assumed a surreptitious form: few political leaders insist upon it publicly even though, since the mid-1980s, all have in fact accepted more. Liberalism as an economic doctrine remains far less widespread in academic and media circles than in English-speaking countries.

To justify reforms, leading Socialists have appealed to the Mendesiste left-wing tradition of economic modernisation designed to challenge 'traditional centres of capitalist privilege'. From the early 1980s, social Catholics like Delors sought a 'Third Way' that would retain elements of *dirigisme* while accepting the predominance of market forces. What was common was the idea of 'reforming' capitalism in alliance with the technostructure of the French state. The idea of regulating and controlling markets in the context of what Jospin labelled a 'modern socialism' was an important element of Socialist Party discourse in dealing with the constraints of globalisation (Jospin 1999; Marian 1999; Cambadélis 1999). Leading Socialists learnt from their defeat in the 1993 legislative elections that a continued *dirigiste* discourse and policy response were crucial to their electoral success by preventing the loss of support to other left-wing parties. In order to reinforce his government's left-wing credentials, Jospin also distanced himself from the 'social democracy' espoused in the Blair–Schröder Paper – attacked as 'social liberalism' by many in the French left – and insisted on the plurality of European social democracy.

Officially, EMU was not to force the left into strategies that pushed 'modernisation' in the direction of unacceptable liberalisation. Jospin (1999) claimed that the *volontariste* state remains a crucial part of 'modern socialism' despite

European and international constraints (also Marian 1999). The left accepts the central role of the market but insists that it must be regulated and 'governed' at both national and international levels. While interventionist strategies of the 'old' left are no longer valid, *volontarisme* remains crucial in three forms: what Jospin calls a 'strategic state', which encourages activity in areas of future growth; an 'investor state', which plays an active role in assuring the improvement of infrastructure, education and research; and a 'facilitating state', which works to improve the quality of the operating environment of companies.

Jospin also placed emphasis on the construction of 'social democracy' at the European level as a means to counterbalance the monetary power of the ECB and to limit the worst effects of globalisation. He stressed improved economic policy coordination in the Eurogroup, especially coordinated reflation, the development of European employment policy, the reinforcement of European social policy, and common European positions on international market regulation. If appropriately counterbalanced by EU-level economic policy coordination, EMU was a means to regain control of, and manage, the forces of globalisation. This strategy reflects the strong negative connotation of globalisation on the French left, demonstrated by the popularity of such books as *L'Horreur économique* (1996) by Viviane Forrester. Equally, it illustrates the relatively positive perception of European integration in the Socialist Party established by President Mitterrand. In the 1990s EMU has been manipulated in the same way as the Single Market Programme from the mid-1980s: as a mechanism to make the economy more competitive while preserving the relatively generous social security system and working conditions (*les acquis sociaux*). The discourse of EMU as a means of reconciling the European social model to the new realities of globalisation – notably in Germany – has been less present in France given the widespread hostility that 'globalisation' inspires.

However, Jospin's Socialist-led government from 1997 placed clear boundaries around this *dirigiste* reflex. The brief return of neo-Keynesianism under Oskar Lafontaine (briefly the Socialist finance minister) in Germany was not matched intellectually in France. The Socialist finance minister, Dominique Strauss-Kahn, joined several Lafontaine initiatives calling for more European-led activism on growth and employment (see, for example, their jointly written article in *Le Monde*, 15 January 1999) and the two ministers issued a joint statement praising the 3 December 1998 drop in French and German interest rates.

At the international level and in business and financial sector forums in France, Strauss-Kahn was particularly active in promoting his government's modernising credentials. He was frequently praised for his ability to present very different messages at different forums. At the twelfth anniversary meeting of the London-based Centre for Economic Policy Research (CEPR) in November 1998, he equated 'modern socialism' with 'modernisation' and, in particular, 'sound' money and finance. He argued that there was nothing socialist about high deficits and debt (Strauss-Kahn 1998). Though his domestic public and party political speeches were decidedly more *volontariste* in rhetoric, the Jospin government accepted the need for continued 'modernisation' in the face of increased competition in the euro-zone and globalisation. It privatised more state assets than all previous conservative governments combined and refused to intervene in highly politicised factory closures (the Renault plant in Vilvorde, Belgium, in 1997) and massive lay-offs (Michelin in 1999) despite considerable pressure from coalition partners and trade unions. In consequence, the government was exposed to accusations that it had accepted the dominant conservative liberalism in economic policy making and allowed an excessive Anglo-American-style liberalisation. In contrast, it had used a 'virtual' activism in EU and domestic social and employment policies in order to legitimise modernisation (Desportes and Mauduit 1999).

EMU AND FRENCH STATE REFORM

Adjusting to independent monetary authority

The early benign economic impact of the euro-zone helped to legitimise the highly controversial transformation that EMU imposed on France, notably central bank independence. Administrative and political opposition to independence was rooted in four factors (Howarth 2001): the republican tradition, notably the indivisibility of French political authority; the perception of the appropriate link between monetary and economic policies; the belief that low inflationary policies do not require independent central banks; and the institutional power interests of the French Treasury. This opposition fed wider public concern about rule by 'technocrats' and lack of democratic accountability.

Compared with other national central banks, the Bank of France was normally considered to be one of the more 'dependent', with monetary power concentrated in the Treasury division of the Finance Ministry (Goodman 1992). In the post-war period, the bank had made repeated demands for increased autonomy, but political and Treasury opposition had been too great. Conservative liberal admiration of the 'German model' did not extend to support for central bank independence. On the left, autonomy was associated with a pre-war privileging of private interests, deflation and inadequate investment. Nonetheless, prior to the Maastricht Treaty the ERM, the stable franc policy and financial market liberalisation had already promoted a shift of relative power from the Treasury to the Bank of France, notably because of the increased importance of interest-rate policy, on which the bank had the greater expertise (Mamou 1987; Dyson *et al*. 1994; Dyson 1997). German insistence on the privileged position of the EU central bank governors in the negotiations on EMU also reinforced the position of the bank in relation to the Treasury.

The rapid move to independence for the Bank of France in 1994 – right at the start of the 5-year second stage of EMU during which independence was to be achieved – was justified as building confidence in the franc in the context of record levels of speculation. The intensity of the 1993 debate on the bill granting independence, opposed essentially by the same politicians who opposed EMU, and the necessary constitutional change – which required a special majority of three-fifths of both legislative chambers meeting at Versailles – demonstrated the unlikelihood that independence could have been achieved without EMU. The legislation on independence had initially been blocked by the French Constitutional Council on the grounds that, under the constitution of the Fifth Republic, a government could not delegate responsibility for the conduct of monetary policy to an independent body.

Article 1 of the bill also attempted to meet republican objections to the ban on 'soliciting or accepting' outside instructions on the conduct of monetary policy by asserting that monetary policy must operate 'in the framework of the government's general economic policy'. The move to independence also provided the opportunity to transfer full power over banking supervision to the Bank of France, opposed by the Treasury and traditionally by much of the political class. However, this move was seen as crucial in rebuilding confidence in banking supervision after the *Crédit Lyonnais* scandal, which had demonstrated the difficulty of maintaining effective Treasury control given the cosy networks of the Financial Inspectorate.

Independence and EMU transformed the role of the Bank of France in domestic policy making. Governor Jacques de Larosière, former head of the IMF, played a crucial role in the discussions on EMU leading to Maastricht, both as a credible interlocutor of the *Bundesbank* and by his efforts, using a very active and public campaign, to convince Mitterrand and others of the need to accept German demands for independence. Bank of France governors had previously been known for their criticism of government policy, especially during the Fourth Republic. However, most demonstrated caution when commenting on government policy making. Following independence, the bank had to accommodate itself to a more active and public role in promoting 'stability' culture in France. Jean-Claude Trichet, the first governor of the independent Bank of France, made several thinly veiled attacks on presidential and government economic and monetary policy statements and economic policy decisions which appeared to threaten the pursuit of 'sound' money policies, the move to EMU, and respect for the Stability and Growth Pact (Aeschimann and Riché 1996; Milesi 1998).

The process of appointment of the bank's Monetary Policy Committee members created the possibility of strongly divergent perspectives on monetary policy making and a less orthodox leadership than that of the *Bundesbank* and, paradoxically, the pre-independence Bank of France. The appointment of six of the nine external members for staggered 9-year terms is shared between the presidents of the National Assembly, the Senate, and the Economic and Social Council. The other three, the governor and deputy governors, are appointed for periods of 6 years. By early 1997, a majority of the committee – five of the six externally appointed members – were known for their anti-EMS credentials and opposition to the excessively high interest rates necessary to keep the franc in the ERM. The leading neo-Gaullist Eurosceptic, Phillipe Séguin, as president of the National Assembly, nominated Jean-René Bernard and Pierre Guillen, who were appointed on

3 January 1997. The latter, a former president of the metal-workers' federation, had actively opposed the Maastricht Treaty. This anti-EMS majority battled unsuccessfully for a rapid drop in French rates. In November 1996 two of the externally appointed members publicly expressed their disapproval of the EMU convergence criteria and argued in favour of an additional criterion emphasising employment levels. Thus, the governing board of the independent Bank of France itself contributed to qualifying the emphasis placed on 'sound' money policies which had been established as its sole official objective in the 1993 statute. Paradoxically, in doing so, it may have reinforced the independent bank's legitimacy on the left.

Bank of France independence also involved a shift in government discourse on monetary policy. In the context of domestic political pressures to stimulate economic growth, there was a strong temptation to use the bank, and notably Trichet, as a scapegoat for the high interest rates in the EMS. Such scapegoating was highly problematic given the bank's fragile legitimacy and public support, compared with its German counterpart. Leading Eurosceptics and opposition politicians frequently attacked Trichet, whose name unfortunately approximates the French word *tricher* ('to cheat'). More problematic were the attacks by President Jacques Chirac and the government of Alain Juppé. In the context of continued doubt about French willingness to maintain high interest rates and commitment to EMU, such attacks prompted speculation against the franc. Thinly veiled personal attacks against Trichet threatened to undermine his professional credibility and public acceptance of independence. Thus on 14 July 1995, in a televised interview, Chirac implicitly, but very clearly, took Trichet to task on two matters: high interest rates and the laxity of banking supervision in the late 1980s and early 1990s when Trichet was head of the Treasury. The Jospin government resisted criticising the ECB or diverging in any way from public support for a strong euro. In part, this stance reflected policy learning. The long experience of foreign-exchange speculation made French governments, particularly Socialist-led ones, highly sensitive to the need for caution when discussing monetary policies. The risk of incurring the sanction of euro-zone partner governments also imposed greater caution. More importantly, the difficult economic and political conditions of the period 1992–7 had been lifted and were unlikely to be recreated in the near future.

The French Treasury had to accommodate itself to a very different kind of policy-making role. The loss of control over monetary policy and banking supervision were only two elements of the gradual decline of Treasury power. Other elements included financial market liberalisation, privatisation and European competition rules. However, the Treasury regained influence in domestic policy making as a consequence of reinforced EU-level coordination of macroeconomic policies in the euro-group and the Cologne process and on the medium-term stabilisation plans which have largely corresponded to conservative liberal reform priorities. The Treasury remains very much the centre of economic intelligence in France. Although the Bank of France has increased its capacities in this field, it still depends on Treasury information in several areas, notably economic statistics and forecasting information. Treasury power was reasserted as the privileged partner in the Franco-German Economic Council, created in November 1987, and, alongside the Bank of France, in the Economic and Financial Committee – the rebaptised Monetary Committee – whose first head was Jean Lemierre, a former Treasury director and Financial Inspector. The appointment of former Treasury director and Financial Inspector Christian Noyer as ECB vice-president, and thus member of both the executive board and the governing council, created a vital link between the French Treasury, the French financial elite and the ECB. Noyer's appointment, although acceptable according to the ECB statute given his experience in the area of monetary policy, was unusual. He was the only member of the ECB Governing Council with no direct professional or academic experience in central banking.

Policy regime reform

The framework of monetary and financial discipline created by the EMS and EMU has been an explicitly manipulated driving force behind financial market liberalisation as well as budgetary, fiscal, welfare state, administrative and labour-market reforms. This connection was made most prominently in the 1994 Minc Report, the most comprehensive package of reform recommendations to date. The EMU constraint has been used by governments as a more politically acceptable way of 'internalising' external economic imperatives represented by globalisation. EMU as a justification for reform was presented as the central message of Chirac's public U-turn on economic policy on 26 October 1995, the Juppé Plan of the following November, and the shift in the Jospin government's budget policy in summer 1997.

EMU as a justification for reform has, however, run up against competing values. A combination of ideologically inspired political opposition to reforms with trade-union opposition to modifications to social security regimes and to privatised public services which disadvantage public-sector employees has resulted in a degree of inertia. Slower than expected change was due less to domestic institutional vetos than to a lack of political will. The political difficulties of reform were manifested in the widespread strikes and public demonstrations of December 1995 and at various times thereafter. Public administration staff cuts – the non-replacement of retiring staff – have been recommended in diverse reports but consistently avoided by governments. In April 2000 Prime Minister Jospin sacrificed his minister of finance, Christian Sautter, and cancelled cuts in the number of tax officers which had sparked nation-wide strikes. The aim of the cuts had been to set a precedent for other ministries. The French public-sector deficit remains one of the largest in the euro-zone, and there is pressure from other member states on France to make more sustainable cuts to public spending. With presidential and legislative elections in 2002, the Jospin government was unwilling to engage in further cuts that would enable it to meet the Stability Pact's aim of a budget surplus during a period of relatively strong economic growth.

French public-sector debt hovers very close to the 60 per cent maximum debt criterion to be respected by countries participating in EMU, which makes more substantial cuts necessary after the 2002 elections.

Careful political management, increased emphasis on negotiation and good relations with trade-union leaders, and gradualism have become core elements of government reform strategies (Marsh 1999). The public reaction to the Juppé Plan of November 1995 demonstrated the dangers of pushing through ambitious reforms without adequate consultation and supportive coalitions. The presence of Communist, Green and left-wing Socialist parties in the Plural Left government made the management of reform particularly hazardous but has equally helped to contain opposition (Cambadélis 1999). Jospin placed considerable emphasis on open debate, although coalition partners increasingly complained that this debate was principally a technique to push through reforms that they found unacceptable. In this context, resort to a government audit in 1997 was necessary to justify continued government spending cuts to meet the 3 per cent criterion. The Plural Left coalition had promised to stop these cuts.

Jospin also created the *Conseil d'Analyse Économique* (CAE), attached to his office. This group consists of 38 academic economists, appointed by the prime minister, who meet once a month to discuss matters chosen by him or other ministers in advance. It was presided over by either Jospin himself or Pierre-Alain Muet, a leading French academic economist and member of his support staff (*cabinet*). The stated purpose of the CAE is to provide an opportunity for open debate on the major economic and social questions of the day prior to government decision-making. Its members produce reports requested by ministers, and these reports reflect, rather than suppress, the diversity of views. The CAE is intended to present a public challenge to the perceived excessively technocratic Treasury control over economic policy (Victor 1999: 427). It plays the role of legitimiser of controversial economic policy decisions and a means to contain the opposition of left-wing academic economists. More generally, the creation of the CAE represents an attempt to respond to those who question the legitimacy of the highly technocratic EMU and the economic constraints that it imposes by demonstrating the continued capacity of the government to take an activist line on economic and social policies.

Financial market liberalisation

Besides monetary policy, the financial market liberalisation of 1984–8 was the first major French policy-regime reform linked explicitly to the operation of the EMS. It was inspired more by Anglo-American neo-liberalism, which shaped the thinking of American-educated members in the Socialist finance minister Pierre Bérégovoy's *cabinet*, than by 'sound' money ideas imported through the operation of the EMS. Still, the decision to maintain the franc in the ERM made financial liberalisation both more acceptable and more likely because French policy had to focus on market-imposed interest rates more closely. The continued participation of the franc in the ERM made the pursuit of low inflationary policies more necessary, whereas the provision of state-allocated credit in the *circuits de trésor* was inherently inflationary. The challenge of controlling inflation provided a useful logic that helped overcome the institutionally rooted reluctance to accept liberalisation in the Treasury, which had blocked previous reform attempts (Loriaux 1991).

Financial market liberalisation in turn reinforced the ERM constraint and increased the logic of moving to EMU. The limited development of French institutional investors resulted in the dramatic growth of French dependence on foreign-held, largely American, debt, which amounted to roughly 40 per cent of total debt by the early 1990s, far higher than any of the larger EU member states. In consequence, French governments had to be particularly cautious about the perceived strength of the franc and attractiveness of French interest rates (Reland 1998). Liberalisation also created new controlling interests – American pension funds – which increased the importance of shareholder value and discouraged interventionist strategies that were inconsistent with this value.

The need to maintain high real interest rates in the context of the asymmetric operation of the ERM encouraged the French to pursue reform and led to the Basle–Nyborg accords on improved interest-rate policy coordination. The German refusal to accept further obligations that would make the EMS a more symmetric system encouraged French interest in more substantial reform. Increased reliance on foreign capital and the desire to build Paris as a financial centre also made capital controls imposed at the national level increasingly problematic. In consequence, France had less to lose from capital liberalisation, which the German government had established as a precondition for discussions on EMU. Nonetheless, French governments remained wary of the impact of liberalisation on exchange-rate stability, given the persistent speculation against the franc well into 1987. Ironically, President Mitterrand had to impose capital market liberalisation on Bérégovoy, the father of financial market reform, in the interests of making progress on EMU (Howarth 2001).

Budget cutting

The 'sound' money policies pursued in the EMS increased pressure on governments to keep public spending under control. Following financial market liberalisation, budgetary restraint was deemed necessary to lower French interest rates. Justification of budget cutting involved a reinvention of discourse appealing to the preoccupation with unemployment. Dramatically reversing the reflationist discourse and criticism of the deficit convergence criterion that characterised his presidential campaign, in October 1995 President Chirac explicitly argued that rapid cuts were necessary to ensure the move to EMU in 1999.

EMU, German insistence on respecting the 3 per cent deficit criterion, and the Stability and Growth Pact placed budget reform high on the agenda. However, even without the external constraints, budget cutting would have been a priority because of record high tax levels and a decreased margin of manoeuvre in budgetary policy. A growing percentage of the total budget consisted of allocated expenditure. In 1993 the budget deficit reached an unprecedented 6 per cent of GDP. In his October 1995 interview, Chirac insisted that low budget deficits were a precondition of job creation, a core argument in conservative liberal discourse.

Governments were forced to examine possible cuts in government and social security spending, a tighter control over local government budgets, and also, more controversially, structural reforms. The ability of the Jospin government to meet the fiscal criteria to ensure that France was an uncontroversial candidate in 1998 depended largely on privatisations and transfers of French telecom profits. More problematically, in 1996 the Juppé government had assumed state control over existing *France Télécom* pensions. In consequence, *France Télécom* transferred 37.5 billion francs to the state budget, which diminished the deficit by 0.45 per cent. Though vital to prove continued French commitment to EMU, it imposed a heavy financial burden on future governments.

Barring substantially higher economic growth rates, further structural reforms are required in order to respect the Stability Pact in the medium term. Budget cuts largely affected the Ministry of Defence. With one of the largest public administrations in Europe in terms of percentage of total jobs, cuts to staff numbers have been widely recommended. The Picq Report of 1994 established the goal of replacing only one in three civil servants retiring from the administration in order to reduce the total number of staff to the 1980 level: a 15 per cent cut. However, in the context of record high levels of unemployment, and the strong and militant trade-union presence in the public sector, led by *Force Ouvrière*, cuts were postponed by the Balladur and Juppé governments. The need to start making politically difficult cutbacks, combined with an anticipated economic downturn, was one major consideration that led President Chirac to dissolve the National Assembly and hold the legislative elections in 1997, a year early. Just prior to these elections the UDF minister of finance, Jean Arthuis, promised to reduce personnel. However, the Plural Left government of Jospin continued to delay total staff cuts. It used staff replacement as a political device to demonstrate its commitment to job creation in the public sector, allied with temporary youth employment schemes.

Improved budget management also came on to the agenda. Bolstered by the Stability and Growth Pact's commitment to budget surpluses during periods of economic growth, Arthuis (1998) called for changes to the budget ordinance of 1959 in order to prohibit a deficit on current expenditure. Government deficit financing would be strictly limited to capital expenditure. This move would have been in keeping with the emphasis that Arthuis as finance minister had placed on the distinction between current expenditure and capital expenditure in preparing the 1997 budget. While this reform proposal had some support in conservative liberal circles, it is unlikely that it would have been proposed in the absence of the Stability and Growth Pact. There have also been growing calls, led by two former finance ministers,

Arthuis (1998) and Alphandéry (2000), to increase parliamentary control over the budget. They sought increased powers and resources for the finance committees of the Assembly and the Senate, in particular to resist more effectively the adoption of supplementary credits by decree. But the well-entrenched opposition to the extension of parliamentary control over the executive prevented any significant early moves in this direction.

The Juppé government was not, however, opposed to the extension of parliamentary control of overall social security expenditure. This increased control involved a major challenge to the powers of the social partners – employers' representatives and trade unions – which previously had the final say over budgets in the mutual fund administrative councils. Opposition to this element of the Juppé Plan was one of the factors that sparked off the December 1995 demonstrations. Nonetheless, the government proceeded with the necessary modification of the constitution on 19 February 1996 and the legal process – a decree of 24 April 1996 – to enable the reform. Decrees were also adopted to reform hospital administration and to control more effectively medical practitioners' standard consulting fees. Additionally, the Juppé government sought, unsuccessfully, to modify pension regimes for public-sector employees by increasing the contribution period from 36.5 to 39 years in line with the private sector. Initial moves in this direction in November 1995, affecting train and metro conductors, were rescinded to end nation-wide strikes.

Before the 1997 elections the Plural Left promised an end to budget cuts. But the Jospin government rapidly abandoned promises to run an activist budgetary policy and continued with cuts in government expenditure, notably in defence. Nonetheless, the Jospin government kept up the rhetoric of margin of manoeuvre – vital for maintaining legitimacy on the left – promising an increase of 1 per cent in government expenditure, whereas the Juppé government had sought an expenditure freeze. In December 1998 the Jospin government announced its annual medium-term stabilisation plan for a sustainable drop in the public deficit. The increase in government expenditure was to be only 1 per cent over 2000–2, or 0.3 per cent per year – a reinterpretation of the previous promise – lowering the public deficit from 2.3 per cent in 1999 to 0.8–1.2 per cent in 2002, depending on growth rates. From the start of 1999, the Jospin government announced that for the 2000 budget there would be no spending increase, an indication that it had decided to defer any increase to the lead-up to the 2002 presidential and legislative elections. The Socialist-led government recognised the unpopularity of cutbacks in its own constituency, much of which works in the public sector. Finance minister Christian Sautter failed in his efforts to decrease the excessively large number of tax administrators due to the unwillingness of the Socialist-led government to push through cuts in the face of stubborn trade-union opposition. He was replaced by the more politically astute former prime minister Laurent Fabius, who put all government cutbacks on hold. Relatively strong economic growth during the first three and a half years of office enabled the Jospin government to delay more substantial, sustainable cuts until after the 2002 elections.

The debate in early 2000 on the unexpectedly large budget revenue – the *cagnotte* – due to stronger than predicted economic growth was revealing. The use of the *cagnotte* became a symbol of the Jospin government's priorities. Rather than using it to further reduce the deficit, Jospin was constrained by the Socialist left and the Plural Left coalition partners to increase government spending. Likewise, the government sought to prioritise income-tax cuts – announced on 31 August 2000 – for the first time in 15 years; French taxes are among the highest in the western world. Tax reductions benefited all income groups, in particular the least well off, as well as companies, with the aim of stimulating further growth in order to lower the deficit. In the 2002 presidential and legislative electoral campaigns, tax cuts were the most important economic policy reform on offer from Jacques Chirac and the Raffarin interim government (cuts in income taxes by a third over the period 2002–7, starting with an immediate cut of 5 per cent, lower corporate taxes and cuts in VAT payments for specific sectors, notably hotels, restaurants and catering).

Labour-market reform

The restriction of interest-rate and exchange-rate policies in the EMS and their loss with EMU, along with the increased wage competition in the euro-zone, placed increased pressure on French governments to modify labour-market policies and increase wage flexibility. Reform took place in the context of high structural unemployment due to the high minimum wage and high social security charges imposed on French companies. It was constrained by the political difficulties of lowering the minimum wage – traditionally, new French presidents and governments raise the minimum wage above the rate of inflation – and by the lack of centralised wage bargaining which makes negotiated solutions more difficult. The attempt by the Balladur government in 1994 to introduce a lower minimum wage for young people met with stubborn student resistance and was dropped.

The combination of these factors led to two major policy responses to the problem of labour-market inflexibility. French governments relaxed rules on hiring by allowing greater scope for the creation of work of a limited duration – *contrats de durée déterminée* – and for part-time work. The Jospin government also created the possibility for greater flexibility in the context of the 35-hour week. It allowed companies, in collective bargaining on the implementation of the 35-hour week, the possibility of freezing wages and spreading the 35-hour week over the period of a year.

'Sound' monetary policies and the EMU constraint

At the European level, French governments of both left and right consistently manifested a desire to modify two core elements of the EMU project – the prevalence of 'sound' monetary policies and technocratic control over monetary policy – with more interventionist EU strategies. Despite the increased influence of conservative liberalism and the determined pursuit of low-inflation policies, this desire was reflected in long-standing French efforts to persuade the Germans to accept a more balanced economic convergence and to increase the obligations of strong currency states – notably Germany – in the EMS to decrease the system's deflationary impact. To reiterate, French interest in monetary cooperation and integration was based on accepting the need for an external constraint; but, equally, French governments opposed an excessively rigorous constraint.

Since the early 1980s, French governments have also actively pursued job-creating reflationary EU strategies. Notable was Chirac's success at the June 1995 Cannes European Council in persuading his European partners to accept a massive EU-wide infrastructural development programme – never put into effect. The continued attempts to modify and counterbalance 'sound' monetary policies were demonstrated by proposals to modify the EMU convergence criteria, to create an EU 'economic government' – including improved economic policy coordination and a strengthened employment policy – and to develop EU social policy. French governments consistently sought to modify the economic policy-making constraints imposed by EMU while accepting the EMU goal itself. These government efforts should also be seen as an important legitimising exercise on behalf of the EMU constraint and 'modernising' reforms, appealing to the strong interventionist tradition in France: part of what Dyson (1999) labels the 'craftsmanship of discourse'.

National politicians, both in government and in opposition, had difficulty accepting the idea, central to 'sound' monetary policies, of the neutrality of monetary policy in terms of employment. Following German reunification, the unique situation of low French inflation combined with record high real interest rates to maintain the franc in the ERM did not help this process of acceptance. From 1991 to 1997, French governments were very critical of the *Bundesbank* and the Bank of France for their excessive caution in lowering interest rates. These criticisms tended to undermine the credibility of French monetary policy.

Modification of the convergence criteria, notably the 3 per cent deficit rule, was a consistent demand of French governments against the background of the economic difficulties of the mid-1990s, the dramatic rise in public-sector deficits, and the political difficulties associated with necessary cuts. The government had accepted the convergence criteria in 1990–1, France being one of the few states that could meet them at the time. French negotiators proposed the 3 per cent deficit criterion rule whereas the German Ministry of Finance had originally proposed a more relaxed calculation of deficits.

The Juppé and Jospin governments accepted the proposal for a Stability Pact, principally as a means to meet the demands of the Kohl government and to counter strong opposition to EMU in Germany. However, they sought to render it as innocuous as possible (Milesi 1998; Schor 1999). The Juppé government wanted to avoid the automatic fines sought by the Germans, giving priority to politically determined fines, in ECOFIN (the Council of EU Economic and Finance Ministers). After prolonged discussions, the French accepted automatic fines. They then sought derogation in the event of economic recession. However, again Germany largely prevailed: derogation was guaranteed in the unlikely event of recession beyond 2 per cent of GDP and politically determined in the event of a shrinking GDP between 0.75 per cent and 2 per cent of GDP. The Germans also succeeded in imposing the goal of budget surplus during periods of economic growth. The addition of the word 'Growth' to the Stability Pact was a French demand to facilitate acceptance of the pact at home.

The Plural Left had promised the rejection of the Stability and Growth Pact as part of their wider push for a *euro-social*. To avoid a crisis that would put EMU at risk, the Jospin government reached a compromise with the Germans at the Amsterdam European Council in June 1997. This compromise involved the symbolic modification of the resolution on the pact by a general and vague resolution on growth and employment, topped by a common preamble which ostensibly granted equal weight to both. The Amsterdam resolution on 'growth and employment' included the 'urging' – no obligation was established – of the European Investment Bank (EIB) to increase its interventions in high-technology and small and medium-sized enterprise projects, as well as education, health, environment and large infrastructure projects on the grounds that these tended to create jobs. In reality, this commitment did not amount to any real change. The EIB already took employment into account in its investment decisions, and there was no increased funding – which the Germans were quick to point out. However, a previously agreed EIB loan for small and medium-sized companies was announced at the Amsterdam summit and presented by the Jospin government as proof that the new employment policy had teeth. The Jospin government's efforts to ensure the participation of the Italians – another Plural Left demand – also reflected the desire to maintain a less rigorous euro-zone and limit German influence. French support for not officially criticising Italy for its excessive deficit in 1999 nor Portugal and Germany in 2002 reflected more relaxed attitudes to the application of the Stability and Growth Pact.

French preference for relaxing 'sound' monetary and technocratic control was reflected in constant demands for the establishment of a European 'economic government': a political counterweight to the ECB to improve economic policy coordination and establish an appropriate policy mix at the European level. Improved European economic policy coordination had been a French policy ambition from the oil crisis of 1973, normally with the aim of encouraging the Germans to reflate their economy – or lead an EC-wide reflation – or improved interest-rate policy coordination in the EMS, pursued in the Basle–Nyborg reforms of September 1987, to increase German responsibility for helping weaker currencies resist speculation. Pierre Bérégovoy first raised the need for a European economic government in 1988 to challenge the obvious predilections of the central bank governors meeting in the Delors Committee. In their draft treaty of January 1991 (*Ministère de l'Économie, des Finances et du Budget* 1991) French Treasury officials insisted: 'Everywhere in the world, central banks in charge of monetary policy are in dialogue with the governments in charge of the rest of economic policy. Ignore the parallelism between economic and monetary matters … and this could lead to failure.'

The draft treaty also proposed that the European Council, on the basis of ECOFIN reports, should define the broad orientations for EMU and the economic policy of the EC. Within these orientations, ECOFIN would coordinate the policies of member states and make recommendations to individual governments while the ECB would manage European monetary policy. Bérégovoy insisted that the French draft treaty did not seek to challenge the independence of the ECB and the pursuit of price stability–which the Germans would have refused to accept. French discomfort with having to accept unqualified central bank independence was reflected in the efforts by Socialist politicians to avoid the issue during the 1992 Maastricht referendum campaign. On one significant occasion during the major televised debate on the treaty in early September, President Mitterrand misleadingly claimed that elected officials would establish the economic policy framework for the formation of monetary policy: an interpretation of the treaty inconsistent with its actual provisions.

Likewise, French governments exaggerated the importance of subsequent developments at EU level to the process of constructing an economic government. Thus the agreement at the December 1996 Dublin European Council to create what the French called a Euro-Council was presented by the Juppé government, and subsequently the Jospin government, as an important step towards economic government. Subsequently, it was downgraded to 'Eurogroup' in response to German opposition to the term 'Council', which wrongly suggested that the new body had legal powers. Each reinforcement of economic policy coordination at the European level, including the Cologne Macro-Economic Dialogue, was seized on by the Jospin government as a victory of the French perspective. While some form of economic government is being created, the overriding goal of coordination has been to ensure the maintenance of price stability rather than the older French objective of stimulating economic growth. However, the decision not to criticise officially Portugal and Germany for their excessive deficits demonstrates that – in the context of slow economic growth and low inflation – the French preference for a more flexible application of the stability pact is winning out.

As chair of ECOFIN during the French EU presidency of the second half of 2000, Fabius blamed the weakness of the euro on the lack of strong political leadership in the euro-zone, the absence of an EU equivalent to the American Secretary of the Treasury. In order to reinforce its arguments, the Jospin government created a group in the Planning Commission, chaired by the economist Robert Boyer, to provide a detailed plan of alternative scenarios for the reinforcement of strategic EU-level economic policy coordination and the construction of economic government (Boyer 1999). Boyer (1998) is a well-known critic of what he labels the 'political and institutional deficits of the euro'.

Economic government as expressed through the creation of a substantial EU employment policy was of particular importance for the Plural Left government as a reinforcement and legitimisation of activist domestic employment policies and a modification of the Stability Pact. The Juppé government had accepted the German refusal to extend the EU policy remit to cover employment in the Amsterdam Treaty. Respecting campaign promises, Jospin reached a compromise with the Germans that involved the creation of the employment chapter, the resolution on growth and employment, and the formulation of a European employment strategy. As already noted, the resolution involved only vague objectives. The employment chapter involved no additional spending or obligatory measures but focused on information sharing, pilot projects and benchmarking, as agreed at the Luxembourg and Cardiff jobs summits. French Socialist ministers consistently stressed, if not exaggerated, the significance of EU policy developments in this area.

The efforts of French governments to establish and then reinforce a European social policy from the mid-1980s can be seen as a strategy to limit the competitive disadvantage, in the context of the single European market, created by expensive French social programmes and generous workers' rights, and by correspondingly high taxes and social charges on companies (Guyomarch *et al.* 1998). EMU reinforced this disadvantage by creating a new transparency in prices and costs. For Socialist governments in particular, the EU social chapter has also been a legitimising device to balance excessive emphasis on economic and monetary integration. French strategy was to establish a higher minimum European standard that acted as a buffer, protecting the French social security system from the competitive impact of globalisation. In contrast, German and British governments sought to minimise European-level developments in this field. Overall, a lowest-common-denominator approach prevailed, challenging only states with the more basic standards – notably Britain. But even these limited developments were frequently presented to the domestic audience as victories for French governments. Tax harmonisation has been another priority of French governments, anxious to challenge more competitive tax regimes that place French companies at a disadvantage and attract French capital.

Interventionist employment strategies

Jospin's rallying cry, the core motif of his 'modern socialism', was 'modernising' interventionism. As applied to domestic employment and social policies it meant 'yes to the market economy but no to the market society' (*'oui à l'économie du marché mais non à la société du marché'*). If the reinforcement of EU-level employment and social policies was a priority for his Plural Left government, domestic policy developments in these areas were of even greater importance. The legitimising 'social democratic' element of Jospin government policy making came principally in the guise of active intervention to create jobs and, in particular, jobs for young people.

By 1997 French unemployment had reached 12.4 per cent and youth unemployment was considerably higher. Since the 1980s, French unemployment rates have been well above the European Union average, although considerably lower than those in Spain and Ireland. There are several reasons to explain this high unemployment rate, both specific to France and more generally affecting most advanced industrial countries, such as the flight of jobs to low-wage economies and the high interest rates maintained in the context of the ERM of the EMS during the 1990s. First, the minimum wage in France (the *Salaire Minimum de Croissance*, SMIC) is set well above what the market minimum wage would be. This discourages companies from hiring and encourages the replacement of labour with automation. Crucially, it keeps the young out of the labour market in disproportionately high numbers. Attempts by the Balladur government in 1994 to introduce a special minimum wage for young people (the *Contrat d'Insertion Professionnelle* (CIP) known commonly as the *SMIC jeune*) met with violent protests by the very same people that this measure was designed to help. Another factor which explains high unemployment is that the provision of workers' social security is linked directly to employment (a Bismarckian system of mutual funds). With the rise of the costs of welfare provision, companies have borne a large amount of the burden. They are therefore careful to avoid unnecessary hiring. Third, the French labour market is notoriously rigid, with strict rules and administrative hurdles to surmount in order to lay off workers. This in turn discourages hiring, as companies do not want to be lumbered with unnecessary staff during periods of economic slowdown. As a result of these factors and the economic slowdown caused by the oil crisis of the mid-1970s, there was a rapid rise in French unemployment from 1975. Increased public spending (including subsidies for financially imperilled companies) during the first 2 years of the Socialist government in 1981–2 stabilised unemployment levels. The end of Socialist reflation resulted in a dramatic rise in unemployment from 1983. This dropped again with economic growth in the mid- to late 1980s. However, French unemployment remained persistently above the levels of most other advanced industrial economies. The rise continued from 1991 to 1997. With the relatively strong economic growth of the late 1990s, unemployment has dropped again. However, the drop was slow in coming and, after the peak of the economic cycle in 2001, remained stubbornly high, at 8.7 per cent according to the government's own (problematic) figures of May 2001 (16.4 per cent for the under-25s).

French governments of both the left and the right have embraced a panoply of schemes to lower unemployment. These include vocational and continuous training (organised by the *Agence Nationale pour l'Emploi*, ANPE, and regional governments) to improve the employability and adaptability of French workers. They also include the direct creation of jobs (either deliberate or not): 24 per cent of the French working population works in the public sector (not including the public economic sector), the highest rate of all advanced industrialised countries. The state has also created many 'special' jobs over the years for young people and the long-term unemployed. A large number of financial provisions encourage companies to hire young people, and the state has paid for apprenticeships as well as bearing the cost of the social charges of young employees for a limited number of years. This has involved even more generous programmes for the DOM-TOM, where the rate of unemployment is considerably higher than in metropolitan France. The state had also sought to promote job-creation by setting up schemes to encourage companies to reduce the number of working hours. This included (from 1987) the possibility of derogatory agreements whereby employers and trade unions were permitted to agree a reduction of the working week (from the maximum 39 hours set by the Socialist government in 1981) but without the reduction of salaries. In December 1996 the Robien law was adopted. This enabled the state to pay, entirely for a certain period and partially for an additional period, the social charges of companies which diminished weekly working hours and employed more workers. This had a positive but limited effect on unemployment.

As part of its efforts to legitimise modernisation, the Plural Left government embraced an even more active employment-creating strategy, promising to create 350 000 jobs in both the public and the private sectors. The targets were met thanks to the establishment of special low-paid and temporary contracts for young people in the public sector (*emplois-jeunes*) and improved economic growth in the private sector. Even with the substantial drop in unemployment over the past 5 years, interventionist employment-creation measures remain a rallying cry for the left. During the 2002 election campaigns, Lionel Jospin and the Socialist Party emphasised the need for additional measures to stimulate job creation, improved job training schemes, and pledged 900 000 new jobs through to 2007, including 200 000 for unemployed workers over 50. The 35-hour week has been the most famous – some would say notorious – policy of the government. It was presented very much in terms of social justice, but, faced with the need to increase labour-market flexibility and to lower unemployment, the government reneged on its promise that wages would not be affected, allowing companies to freeze pay in the context of collective agreements with trade unions.

In addition to legitimation, the logic of this activism can be explained in terms of several factors. The first is the evident failure of other, mostly voluntary, policies adopted by previous left- and right-wing governments. Second, there has been an element of party politics in these reforms: the Socialists have a more interventionist tradition than the right. However, especially under the privatising and budget-cutting Jospin government, substantive differences between the two parties in economic policy have diminished considerably. An activist employment policy has been a way to mark a difference between the Jospin government and its conservative predecessors. A third factor is more ideological. In opposition, after their disastrous defeat of 1993, the Socialists swung to the left, and radical action on employment became a pressing concern. In April 1997, despite strong opposition from the right wing of the party (including the future prime minister, Jospin, and minister of finance, Strauss-Kahn), the Socialists voted for their interventionist policies. A fourth factor is party political: after the announcement of the legislative elections, the Socialists joined the Communists, the Greens and the MDC to write a common election manifesto, which encouraged the Socialists to accept a more radical employment policy than they might otherwise have done. A fifth factor is that in government, the Plural Left has modified (often cancelled) most of the more radical policies that it had promised in its election manifesto and immediately following its election, only pressing ahead with the less expensive ones, such as the reduction of the working week, which would not contribute to the public-sector deficit. Political leadership can be considered as a sixth factor: notably, the force and political influence of Martine Aubry, the minister for social affairs and employment until 2000. She insisted upon the economic and political logic of the project despite the opposition of the *patronat* (CNPF), certain trade unions, most French economists, the top bureaucrats in the ministry of employment and in the Treasury, and Dominique Strauss-Kahn, the Socialist finance minister. A seventh factor was the government's need to demonstrate activism in order to calm the gradual rise in political action by the unemployed, whose demonstrations and occupations of benefit centres enjoyed the support of the large majority of the French population.

The 35-hour-week policy also represents the inability of French governments to push ahead rapidly enough with a more far-reaching reform of the labour market. Indeed, the policy has been praised by some as involving 'increased flexibility' through the back door: companies have been allowed to freeze wages and to increase the flexibility of working time. Over the past decade there has been growing pressure for reform. In 1997 a secret reform proposal written by two Financial Inspectors on overemployment (waste and inefficiency) in the public sector was suppressed but was leaked to the weekly newspaper the *Le Canard enchaîné*. The EMU deficit criterion prevents the government from adopting expensive programmes (the 35-hour week costs little) and encourages cuts in the public sector. However, efforts to make cuts have been blocked by trade unions, led by *Force Ouvrière*, with a very strong presence in the public sector. It is unlikely that the unemployment rate will drop sustainably because of the 35-hour week project. Furthermore, the gradual liberalisation of the economy, and above all privatisation, create an increasingly liberal spirit and gives the government increasingly less margin to manoeuvre in adopting more significant labour-market reforms in France in the years to come. However, the relatively strong economic growth of the past 5 years has taken the pressure off the government for the near future and has worked, if only temporarily, to increase the legitimacy of the 35-hour week. During the 2002 election campaigns, President Chirac and the Raffarin interim government pledged to reconsider the application of the 35-hour-week policy to certain sectors of the economy, but such a reconsideration is far from being a priority for the current conservative government.

Continuing generous social policies

The Plural Left government also placed considerable emphasis on social policy, although here rhetoric was not matched by large increases in spending. By 2001 the creation of 'universal health coverage' (*Couverture Maladie Universelle*, CMU) was the most significant social policy development. It financed the complementary healthcare of some 6 million of France's poorest people. While this policy improved the left-wing credentials of the government, the way payment for this programme was organised demonstrates another underlying reform agenda that could transform the French social security system. The CMU's funding – a total of 9 billion francs – comes from the state, which contributes 1.7 billion francs, as well as from mutual funds and insurance companies. The government wanted to minimise the budgetary impact. Equally, the mutual funds sought to minimise contribution increases. Thus, private insurers took the opportunity to strengthen their position in the social security system, which could be a major market for them. This development should be seen in the context of cautious steps by Jospin to allow private insurers to cover extra-complementary (*sur-complémentaires*) pension regimes, adopted in October 1998. Very controversial on the left, these initiatives seemed to represent a first step in the development of Anglo-American-style pension funds, rendered more politically acceptable by 'socialist' frills: no fiscal advantages for higher-income earners and fund management by the 'social partners'.

The Jospin government's tax reform also displayed this Janus-like characteristic in the face of growing pressures from the SEM and EMU to adopt a more competitive regime. On the one hand, the newly elected government adopted a series of tax measures designed to demonstrate its reformist left-wing credentials: a rise in the tax imposed on the most wealthy, a major increase in the CSG (*Contribution Sociale Généralisée*) created to help cover the social security deficit, a slight increase in savings taxes, the progressive reduction of healthcare contributions (*cotisations-maladie*), a temporary 2-year increase in company tax and the targeted drop of certain VAT rates to benefit low-income earners. The Jospin government argued that France had progressed far enough in the European race to lower taxes – even though French corporate tax rates remained among the highest in the EU. Notably, however, no new capital taxes were introduced, and few of the measures had a significant redistributive impact. At the same time, the government proceeded cautiously, despite considerable opposition on the left, with the lowering of the relatively high tax on company stock options. The Fabius income-tax cuts of 31 August 2000 benefited all income groups – although the CSG was cancelled for the lowest-income earners – as well as companies. The Raffarin government has promised to continue with significant corporate and income tax cuts.

FRENCH SOCIAL SECURITY: UNDER GREAT PRESSURE

Croizat, a moderate Communist deputy who became minister of labour in the *Libération* government in 1944, subsequently compared the French welfare state to a palace that could contain everyone: 'You know what happened to our palace: a number of small and separate pavilions were substituted, some by conversion, others without roofs, some furnished, and others not. We live in these modest lodgings. Afterwards we tried to install every comfort' (cited in Ambler 1990). The French welfare state is based on a system of social insurance funds (*mutuels, caisses*) – the origins of which stretch back to the late nineteenth century – into which employers and employees make contributions. Each sector of the economy (mining, textiles, and so on) established its own set of funds, which by the 1960s had to be divided to cover retirement, sickness and health and family benefits. The 'social partners' – employers and employees – meet in corporatist representative bodies called the Councils of Administration which set the guidelines for the management of the funds. Since the 1960s the trade unions and business have had equal representation. The day-to-day management of the funds is left to professional administrators, although they owe their jobs to the members of the councils.

Given that some mutual funds were poorer than others – in particular those in sectors of the economy in decline, such as mining – the state stepped in during the 1950s to establish a system of interfund solidarity. A special transfer organisation was created in the Fourth Republic to move surpluses among the 58 different occupational funds that had been created. Wealthier occupational funds were required to give a certain percentage of their 'surplus' funds to this transfer organisation. Because a large and growing section of the French working population were not in the salaried employment of companies, the state stepped in to extend coverage. The Pleven Law of 1956 created a special national solidarity fund to be paid from state revenues in order to provide additional means-tested payments to low-income non-contributors. The more general objective of the law was to ensure the provision of minimal levels of coverage for all working people. A series of reforms in the 1960s and 1970s gradually filled in the gaps in welfare provision and extended the controlling (regulatory and inspection) role of the state.

The French welfare state was expanded by successive conservative governments in the 1960s and 1970s – providing an insatiable middle-class demand for improved security – to become one of the most generous systems in the world. In 1970 France spent a larger percentage of its national wealth on social security provisions than any advanced industrial country. By 1980 only three countries spent more than France, in terms of GDP, on social spending (the Netherlands, Denmark and Sweden) (see Table 8.1), while France spent by far the most as a percentage of state spending (58.1 per cent versus 51.9 per cent in Sweden). Thus when the reforming Socialists came to power in 1981, they could add little to the system. Nonetheless, in 1988 they extended 'solidarity' further than ever, creating the RMI (*revenu minimum d'insertion*) or a minimum income guarantee that was provided only if the recipient accepted skills training to improve his or her chances of obtaining employment. RMI payments were scaled down and made more difficult to obtain by the Juppé government in 1995.

Like all governments in Western Europe, the French have been faced with the ever-rising costs of social security provision as demand has grown (with increased expectations and the ageing of the population) and – in the case of medicine – treatment has become more expensive. The power of the trade unions (over the management of mutual funds) and the medical unions made spending cuts very difficult. However, with an escalating public-spending debt and EMU requirements for sustainably lower deficits, social security spending cuts became increasingly difficult to put off. The French Finance Ministry prepared numerous reports warning of the need for significant

Table 8.1 Public and social expenditure as a percentage of GDP, 1980–98: France and selected advanced industrialised economies

	Public expenditure (1980–93)			Social expenditure (1980–98)			
	1980	1990	1993	1980	1990	1993	1998
France	46.1	49.8	54.9	22.5	26.5	29.3	28.3
Denmark	56.2	58.3	62.3	26.8	27.8	32.4	29.8
Germany	47.9	45.1	50.0	25.7	23.5	26.4	27.3
Italy	41.9	53.2	56.2	21.2	24.5	25.7	25.1
Netherlands	54.9	54.1	55.8	28.3	28.3	28.8	23.9
Sweden	60.1	59.1	71.3	25.9	33.1	36.7	31
UK	43.0	39.9	43.5	16.4	22.3	26.5	24.7
USA	31.8	33.3	34.4	13.4	14.6	15.4	14.6

Source: OECD (2001).

reforms to social security provision in France in order to keep the public deficit under control.

The Juppé Plan of 15 November 1995 (discussed above and in Chapter 4) entailed the most far-reaching reforms to social security since the Jeanneney reform of 1967 in order to contain rising social expenditure, and involved elements to which some of the trade unions and the medical establishment were bound to be opposed. Its principal objective was to keep medical spending in hospitals under control. This involved modification of the control of the regional social security funds (*caisses*) in order to diminish the influence of the social partners (notably the trade unions and the doctors) and increase parliamentary (in other words, state) control. It also involved establishing improved controls over hospital expenditures and decreasing family allowance. The plan's contents were based largely upon previous reports on social security reform which had never been put into effect, notably the 1994 Briet Report. A great deal of importance was attached to the plan because it was closely linked to the core strategy of the government and its ability to rein in public spending in order to meet the convergence criteria of the Maastricht Treaty and to participate in Stage Three of the EMU project.

THE *INSPECTEURS DES FINANCES*: AN ECONOMIC POLICY-MAKING ELITE

From the late nineteenth century onwards the Financial Inspectorate (*Inspection des Finances*) has been considered one of the most, if not *the* most, prestigious of the *grands corps*. This prestige is due largely to the central importance of the Ministry of Finance in the government administration. As the best-trained and best-connected members of the ministry, *inspecteurs* tend to monopolise the senior financial administrative positions. The centrality of the Ministry of Finance in the government administration and the *inspecteurs'* experience in matters of financial administration have also enabled them to colonise other ministries and important positions in the large public enterprises and banks. It is therefore fair to say that the French economic policy-making elite consists largely of *inspecteurs* even though they may not occupy some important positions in the ministry and other more senior positions in the French administration.

This influence stems from three closely related 'paradoxes' concerning the development of the inspectorate, as outlined by Pierre Escoube in his book *Les Grands Corps de l'État* (1971). First, while the inspectorate was originally created in 1830 as a mere service of the Ministry of Finance to inspect government finances, economic and political developments have transformed it into the most prestigious of the *grands corps*, largely as a result of the increased importance of the Ministry of Finance arising from the increased involvement of the government in the French economy and the growth of the welfare state and a concomitant need for tighter control over government finances. The Ministry of Finance occupies a central position in the administration largely because all the other spending ministries depend upon this ministry for credits. It is also responsible for the operation of the financial business of the state, monetary and financial policy and – since the incorporation of the ministry, and then Secretariat of State, for Economic Affairs – general economic policy. The Ministry of Finance is thus often labelled a 'superministry'. This has widened the control of those *inspecteurs* who fill senior positions in it and in turn has further strengthened the prestige of the *corps*.

As a second paradox, the inspectorate became a *grand corps* and the *inspecteurs* widened their influence and control over policy because many of them ceased to serve as mere inspectors and gained control of key posts in the economic and financial administration. The status of the inspectorate as a *grand corps* has further increased its prestige and thus widened and strengthened its influence at the expense of the two other *grands corps*, the *Conseil d'État* and the *Cour des Comptes*. Only students at the top of their class at the *École Nationale d'Administration* (ENA) can enter the *grands corps* and of these, the tendency has until recently been for the best to enter the inspectorate.

The third paradox is crucial to any explanation of the growing power and prestige of the inspectorate. In order to have a successful great career in the inspectorate, it is important to enter it but even more important to leave. Although it provides valuable experience of the financial administration of the state, the relatively mundane nature of work in this *corps* means that ambitious and highly motivated members are unlikely to stay long beyond their required 5 years. Moreover, as with the other *grand corps*, the lack of prior special training in the functions of the *corps* permits members of the inspectorate to be considerably more mobile than those in the technical *corps*. The top grades of the inspectorate admit only the best and most motivated students and membership fosters a sense of elite camaraderie and establishes working relationships that will be of great use later in the *inspecteurs'* careers after they have left the *corps*.

The importance of these connections to an *inspecteur*'s successful career is magnified by the highly fragmented nature of the French administration both inside and beyond the Ministry of Finance. The French administration is highly centralised, yet focal points of decision making are widely dispersed. Attempts to create formalised coordinating committees have been of limited success. The *grands corps* thus play a crucial, some have called it an imperialistic, role in the coordination of policy (Cheverny 1966). The Ministry of Finance is itself far too large to be a cohesive and monolithic organisation. Rather, it is organised into federated divisions which are further subdivided into autonomous bureaus. Ministers of Finance prefer to appoint well-connected administrators because they know that their connections will greatly facilitate the development of coherent policy and the coordination of that policy, which largely takes place in an elaborate network of informal and *ad hoc* interdepartmental committees and interministerial councils. Moreover, the appointment of a well-connected group of *inspecteurs* to the cabinet increases the ability of the minister of finance to achieve his objectives in his constant battles with other ministers over the size of their budgets and the specific allocation of their expenditure.

All ministers need to appoint bureaucrats to their cabinets because they need people familiar with the technical aspects of the ministry's work. In the cabinet of the minister of finance, these bureaucrats – called *conseillers techniques* – will almost always be *inspecteurs*. Indeed, the Ministry of Finance is 'the clearest example of a ministry that admits few outsiders, either into the highest posts in the ministry or into the cabinet' (Suleiman 1974: 252).

The tight network of well-positioned *inspecteurs* forms a force within the administration which can severely restrict the power of ministers in a wide range of ministries. Ezra Suleiman has noted that 'ministers are, for all intents and purposes, powerless to remove and replace higher civil servants despite their legal power to do so ... like a commander-in-chief who is powerless to change his commanding officers' (1974: 274). This is not to claim that ministers cannot or will never remove *inspecteurs* – they have done so – but rather that they must tread very carefully and receive the tacit approval of the *inspecteurs* when they do so. Extensive pressure from the *corps* will also ensure that an *inspecteur* will normally be appointed to an available division directorship.

The influence of the *inspecteurs* is such that the formation of the minister of finance's *cabinet* must meet with the general approval of the division directors, who are all *inspecteurs*. Moreover, the minister normally leaves to the *directeur de cabinet* – also an *inspecteur* – the responsibility of choosing the *conseillers techniques*. In the final analysis, this is not, actually, such a bad policy, seeing that the division directors are generally regarded as experts in their domains, and likely know best who to appoint to follow the work of their divisions.

The *conseillers techniques* have, therefore, a dual loyalty: they are obedient to the minister while maintaining a natural allegiance towards their division. This promotes coordination because the *conseillers* are intimate with the workings of the divisions yet at the same time have the opportunity to gain a better appreciation of the minister's approach to different policies and help to modify this approach. They can better advise the minister on what policies should be carried out and they help to keep conflicts between the minister and the directors under control and ensure the removal of any major obstacles to the smooth functioning of the ministry. Ministers of finance recognise the crucial importance of working with the *inspecteurs* because disputes cause undesirable delays. This gives the *conseillers techniques* a great deal of power to oppose a minister's project in the name of the 'ministry' (i.e., the division director) concerned. In most such cases this encourages the minister to drop or modify the project without a time-consuming debate. In those cases when the *conseiller* supports the project, he can promote it within the ministry. The dual loyalty, therefore, usually serves the interests of the minister, even though in certain cases the cabinet members are 'doing more to represent their division directors – whose work they were ostensibly supervising – *vis-à-vis* the minister than vice versa' (Suleiman 1974: 257). The influence of the directors in the other ministries is considerably less than in the Ministry of Finance, a fact which well reflects the entrenched position of the *inspecteurs*. Correspondingly, considerably less criticism – particularly public criticism – is directed at the minister by the division directors of this ministry than in other ministries.

After 5 years within the inspectorate, members are entitled, through a policy called *détachement*, to leave the *corps* and take on higher positions within the Ministry of Finance, in other ministries, or in the *cabinet* of the minister of finance, other ministers, the prime minister and even the president. They continue to belong to the *corps* but render little service to it. Penetration of these higher positions is systematic. Pierre Lalumière (1959) outlines the necessary steps that ambitious members of the inspectorate must take in order to obtain a post as director in the Ministry of Finance, which is the very top of the career ladder.

This career pattern is systematic for two principal reasons alluded to above. First, the *inspecteurs* already include some of the best educated and brightest students in the country. Many thus feel that it is logical that they are promoted and trained further to fill the senior positions in the financial administration. Second, and perhaps equally important, is that *inspecteurs* are part of a tight elite network which is of great use in the fragmented French administration in terms of the better coordination of policy.

During the first decade of the Fifth Republic, 70 finance inspectors left the *corps*. Nineteen took over divisions or subdivisions of the Ministry of Finance; 12 went to senior administrative posts in other ministries; 12 joined ministerial *cabinets* (6 joining the minister of finance's cabinet or that of his minister for the budget); 17 became managers of public corporations (8 in banks); and 6 took posts abroad (including 3 in the European Community). *Inspecteurs* hold a semi-monopoly of top posts in the Ministry of Finance. In 1970 the *inspecteurs* were at the head of all six of the ministry's major divisions (*directions*): the budget, the Treasury – which are the two main centres of power in the ministry – public accounting, tax, price and economic forecasting. In the state banking sector, the governors and deputy governors of the Bank of France were all inspectors, in addition to the heads of several of the largest public-sector banks (*Crédit Foncier*, the *Caisse des Dépôts et Consignations*, *Crédit National*, the *Caisse Nationale de Crédit Agricole*), and the large deposit banks nationalised in 1945: the *Crédit Lyonnais*, *Société Générale* and *Banque Nationale de Paris*. Numerous *inspecteurs* also resign from the administration to assume top positions in the largest private banks in France (in 1970 *inspecteurs* were at the head of the *Banque de l'Indochine*, *L'Union Parisienne*, *Banque Rothschild*, *La Banque de Paris et des Pays-Bas*, *Banque Worms* and *Banque Lazard*). There are also *inspecteurs* among the presidents, directors-general and directors of financial services of the largest industrial societies in France, including Péchiney, Alsthom, Progil, Saint-Gobain and Wendel.

Moreover, the *inspecteurs* have colonised other ministries, filling both directorships and *cabinet* positions. In 1969 a total of 21 directorial or directorial-adjoint posts were held by members of the inspectorate. In the same year, of a total of 54 *cabinet* posts, 31 were held by *inspecteurs*. Although this may not substantially augment the extensive influence of the *inspecteurs* over economic policy, especially given that financial controllers are already attached to all the other ministries to constantly supervise expenditure, their spread throughout the administration both strengthens their aura of elitism and widens an already extensive network. Many ministers choose to appoint one or more *inspecteurs* to their *cabinets* or directorships in their ministry even if they do not have the technical qualifications for the post, in order to maintain good relations with officials within the Ministry of Finance and to exert influence at the right times and places. Well-known *inspecteurs* include François Bloch Lainé, François Xavier Ortoli, the former minister Elisabeth Guigou and the current governor of the Bank of France, Jean-Claude Trichet.

Prior to EMU, French monetary policy (both domestic and international) was decisively influenced by *inspecteurs* as they held virtually all the senior positions in the responsible bodies: the Treasury division of the Ministry of Finance, the Bank of France and the *Caisse des Dépôts et Consignations*. *Inspecteurs* were usually appointed as governor and deputy governors of the Bank of France, in part because this increased the probability that the central bank and the Treasury division see eye to eye on monetary issues and would be able to work closely together on the four committees through which they jointly managed monetary affairs: the Banks Control Committee, the National Credit Council, the Stock Exchange Committee and the Franc Area Monetary Committee.

While the *inspecteurs* form an economic policy-making elite, there are numerous factors which limit the extent to which they can actually influence policy. These include the strength of the minister of finance; the will of the prime minister and the president and their *cabinets*; and those economic policy-making bodies which largely exclude the inspectors, notably the Planning Commission. As noted earlier in this chapter, the influence of the *inspecteurs* over monetary policy has been largely eliminated by the move to EMU. The minister of finance has some leeway *vis-à-vis* the *inspecteurs* but for the reasons given above, this is quite limited. Nonetheless, he does have the final say. With regard to important decisions which involve the prime minister, the cabinet (*Conseil des Ministres*) and the president, the influence of the *inspecteurs* will be further diminished, although they will continue to forward those policy options that they consider suitable. The Economic Interministerial Committee meets weekly, usually under the chairmanship of the prime minister. The finance minister is the only other permanent member. Other ministers and senior civil servants attend when they are invited to discuss particular relevant issues. The principal function of this committee is to resolve conflicts between the prime minister, the minister of finance and the spending ministers with regard to budgeting which cannot be ironed out at the administrative level. The position of the budget division of the Ministry of Finance (usually headed by an *inspecteur*) will determine the general framework of the conflict which will be decided upon by the prime minister, or by the president if the minister of finance chooses to appeal against the prime minister's decision. The minister of finance, however, wins about 90 per cent of his conflicts with the spending ministers. The president has long had an important role in most major economic decisions, such as the devaluations of the franc in the 1980s. The influence of particular *inspecteurs* can still be considerable at this level, however, as in 1969 when de Gaulle invited two directors of the Ministry of Finance (as opposed to the minister himself) to outline their views on the economic crisis and to present concrete proposals and then adopted their recommendations.

The Planning Commission is perhaps the only economic administration that has escaped colonisation by the *inspecteurs*, although, even here, M. Ortoli, an *inspecteur*, was put in charge in 1966. The commission is not part of the Ministry of Finance nor does it fall under the authority of the minister. Nonetheless, it retains only a limited independence *vis-à-vis* both the minister of finance and the prime minister. While the Ministry of Finance and individual *inspecteurs* may have only a limited control over planning, successful implementation depends largely upon coordination with the Ministry of Finance. In this regard, the Forecasting Division (*Direction de la Prévision*) and the National Statistical and Economic Studies Institute (*Institut National des Statistiques et des Études Économiques*, INSEE) play a particularly important role. Moreover, the Ministry of Finance retains final say over funding of the different elements of the latest plan, although after the lengthy procedure of consultation and formulation it is difficult to make substantial alterations. The spending ministries are largely confined to the limits imposed by the ministry and the plan, although another *inspecteur*-led body, the *Caisse des Dépôts et Consignations*, which is the plan's investment bank, will usually supply the funds to make up the difference between what is authorised and what is spent.

To conclude, we should note one other characteristic of the *inspecteurs*: they do not form a uniform body. Despite their similar background and their mutually supporting connections, *inspecteurs* may disagree significantly on policy for both technical and ideological reasons. Thus, while the *inspecteurs* can be described as an economic policy-making elite, this elite is itself fragmented. Nonetheless, for this reason and because of the closed-shop nature of appointments to the senior financial administrative positions, there are many critics of the *inspecteurs'* semi-monopoly over these positions as well as their colonisation of other ministries. Many argue that more opportunities should be provided to *administrateurs civils* – that is, non-members of the *grands corps* – to enter higher administrative positions. During the wave of administrative reforms in the 1960s, governments repeatedly stressed their commitment to appointing more *administrateurs civils* to posts immediately below the heads of division (*directeur-adjoint*, *sous-directeur*, *chef de service*). In the Ministry of Finance, these attempts made little headway against the firmly entrenched position of the *inspecteurs* and the extent of their influence. Even though certain *administrateurs civils* may acquire greater knowledge of and experience in the details of their division, concern for the effective coordination of policy and agreeable relations with the *inspecteurs* largely binds the hands of ministers of finance, who continue to appoint *inspecteurs* to senior positions in the financial administration.

9

FRANCE, EUROPE AND THE WORLD

Despite the end of the Cold War, the collapse of the former Soviet Union, the considerable loss of policy-making powers to the level of the European Union and the disastrous economic and political difficulties in nearly all of France's former colonies, there has been a remarkable continuity in French foreign policy over the past four decades. The underlying themes of this policy are the continuation and expansion of the diplomatic, military, cultural, linguistic and economic importance of France in the world and the maintenance of an independent diplomatic margin of manoeuvre in relation to the United States, either on its own or through European cooperation. This chapter examines recent developments in French foreign policy. We argue that the traditional themes of French diplomacy have continued to apply in the post-Cold War world and in the context of an ever more integrated European Union. However, through an analysis of the recent Jospin Government's European policy, we also argue that the traditional Gaullist vision of desirable European cooperation faces unprecedented challenges at the start of the twenty-first century.

MAJOR THEMES OF FRENCH FOREIGN AND DEFENCE POLICY FROM 1944 TO THE PRESENT

The roots of current French foreign and defence policy lie in the Second World War, de Gaulle's poor relations with the Americans and his desire to maintain and promote the *grandeur* of France. The underlying theme of French foreign policy from the time of Liberation until the end of the Cold War was the establishment and maintenance of the diplomatic and military prestige of France. France alone or through Europe was to be a 'third power' between the USSR and the USA. On the diplomatic front this involved insistence upon French independence from American foreign policy and the maintenance of cordial relations with the Soviets. France consistently maintained political and economic relations with the Soviet Union after the various Soviet invasions of East European satellites and of Afghanistan in 1980. French foreign policy also involved the maintenance of French influence in Europe through the diminution of potential German economic and diplomatic power within the context of European cooperation and the extension of French influence at the international level through European means. European construction was used to constrain German power: the consensus of the 1950s and 1960s was that France was and should be superior politically and militarily even if its economy had been surpassed by the German *Wirtschaftswunder*. However, this balance was challenged increasingly during the 1970s and 1980s. The French sought to secure a strong international diplomatic presence through the maintenance of a permanent seat on the UN Security Council, the obtaining of which was a great victory for French diplomacy in the aftermath of the Second World War. The permanent seat gave French governments the opportunity – frequently used – to question American leadership in the non-communist world. The French also sought to maintain a zone of influence in the developing world (notably the former French colonies in Africa). French governments sought to maintain these colonies but it became clear by the 1950s that it would be too costly to do so (because of wars against independence fighters and the necessity of social investments). France was beaten out of Indochina and North Africa and de Gaulle granted independence to most of the remaining French colonies in Africa in 1960. A handful of colonies were transformed into overseas *départements* and territories (the DOM-TOM) which ensured France's continued presence in the four corners of the world. The French presence – economic, political, military and even cultural – in several former colonies was largely eliminated and they entered, at least temporarily, into a Soviet or Chinese sphere of influence (and in Indochina, initially, an American sphere). Successive French governments, however, maintained a strong presence in most of the former colonies in Sub-Saharan Africa. To reinforce this presence and maintain or rebuild French political and cultural ties to other former colonies, in 1986 President François Mitterrand created the *Francophonie* organisation – similar to the Commonwealth – a forum for bilateral and multilateral cooperation in a range of areas.

An important element of French diplomacy since the Second World War has been cultural. French governments have spent a great deal of money – more in total than any other country – promoting the national culture and language throughout the world. After economic exploitation, colonisation had a strong 'civilising' element to it which involved sharing the benefits of French culture. After decolonisation, French governments maintained well-funded educational and cultural programmes with both Francophone and non-Francophone countries and the *Alliance française* was created.

On the military front, the French sought to maintain a strong army and, from the mid-1950s, to establish and maintain an independent nuclear power, effectively a French nuclear deterrent under the wider and more menacing American umbrella. Although the first French atomic weapons test took place in 1960, thus associating the birth of nuclear weapons with de Gaulle, the nuclear programme was started by governments of the Fourth Republic. A strong and largely autonomous strategic military capacity required obligatory military service, which lasted until the mid-1990s, and high public expenditure throughout the Cold War period and France consistently spent more as a percentage of GDP on defence than any other West European country, reaching 12.4 per cent in 1952. France became a member of the North Atlantic Treaty Organisation (NATO) from the creation of this defence alliance by the Treaty of Washington in 1949. Successive French governments of the Fifth Republic sought to reduce American dominance in NATO and increase French influence, notably through the appointment of a European (read French) head of SACEUR (the Strategic Allied Command in Europe). Faced with American refusal to meet this French demand, President de Gaulle ended French participation in NATO Mediterranean naval cooperation in 1965 and in 1966 he withdrew France from the military command structure of the organisation. French governments sought to establish a European defence outside of NATO in the context of the largely defunct body of the Western European Union (WEU) which stemmed from the Brussels treaty of 1948. This European defence was to be led, it was assumed, by the French and with a French-controlled (European-financed) nuclear deterrent. However, at the same time, French governments were unwilling to surrender the national veto over the operation of a European defence (an apparently contradictory policy, unless France were to replace the United States as the military hegemon). Eventually, French efforts led to the establishment of several forms of European military cooperation outside the NATO framework including a joint European military battalion called Eurocorps based in Strasbourg. Nonetheless, French forces continued to engage in joint manoeuvres with NATO forces and European military cooperation fell far short of a common European defence arrangement outside the NATO framework.

In the economic sphere, French governments sought, through a very aggressive economic diplomacy and active industrial policy, to improve France's position as an internationally significant commercial power. During the 1970s, under presidents Pompidou and Giscard, a domestic industrial policy of 'national champions' involved government-led mergers designed to create massive French companies – for example, the chemicals giant Rhône-Poulenc – which could take on the American and Japanese competition. Anxieties about the greater power of West Germany have always been rife in French governments preoccupied with the comparative weakness of the French economy and the consequent waning of France's diplomatic influence. Despite these fears, the French economy became the world's fourth largest by the 1970s, surpassing that of the UK. Unlike governments in the UK, however, French governments were cautious about freeing international trade, in part because of the weakness of several sectors of the French economy and in part for ideological reasons (after the Second World War economic liberalism was adhered to by only a small minority of the country's political class). French governments, therefore, only supported a very limited freeing of trade at the global level. They generally followed the policy of freeing trade within the

European Community in order to improve the competitiveness of French companies. However, French governments were reluctant to accept many of the liberalising implications of European competition policy, including the dismantling of several state-run monopolies and an end to significant subsidies to leading national companies. As with diplomatic and defence policy, the French also sought to extend their economic power through the medium of Europe and the development of the European Economic Community's (EEC) single international commercial policy, thus carrying greater weight in trade negotiations with the Americans and Japanese. French interest in the Common Commercial Policy corresponded to traditional *realpolitik*. Given the demographic and economic realities of the world, France recognised the inevitability of its shrinking influence in world economic affairs. Equally, French governments were interested in industrial cooperation with European partners (for example, the fields of aerospace and information technology, as with the ESPRIT programme) but normally only if such cooperation was clearly in the interests of French companies and it could be directed by France.

The above themes of French policy have been transformed but not rejected since the end of the Cold War. French governments have continued to insist upon a foreign policy independent from that of the United States, frequently opposing American initiatives (as in ex-Yugoslavia and post-Gulf War Iraq) and challenging America's role as the sole remaining superpower. Since the end of the Cold War, the French political class has also greatly feared a resurgent Germany coming increasingly to dominate in Central and Eastern Europe and, at the international level, the creation of a tripolar world with American, Japanese and German poles. During the 1990s the existence of a newly reunified Germany has reinforced the perception of the need to contain German power within the EU. French governments have also sought to improve their links with the Central and East European countries (CEECs) and former Soviet republics and the Russian Federation, above all in terms of administrative and political cooperation. However, France invests much less in the region than the Germans, Americans, Japanese and British, which weakens the potential growth of French influence. In the world of international diplomacy, France continues to hold on to its permanent seat in the UN Security Council but it must now face growing challenges to its privileged status coming from many quarters and, in particular, from German governments which seek to share the British and French permanent seats, through the creation of two European Union seats occupied on a rotational basis.

French influence in the developing world continues to be threatened by regime change and errors of French diplomacy including highly suspect interventions in several countries such as Rwanda and Zaire (Congo). French relations with several corrupt regimes possessing little in the way of democratic legitimacy have been widely condemned as have the special mutually beneficial relations between certain African leaders and certain leading French politicians (including the former Central African Emperor Bokassa and President Giscard d'Estaing and Gabon's president El-Hadj Omar Bongo and President Chirac). The former colonies of French West Africa expressed considerable frustration with France at the time of the devaluation of the CFA, the West African franc, in 1994, a necessary step for the development of their economies, but particularly opposed by an elite which saw its power of purchase plummet. Despite the continuation of very high public expenditure on cultural diplomacy in general and the *Francophonie* in particular (which has resisted substantial budget cuts during a decade of constraint), French cultural and linguistic influence has continued to diminish. English has replaced French almost everywhere as the first foreign language, even in former French colonies or where France maintains a strong influence. Most symbolically, the Algerian government, despite very strong links with French governments, decided in 1997 to adopt English as the first foreign language and embraced a policy of arabisation of street signs. Suppressed economic growth and investment during the first half of the 1990s contributed to the French government's delay in introducing and promoting the Internet, on which it has now started to catch up. Europe continues to be seen as a potential vehicle for French diplomacy, most recently in terms of the euro, always presented in France as the most effective way to challenge American monetary hegemony.

French efforts to maintain pre-eminence in the military sphere appear to have only partially paid off in terms of international power and prestige, because a country's military power, including its nuclear capability, has been perceived as much less important since the end of the Cold War, so much so that some question the usefulness of France's nuclear deterrent in the context of the world today. These reservations notwithstanding, France has maintained its nuclear weapons policy unchanged since the end of the Cold War, as demonstrated most controversially by the 1995–6 French nuclear weapons tests (see Exhibit 9.1).

Exhibit 9.1: The controversial 1995–6 French nuclear weapons tests

The French aim of maintaining its independence in nuclear weapons technology in part explains the announcement by President Chirac shortly after his May 1995 election victory that France would restart underground nuclear tests in the Moruoa Atoll in French Polynesia. In resuming these tests the French broke a moratorium on underground nuclear testing and incurred the anger of most of the world which led to boycotts of French products in several countries, notably New Zealand and Australia. However, French testing made sense for strategic, technological, economic and symbolic reasons. It was justified on the grounds that France needed to conduct a few additional tests in order to finetune its computer test simulation technology, in which a great deal of money had been invested and which had been developed completely independently of American research. In symbolic terms, renewed testing was arguably an important statement from a neo-Gaullist president who was about to end military conscription, long an important element of the republic, and bring France back into the military command structure of NATO, an organisation previously criticised for being dominated by the Americans.

In the 1990s, as part of a more general drive to lower the public deficit, French governments began making significant cuts to defence spending. At the same time, state-owned or subsidised arms companies lost much of their competitive edge at the international level due to a combination of American mergers and the glut of less expensive arms produced by the Russians and Chinese. French governments have had to accept the necessity of increased cooperation with other European countries in the production of some military hardware and even the merger of French and other European armaments companies in order to achieve economies of scale.

In the post-Cold War period, French governments have continued to demand the reduction of American leadership in NATO and the construction of an autonomous 'European Security and Defence Identity' (ESDI) (or Common European Security and Defence Policy, CESDP) as a stepping stone towards a distinctively European defence organisation. The Americans and British have been reluctant to accept French demands. (The progress in the construction of a CESDP is discussed later in this chapter.) In the early to mid-1990s, French hopes for a more successful EU collective diplomacy (through the Common Foreign and Security Policy (CFSP)) were dashed in the former Yugoslavia. European efforts to formulate a common policy of intervention failed, principally because of the widely divergent European positions on the situation. American presence and leadership proved necessary to bring the Serbs to the negotiating table. Much to the surprise of both French and foreign observers, in December 1995, President Chirac announced that he intended to bring France back into the NATO military command structure and the Mediterranean fleet. The French sought to take advantage of the dramatic reduction of American troop levels in Western Europe to reassert French leadership in the organisation and lead the construction of the 'European arm' of NATO. Once back inside, France immediately began to insist – very publicly yet unsuccessfully – upon the appointment of a European (again ideally French) replacement of the American Wesley Clark as head of SACEUR and other key NATO command positions.

As mentioned above, economic strength is of greater importance to the overall diplomatic position of countries in the post-Cold War period. France is well placed in this context, despite the relative backwardness of particular sectors of its economy, notably the weakness of its Information Technology sector. At the European level, French politicians appear to have become less fearful of a resurgent Germany, having seen that country lumbered with the costs of reunification and suffering slow growth and rising rates of unemployment. Despite the strong French position in the international division of labour and international trade, French governments have continued to be reluctant to accept increased free trade at the global level, held back by powerful political lobbies, above all French farmers and a population generally sceptical about the merits of free trade. A Socialist government under Pierre Bérégovoy blocked a December 1992 agreement between the EU Commission and the USA which was to bring to a conclusion the international trade talks of the Uruguay Round of the GATT (General Agreement on

Tariffs and Trade). The French farming and cultural lobbies were particularly anxious about elements of the agreement affecting them and the Socialist government was preoccupied with the upcoming March 1993 parliamentary elections. The Bérégovoy and subsequent Balladur governments delayed the ratification of the Uruguay Round until October 1993, insisting on special concessions for oilseed producers and the cultural industries.

THE FRENCH APPROACH TO EUROPEAN INTEGRATION

Since the early 1950s, most of the French political and administrative elite has seen improved European cooperation and limited European integration as a useful channel for the pursuit of French diplomatic and economic interests. French policy reflects long-standing *realpolitik*, discourse, and identity on European matters (Dyson 1999). While there has always been a small number of idealists (Euro-federalists) in French policy-making circles, most of the elite has been motivated entirely by the pursuit of national interests. Support for European integration has, thus, always been 'limited' and almost always in favour of intergovernmentalism. The emphasis that de Gaulle placed upon *Europe des patries* – that is, a Europe of nation-states rather than a supra-national Europe – has infused all French policy making. The French understanding of acceptable cooperation and integration has shaped most of the major European developments over the past 40 years, albeit through compromise agreements with the Germans.

The European Coal and Steel Community (ECSC) was created to ensure the supply of German (Ruhr) coal to French steel factories and contain German rearmament. The European Defence Community (EDC) was proposed by the French as a worried reaction to the necessity of German rearmament insisted upon by the Americans. The EEC was embraced by the policy-making elite as a means of imposing greater free trade and competitiveness upon certain powerful hostile economic interests and a reluctant political class, in order to strengthen French industry further. However, an awareness that West Germany would likely benefit more from the creation of the Common Market led the French to insist upon the corresponding creation of the Common Agriculture Policy (CAP). This policy ensured an open European market for agricultural produce as well as the Europeanisation of price setting and agricultural subsidies, which in effect amounted to German subsidies for French farmers and agricultural modernisation.

In the early 1970s, the French sought to limit the impact of the instability of the American dollar upon the French economy through the creation of European monetary mechanisms which would provide for stability between the exchange rate parities of participating European currencies. Negotiations on EMU, begun in 1970, collapsed, given French refusal to accept economic policy convergence among participating countries prior to the start of monetary union. Above all, the French wanted European monetary support mechanisms that would force the central banks of strong currency countries (notably Germany) to come to the aid of weak currencies in the system (notably the French franc). The 'Snake' monetary mechanism, established in 1972, failed to provide sufficient support for weak currencies and the franc was forced out of the system on two occasions over the following 3 years. The German mark was the anchor currency of the Snake and those countries unable or unwilling to maintain inflation at low German levels – notably France – found it difficult to maintain a stable exchange rate *vis-à-vis* the mark. The government of Raymond Barre made a strong commitment to lowering French inflation and President Giscard d'Estaing reached an agreement in 1978 with the German chancellor Helmut Schmidt on the creation of a new European monetary system (the EMS) which would provide greater financial support for weaker currencies in order to maintain greater stability within the system and overcome some of the asymmetry of the Snake mechanism. However, the EMS in operation remained a fundamentally asymmetric system, with the German mark at its centre and the German Bundesbank setting monetary policy that the other countries were obliged to follow. The French continued to demand reforms to the system throughout the 1980s. However, the Germans were unwilling to provide the kind of guaranteed monetary support to weak currencies that would have been necessary to transform the system into a truly symmetric one. French frustration with the EMS translated into growing interest in EMU – one that entrenched German low inflationary principles but also forced the Germans to share monetary power at the European level. Thus the history of French policy on monetary cooperation and integration at the European level can be seen in terms of French efforts to maximise both international and European monetary power by decreasing the impact of American economic and monetary polices upon the French economy through European monetary mechanisms and decreasing the impact of German economic and monetary policies through reforms to increase support for weak currencies in the EMS and finally EMU itself (Howarth 2001).

French support for the Single European Act (SEA) of 1986 and the Single European Market Programme reflected the acceptance of the Socialist government of the day that French industry could not be strengthened by national subsidies and domestic reflationary measures, in large part due to the difficulties that such measures created for continued French participation in the EEC and the EMS. The rigours of greater European competition combined with joint European industrial and high-technology schemes and European-level mergers were seen as necessary for the restructuring of French companies. In the meantime, Socialist policy-makers believed that the Common External Tariff would protect the French social model from an onslaught of competition from low-wage countries. The French perception of the Single European Market (SEM) differed considerably from that of the British, which stressed liberal economic arguments in favour of free trade.

Despite its consistent pursuit of national interest, the political and administrative elite has met stubborn domestic political and public opposition to the inevitable encroachments made on national policy-making autonomy on all but the most clearly advantageous developments in European cooperation and integration (notably, the ECSC and the CAP). The establishment of the EEC, EMU and the EU was opposed by large sections of the French political class and population (with only a wafer-thin majority in favour of the Maastricht Treaty in the September 1992 referendum) while the establishment of the European Defence Community (a French initiative in the Pleven Plan of 1950) was blocked by a negative National Assembly vote in 1954.

Limited supranational developments have been perceived and defended as necessary in the context of major gains for France. In other words, concessions to German demands for greater political integration have been minimal, limited principally to package deals leading to the substantial treaty reform sought by the French. Thus, the nationalist reaction to the ECSC which created a High Authority with significant power led the French government to insist upon strengthening the Council of Ministers, an intergovernmental forum, as the major decision-making body of the EEC. Attempts to move towards weighted majority voting in the council were subsequently blocked by de Gaulle (the 'Empty Chair Crisis'), but it is very likely that less overtly 'nationalist' French leaders would have done the same. The adoption of Qualified Majority Voting (QMV) in the SEA was seen as necessary to overcome the potential obstructionism to the creation of the SEM by competitively weaker countries. Likewise, the extension of QMV, in the Treaty of European Union (TEU), to the establishment of certain social rights at the European level, was seen as necessary in order to build a European social policy. This was supported as it would raise the social costs in countries such as Britain in order to reduce their competitive advantage and prevent the phenomenon of 'social dumping' – the term frequently used in France to refer to the feared possibility that companies would move their operations from countries with more generous social provisions and higher taxes (notably France) to take advantage of the lower costs and lower levels of taxation found in certain other EU member states. The complete loss of national control over monetary policy in the EMU project was seen as an acceptable price for ending German monetary dominance in Europe.

Granting the European Parliament (EP) final say over the EC budget in 1975 was supported only reluctantly by the French. Direct election of the EP met with substantial domestic opposition and was accepted largely because enough French opponents were convinced that the EP would not be able to do much with its increased legitimacy. The limited extension of EP powers in the SEA (the cooperation procedure), the TEU and the Treaty of Amsterdam (the creation and extension of the co-decision procedure) again reflected the demands of Germany and other countries and were accepted only reluctantly at each step by the French, in the context of advantageous package deals. French opposition to the extension of EP powers demonstrates the widespread bias of the Fifth Republic against strong parliamentary control over the political executive. French efforts to respond to complaints regarding the European democratic deficit have been half-hearted and have focused upon strengthening the powers of the French National Assembly rather than the European

Parliament: namely, the creation of Article 88.2 of the French constitution which requires governments to consult the National Assembly and the Senate on French positions prior to votes in the EU Council of Ministers.

Recent developments confirm France's bias in favour of intergovernmentalism. The acceptance of the term 'European Union' to describe the three pillars created in the TEU demonstrates a willingness to support empty terms with a 'federalist' connotation rather than any commitment to create a real federal state. The French joined the British in insisting upon the maintenance of member state vetoes on all advances in policy cooperation covered by the two new pillars: CFSP and Home and Justice Affairs. Despite France's problematic relationship with NATO – both outside and now within its military command structure – and its efforts to build European defence cooperation outside the framework of NATO, few leading French politicians are eager to modify the purely intergovernmental nature of cooperation in this area, which effectively means little significant cooperation. Limited progress of common policy-making in Home and Justice Affairs has been achieved on an intergovernmental basis. The French have accepted the implications of the free movement of people by agreeing to common visa and asylum policies but only on the basis of unanimity in the Council.

THE EUROPEAN POLICY OF THE JOSPIN GOVERNMENT (1997–2002): A NEW TWIST TO OLD FRENCH GAMES[1]

The Jospin government's European policy demonstrates considerable continuity with the policies of previous French governments. The extent to which this government's policies differed from its predecessors can be explained principally in terms of the rapidly changing European political and economic environment of the late 1990s. Although the Gaullist paradigm remained very influential from the mid-1980s, it was progressively modified during the two terms of President Mitterrand, who was willing to accept a far greater loss of autonomous national policy-making powers than his predecessors, as well as under the neo-Gaullist President Jacques Chirac, in power from 1995. Even with the advance of European integration in the 1980s and 1990s, most developments – for example, the extension of qualified majority voting (QMV) in the council, the strengthened role of the European Parliament in the EU legislative process, the extension of EU citizenship and mobility rights and EU social and environmental policy – were considered acceptable because they reinforced or at least did not significantly undermine traditional perceptions of French state identity. Moreover,

[1] Much of this section is reproduced with permission from Howarth, D. 2002: *Modern and Contemporary France*, Vol. 10(3), pp. 353–69; http://tandf.co.uk

changing perceptions of the appropriate role of the French state in the economy encouraged new developments in French European policy – notably agreeing to the Single European Act (SEA) of 1986 and the Single European Market programme (SEM) – which in turn contributed to a change in dominant French perceptions of state identity.

However, by the early 1990s, European policy developments began to conflict significantly with dominant perceptions of French state identity and ideational constructions, making the challenge to the Gaullist paradigm more difficult for all the political parties to accept and legitimise in public discourse. The operation of the European Competition Policy began to conflict with dominant French perceptions of appropriate state intervention in the economy and French governments of both right and left maintained a spirited defence of public utilities against considerable pressure from the European Commission and certain other EU member states. The decision to pursue EMU – imposed by President Mitterrand and opposed by the large majority of the French political and financial administrative elite – and the economic policy constraints it entailed significantly destabilised French republican views on state 'sovereignty' and central state control over the levers of economic policy (Howarth 2001). The controversy encouraged the 'craftsmen of discourse' to emphasise the traditional justificatory idea of achieving French *grandeur* through European means (Dyson 1999). Nonetheless, the Cresson and Bérégovoy Socialist governments and the Balladur and Juppé RPR–UDF governments all suffered from political difficulties created by the increasingly apparent conflict between dominant state identity and European policy developments. Crucially, the legacy of the Gaullist paradigm weighed heavily on successive governments, preventing them from conceptualising a highly supranational end-goal of European integration.

By the June 1997 elections, the contradiction between traditional Gaullist perceptions of French state identity and perceptions of European integration as an extension of that identity on the one hand, and European integration and the actual constraints imposed by integration on the other, was aggravated by constraints imposed by the operation of SEM and EMU. (The manner in which EMU has shaped French state identity and French policies is explored in Chapter 8.) Furthermore, new challenges germinating under previous governments arose during the life of the Jospin government. German governments began to demonstrate a greater willingness to question the 'historic compromises' upon which European integration had been based (and made acceptable in many French minds) which created strains in the Franco-German relationship, the axis that had historically driven integration. Progressive deepening of European integration presented difficult questions about its future direction that previous French governments had preferred to leave unanswered. EU enlargement to Central and Eastern Europe was increasingly perceived as a historical necessity, even to French policy makers, who had initially opposed enlargement as damaging to both the Gaullist vision of the small and intergovernmental European Community and other French interests, notably agricultural. Enlargement to Central and Eastern

Europe posed a significant challenge to institutional structures and policies which had, for the most part, previously been in line with French preferences.

It would be wrong, however, to claim that all European-level developments in the 1990s posed challenges to traditional French perceptions. The transformed European and international geo-strategic situation since the end of the Cold War and the development of American, German and British security policies created new opportunities for partial fulfilment of the security and defence dimension of the Gaullist paradigm, linked to the traditional French wish to strengthen the international role of the European Community/Union (*Europe de la Puissance*).

It is also clear that some of the Jospin government's policy developments were heavily influenced by partisan politics and only came about because of the change of government in June 1997 – for example, the insistence of the Plural Left on the creation of the Employment Chapter of the Amsterdam treaty, which was a policy that the previous Juppé government had wanted but was willing to do without. Moreover, various domestic political factors made Jospin's European policy and policy making unique: the constraints of coalition politics, the politics of cohabitation and the occasionally significant role played by the president in shaping French policy, and the ideological factors that pulled the Plural Left's preferred European policy themes to the left.

A word of caution. To examine the European policy of the 'Jospin government' *per se* is problematic given the extent to which President Chirac was responsible for shaping France's vision on European policy developments and had a direct say in these developments (as guaranteed by the French constitution's provisions on the role of the president in international affairs, the precedent established by earlier French presidents and in particular by former President Mitterrand during previous periods of cohabitation). The problem is all the greater given that Chirac's policy and that of the Jospin government differed on a few important matters. In most respects this was more a difference in style than in substance, reflecting deeply embedded French perceptions and mutual difficulties in meeting challenges to these perceptions. However, on some issues – notably social and employment policies and the political management of the euro-zone – the Jospin government clearly did leave its mark and President Chirac's position conformed largely to the government in these areas, as long as his overriding objectives were met. Notably, Chirac was able to insist that the Jospin government agreed to the Amsterdam Treaty despite having its conditions for acceptance watered down a great deal due to German and British obstructionism. However, it is also problematic to claim that the Jospin government would have been willing (without presidential interference) to block the adoption of the treaty. On some policies difficulties arose, either because of slightly differing visions (President Chirac is, after all, a neo-Gaullist and draws, at least more publicly, on the Gaullist legacy) or more likely because of politically motivated conflicts and problems of coordination between Matignon (the prime minister's office) and the Elysée (the president's office). For example, in March 1999 President Chirac – presenting himself as the defender of French farming interests – succeeded in watering down the

CAP reforms previously agreed by the Jospin government in negotiations with its EU partners. Moreover, the problematic management of the French EU Council presidency of the second half of 2000 can be blamed in part on coordination problems between Chirac and the government. However, the aim of this chapter is not to explore the dynamics of cohabitation with regard to French European policy in large part because in terms of substantive French European policy the impact of cohabitation was limited and similar positions were common.

STRAINS IN THE FRANCO-GERMAN AXIS: THE RISE OF GERMAN UNILATERALISM

French governments have always used the strong bilateral relationship with Germany, institutionalised by the 1963 Elysée Treaty, in order to forward French preferences on European and other international policy developments (Cole 2001; Pedersen 1998). Prior to the end of the Cold War, the French dominated this relationship, assuming a relatively compliant Federal Republic that would avoid direct confrontation with France on most policy issues. Likewise, French governments expected to be consulted on German policy proposals. The French and German governments were the principal agenda setters for most major European developments, as seen during the discussions and negotiations leading to the Maastricht and Amsterdam Treaties, when the French and Germans agreed on most matters bilaterally prior to the intergovernmental conferences. However, the French and Germans were not always able to impose their collective will on the other member states and dissension often existed between the two countries on major issues – although this dissension was never allowed to fundamentally undermine the strength of the relationship. Kohl's relationship with the RPR–UDF governments between 1993 and 1997 and with President Chirac from 1995 was considerably less close than had been his relationship with President Mitterrand. The Kohl government became increasingly vocal in its criticism of the structure of the EU budget, the size of the German net contribution and CAP spending. Furthermore, the Juppé government only accepted the Stability Pact after a very bitter public row with the Germans. Despite the establishment of bilateral positions on treaty reform, the negotiations during the 1996–7 Intergovernmental Conference (IGC) were also noteworthy for difficult Franco-German relations.

During the Jospin government, the Franco-German relationship was put under greater strain than previously owing to changes in expectations on both sides. Some observers have argued that the period was noteworthy for the French failure to rise to the challenge of the new balance in the relationship since German reunification (Drake 2001). The new Jospin government attempted to use the bilateral relationship to force through changes in the Amsterdam Treaty. Jospin met with Kohl at Poitiers on 12 June 1997 with a list of specific demands for changes to the treaty and, although most of the

French demands were not met, Kohl helped Jospin achieve a face-saving compromise. The relationship was further placed under strain over the reinforcement of 'Economic Government' and the choice of the first president of the ECB, which caused a prolonged debate with the Germans and bitter disputes, as at the March 1998 Brussels summit.

Many observers thought that the arrival to power in September 1998 of Gerhard Schröder's Socialist (SPD)-led government would result in improved Franco-German relations, given the similar ideological leaning of the Jospin and Schröder governments and the partisan make-up of the coalitions (both containing Socialist and Green parties). Moreover, Oskar Lafontaine, as the former leader of the SPD and now finance minister, had developed close links with the French Socialists and in particular the French finance minister Dominique Strauss-Kahn. However, history has also shown that the closest Franco-German relations have not necessarily been those between parties of similar partisan stripe. Initially the relationship appeared strengthened, thanks to a flurry of bilateral diplomatic activity and the close relations between the two finance ministers, who made joint declarations on the need for a coordinated EU growth strategy and a more interventionist employment policy. However, the Franco-German relationship cooled considerably following Lafontaine's forced departure from government and the announcement on 6 June 1999 of the Blair–Schröder pact on a 'Flexible and Competitive Europe' which directly contradicted the more interventionist strategy of the Jospin government. Schröder himself was known as having closer ties with New Labour and his vision of *Neue Mitte* seemed to echo Blair's 'Third Way'.

The Franco-German relationship reached what many observers have labelled a nadir during this period owing principally to the greater willingness on the part of the Schröder government to assert German preferences unilaterally. The 'normalisation' of German foreign policy – with Germany pursuing its national interests just like France or the UK – was seen as a threat to traditional French perceptions of European integration as an extension of French state preferences. The Schröder government demonstrated a greater willingness than previous German governments to question the 'historic compromises' upon which European integration had been based (and made acceptable in many French minds). Schröder asserted that Germany should stand up for its own interests and questioned the 'coordination reflex' which had defined German policy-making since the end of the Second World War, suggesting that Germany would not refrain from pursuing its interests unilaterally rather than in the traditional Franco-German tandem. Some observers have argued that the inexperience of the SPD government with EU diplomacy and the niceties of Franco-German relations – the SPD had been out of power at the federal level for almost 16 years – meant a certain degree of initial clumsiness of language (Cole 2001). Some have also argued that Schröder's confrontational style played to a domestic political audience hostile to EMU.

The most intense debate between the Germans and the French took place during the German presidency of the European Council in the first half of 1999, when Schröder sought to reach an agreement on budget reform that would prepare the way for EU enlargement. Schröder, actively supported by the British and the European Commission, demanded far-reaching CAP reform including the partial renationalisation of the policy. He also demanded a British-style budget rebate given the massive size of the German net contribution to the EU budget (in 1998 10.9 billion euros versus France's net contribution of 0.8 billion). Both proposals were unacceptable to the Jospin government: gradual CAP reform to cut expenditure was acceptable but not any fundamental challenge to the continued existence of the policy. Likewise, a decreased German net contribution would translate into either less money for the European budget or compensatory increased contributions by other countries, notably France. Previously – in 1988 and 1993 – budget reform was managed to a large extent in the context of the Franco-German bilateral relationship. French governments accepted the need for reform in order to prevent excessively large increases in CAP expenditure, while German governments never aggressively challenged their large net contribution, which dated back to a historic compromise that involved German financial support for French agricultural modernisation in exchange for French support for the creation of the Common Market. Fortunately for the Jospin government, there were clear limits to Schröder's aggressive unilateralism, and the German chancellor backed down on most of his demands. CAP reforms were significant and included large cuts in support prices for several major foodstuffs which the French recognised as necessary to decrease overproduction, but the Jospin government succeeded in blocking any renationalisation, and no rebate for Germany was agreed.

The Schröder government's unilateral pursuit of its own agenda was also evident in a challenge to the former consensus that had been in place since the resolution of the Empty Chair Crisis in 1966, of not pushing France too far and too fast on European integration. The so-called 'Euro-visions' debate started on 12 June 2000 when Joschka Fischer, the German foreign minister, in a speech at Humboldt University in Berlin, outlined his vision of a European federal state and the need for rapid progress in this direction. The difficulties for the Jospin government (and Chirac presidency) in responding with a clear French vision of future integration are explored in the following section. Difficulties in the Franco-German relationship were also a major contributing factor to the French council presidency's disastrous handling of the treaty reform negotiations leading to the December 2000 Nice summit. Many of the difficulties centred around the French refusal to accept German demands for a larger number of votes in the council than France and the other large member states on the grounds of Germany's larger population. The French held firm to the principle of parity.

The Jospin government (and Chirac presidency) were consistently effective in preserving the status quo ante where this clearly worked to France's advantage and conformed to traditional French perceptions of European integration as an extension of French policy preferences: on the budget, the CAP and parity in the council the Germans backed down, but only after unusually bitter and unseemly public battles. There were also clear limits to the Schröder government's unilateralism and in security and defence policy the bilateral relationship appeared strengthened. Prior to June 1997 German policy had moved markedly closer to French policy on the reinforcement of the European Security and Defence Identity (see below pp. 205–7) and Schröder did nothing to modify this *rapprochement*. The Franco-German relationship also remained firmly embedded institutionally. Indeed, following the difficult experience of the Nice Treaty negotiations, the Jospin government sought to rebuild the Franco-German relationship with more frequent ministerial-level meetings in 2001 designed to re-establish the habit and predictability of good relations. On 12 June 2001, at the 77th Franco-German summit held in Freiburg, Germany, the strength of the bilateral relationship appeared reconfirmed: Chirac and Schröder agreed to a joint declaration stating their confidence in the adoption of the Nice Treaty despite its rejection in the Irish referendum a few days earlier, and asserting that the Irish vote would not alter the timetable for EU enlargement (*Financial Times*, 12 June 2001). However, profound differences in French and German visions of the EU's future remained and could less easily be negotiated out of the way.

THE CHALLENGE OF THE FUTURE

The Jospin government and the Chirac presidency had great difficulty conceptualising the future of European integration. The French Gaullist vision of a small and largely intergovernmental community had been gradually rendered redundant by successive enlargements and the progress of European integration. However, the French had always refused to nullify the Luxembourg Compromise which guaranteed the national veto on matters of 'national interest'. Moreover, French governments had been able to avoid any serious reconceptualisation of the desirable end-goal of European integration. President Mitterrand, himself, had been notoriously sibylline about his vision of the European Union's future. This avoidance can be explained in large part by strong support for intergovernmentalism in most political parties, often linked to the deeper republican tradition of the 'one and indivisible republic' and the widespread Euro-scepticism which discouraged forward thinking. Some initial attempt at reconceptualisation had started to take place in the mid-1990s. Arnaud (2000) and Drake and Milner (1999) argue that thinking in favour of further European integration had gained the upper hand in the French policy-making elite, with even a willingness to consider, if not accept, words such as 'federalism' and 'constitutionalism' (Arnaud 2000; Drake 2001). The new consensus that had developed accepted stronger EU institutions and the limited further transfer of policy-making powers. However, this reconceptualisation was limited: many of the new ideas were vague and the Euro-sceptic and intergovernmentalist impulse remained strong.

The Jospin government found it increasingly difficult to avoid reconceptualisation, for several reasons. First, ever further integration through the

Maastricht, Amsterdam and Nice Treaties and the coming into effect of EMU, combined with the perception of an incomplete European Union, led many in France and other EU member states to ask more questions about the future. Second, the imminent EU enlargement to Central and Eastern Europe, which became increasingly difficult to delay, encouraged political leaders to think harder about the shape of a much larger European Union – its policies and institutional structures but also its more general design. Third, unlike previous German politicians in government, Fischer and Schröder demonstrated their willingness to place the French government on the spot, forcing a public clarification of their vision. Some observers have argued that German unilateralism in starting the 'Euro-visions' debate was of little surprise given the leadership vacuum in the realm of ideas and the delays in the enlargement process (Drake 2001). Following the December 2000 Nice summit, the Jospin government also had little choice but to start thinking more seriously about further integration. The Schröder and d'Alema (Italian) governments succeeded in achieving an agreement at Nice on another intergovernmental conference for 2004 which they hoped would lead to the creation of a more federal European constitution.

Despite these external pressures, the French demonstrated their limited capacity to spell out a convincing vision of the EU's future. President Chirac responded to Fischer in his 27 June 2000 speech ('Our Europe') to the German *Bundestag*. He called for a rather impressive-sounding reworking of the EU's institutions, with a 'pioneer group' of member states pushing ahead with advanced integration, especially on tightened economic policy coordination of the Euro-zone countries in the Eurogroup. However, some observers have noted the contradictions in the president's speech, emphasising both traditional neo-Gaullist themes and further integration (Dinan and Vanhoonacker 2000). The Jospin government was even more limited in its response to Fischer and Chirac. Foreign Minister Hubert Védrine provided a constructive criticism of Fischer's ideas while European Affairs Minister Pierre Moscovici claimed that Chirac's views would not determine the Jospin government's approach to treaty reform (Drake 2001). A year later, both Chirac and Jospin responded to Schröder's May 2001 call for a federalist EU constitution – on 9 May (Europe Day) and 27 May respectively. Chirac presented again his poorly spelled-out vision of a small 'pioneer group'. Jospin cautiously greeted the German chancellor's proposals on overhauling the EU's powers and institutions. However, in his clearest statement to date on the future of the EU, Jospin presented a largely intergovernmentalist vision, stating that Schröder's idea of turning the European Union into a more federal structure was anathema to most of France's political class.[2] The prime minister also refused to endorse Chirac's 'pioneer group' on the grounds that it was too exclusive and went against the grain of the flexible multispeed integration that had been the thrust of French policy since 1994 when Edouard Balladur outlined his 'concentric circles' policy.

---

[2] For an outline of Jospin's 27 May 2001 speech see http://news.ft.com/ft/gx.cgi/ftc?pagename=View&c= Article&cid=FT3HE10IANC&live=true&tagid=YYY9BSINKTM&useoverridetemplate=IXLYHNNP94C

Despite the differences in their speeches, the president and the prime minister both drew on former commission president Jacques Delors's intergovernmentalist vision of a 'European Federation of Nation States'.

There are diverse views about the French council presidency's handling of treaty reform in the lead-up to the Nice summit, some of them highly critical (see, for example, Ross 2001). President Chirac, in particular, was widely criticised for his poor diplomacy, while difficulties were created by France's stubborn pursuit of national interests: its insistence on parity with Germany in the council and on the reweighting of votes that would maintain the relative influence of the large member states in the council following enlargement. Nonetheless, the French accepted several reforms to make enlargement work that went against the intergovernmentalist grain: the substantial extension of QMV; the eventual loss of one of France's two commissioners; and the reinforcement of the flexibility ('strengthened cooperation') provisions to allow a number of countries to proceed with integration if this met the approval of a qualified majority of the member states. Some observers also argue that the French council presidency promised too much and delivered too little (see, for example, Ross 2001: 6). Other observers present a more balanced picture, arguing that the outcome at Nice was the best that could have been hoped for given a narrow margin of manoeuvre, pressure to conclude the IGC negotiations, conflicting national demands on necessary institutional changes (postponed from the Amsterdam summit) – which were by nature divisive given what was at stake – and the relative power and status of existing and future member states (Galloway 2001; Ludlow 2001; Vignes 2001). It can also be noted that the council presidency was afflicted from its outset with a defensive tone and incoherent thinking (Goulard 2000), which was made worse by the coordination problems between Chirac's office and the Jospin government.

REINFORCING EUROPEAN SECURITY AND DEFENCE COOPERATION

It would be wrong to claim that all European-level developments posed challenges to traditional French perceptions. The transformed European and international geo-strategic situation since the end of the Cold War and the development of American, German and British security policies created new opportunities for the partial fulfilment of the security and defence dimension of the Gaullist paradigm, linked to the traditional French preference for reinforcing the international role of the European Community/Union (*Europe de la Puissance*). In the context of a much-enlarged EU, the impracticability of the classic Gaullist vision of a French-led European security and defence policy was generally accepted. A Common European Security and Defence Policy (CESDP) could only work with British participation and joint leadership and, following the reconceptualisation of German security policy (Hyde-Pryce and Jeffery 2001), German participation and joint leadership also had to be incorporated into the French vision. Another central element of the Gaullist paradigm – the development of a purely European security policy outside the US-dominated NATO – had already made considerable progress prior to June 1997. Developments included the Maastricht Treaty provisions creating the framework for a Common Foreign and Security Policy (CFSP) and allowing the EU to call upon the European defence organisation (the West European Union, WEU) to engage in certain military missions: the January 1992 agreement at Petersburg concerning European peacekeeping and humanitarian missions; the incorporation of the Petersburg tasks into the CFSP at Amsterdam; the agreement on a provision that the European Council could alone decide on the development of a common defence policy (thus avoiding the need for further treaty reform to achieve this); the development of the CFSP's secretariat and leadership (a Mr CFSP) and the possibility of the development of a European Rapid Reaction Force (ERRF). The decision by Chirac, announced in December 1995, to reintegrate France into the military command structure of NATO should thus not be seen as an alternative to the construction of a CESDP but rather as part of a more general French strategy to challenge American military leadership in Western Europe.

The Jospin government and Chirac presidency continued French diplomatic efforts to reinforce the CESDP (Howarth 2001). The creation of a Mr CFSP (the EU High Representative on Foreign and Security Policy) and specific agreements on the reinforcement of the council body responsible for coordinating member-state security information were achieved by mid-1999 (the Cologne summit). At Saint-Malo, in November 1998, the Jospin and Blair governments agreed upon practical measures to bring about a European Rapid Reaction Force (ERRF) of 40 000 to 60 000 troops to engage in the CFSP missions (approved at the December 1999 Helsinki summit). Although the subsequent implementation of this agreement was patchy, the promise of future developments encouraged the Jospin government to dismantle the Eurocorps, the former vehicle of EU-sponsored military missions in which previous French governments had invested so much diplomatic effort. Another crucial lacuna in the development of an autonomous European security policy was inadequate military hardware for major interventions, especially communication technology and long-range air transport for military equipment and thus reliance on NATO (i.e. American) means and American approval of their use. Effectively, this gave the USA control over EU missions. Given relatively small European defence budgets, the French spearheaded efforts to establish joint military hardware programmes with other EU member states (including, for example, a military radar project agreed with the Germans). More generally, EU security cooperation was successfully reinforced during the Jospin government, as demonstrated during the Kosovo crisis of 1999 despite major disagreements over NATO strategy and continued problems with information sharing.

Progress on CEDSP was one of the major successes of the French council presidency. In the lead-up to the Nice summit, the French sought unsuccessfully to extend the kinds of military intervention that could be undertaken by

EU-sponsored troops to more aggressive missions. The Jospin government, like previous French governments, also pushed actively for the incorporation of the West European Union (WEU) defence organisation into the EU, which was finally achieved in the Nice Treaty. However, Article 5 of the WEU treaty – which provided the guarantee of mutual joint defence covered since 1949 by NATO's own Article 5 – was rejected by Britain. The Nice Treaty also incorporated the ERRF and various other agreements reached during the French council presidency, including the creation of the Political and Security Committee to be responsible for both the CFSP and CESDP and the formulation of joint actions. However, the Anglo-French debate on the relationship of NATO and the EU's military capacity remained: the French insisted that the ERRF would be coordinated with NATO but independent and the British insisting upon its subsidiary, dependent status. However, the British proved useful allies to the French, who consistently refused to accept the extension of QMV on foreign and security matters against German demands for more supranationalism in these areas. Neither the Jospin government nor the Chirac presidency were willing to reconceptualise the problematic French policy – which had frequently resulted in the failure of the European partners to agree on effective joint action – of maintaining the national veto on the CFSP.

CONCLUSION

This analysis of Jospin government European policy has highlighted the considerable continuity in dominant French perceptions of desirable European policy developments and the extent to which the Jospin government reasserted established French preferences. In Chapter 8 we saw how the government had some success in meeting the challenges of economic and monetary integration with a positive response for example, on EU employment policy (the Luxembourg and Cardiff processes) and strengthened economic policy coordination in the upgraded Eurogroup without abandoning traditional French priorities and the objectives of the French Socialist Party and Plural Left government. Widening cracks in Franco-German bilateralism proved uncomfortable for the Jospin government on several issues and contributed to the French council presidency's difficult handling of the treaty reform negotiations leading to the December 2000 Nice summit. A more assertive Germany forced a reconceptualisation of traditional assumptions concerning France's privileged position in the process of European integration. However, a strong German leaning towards bilateralism meant that the Schröder government was worse in its bark than its bite, and in some areas, notably on security and defence policy, German positions converged with French positions and Franco-German policy coordination was reinforced. Despite the dogged pursuit of national interests, the Jospin government succeeded in accepting, and the French council presidency in managing, significant changes to the EU's institutional structure that were intended to decrease the likelihood of gridlock in the EU decision-making process following enlargement.

Despite some changes in the French outlook towards the European Union and the process of integration, the Jospin government refused – failed – to engage in any serious and public reconceptualisation of the end-point of European integration. There were signs that the government was beginning to encourage such a reconceptualisation following the Nice summit. On 11 April 2001 the Jospin government launched a 'national dialogue' to consider the desirable future of European integration. The political mood seemed right to embark on a national debate: the government had little domestic political difficulty ratifying the Nice Treaty in 2001 and public support for further integration (albeit vague and not very profound) was at its highest for many years. However, in the lead-up to the 2002 presidential and National Assembly elections, neither the Jospin government nor President Chirac demonstrated a willingness to engage in any serious reconceptualisation and it is doubtful whether the Chirac presidency and Raffarin government will do so prior to the 2004 intergovernmental conference.

Indeed, intergovernmentalism has shaped French government policy during the 2002 Convention on Europe's Future, presided over by former President Giscard d'Estaing. The principal institutional innovation sought by President Chirac has been the creation of a stronger, more visible council presidency. Such an institutional change will serve to reinforce the leadership role of the intergovernmental council at the expense of the supranational commission.

10

CONCLUSION

Vive la France, quand même!

'Most Europeans, when asked who runs Europe today, correctly point to Berlin ... hélas. *Where would Europeans most like to work, given the chance? London. What is the capital of European fashion? Milan. And so on. What, then, of France? What of Paris, wedged into its unhealthy little site near the Seine estuary on the western edge of a continent whose peoples all talk to each other in English? Well, in this new Europe of states and regions, councils and commissioners, subsidies and subsidiarity, Paris, quite simply, is* Europe – *the once and future (?) heart, soul, and symbol of a continent in urgent need of all three. If only French statesmen could stop preening and pronouncing, they might see this. France has lost a world, but it has a continent to gain. For the French are right – France is rather special. Everyone secretly knows this, even the English' (Tony Judt, 'The French difference'.* The New York Review of Books, *12 April 2001, p. 21).*

France is said today, once more, to be in a crisis. *Malaise* is a word pronounced readily when one talks of France. Yet, is any of all this new? If one looks at France's history from the time of the French Revolution onwards, the country has always been in a crisis of one kind or another. Thus, it is not the perceived existence of a crisis that is of interest today, but the kind of crisis. Enough has been said about *fracture sociale*, internal cleavages, and *insécurité* in Chapter 2. Here it might be more appropriate to take a wider look at France's place in the world and at how France's citizens see this role today. What strikes one in reactions towards the European Union, at least since German unification, attitudes towards the United States, and reactions to so-called globalisation, is an unmissable fear of the world outside. But it would be wrong to interpret this as simple xenophobia or excessive nationalism and the like. As their President at the time, François Mitterrand, told the

European Parliament in 1995, the French people are neither more nor less nationalistic than other peoples. The differences in manifestations of national feeling among nations have usually more to do with how respective nationals see their role in the world arena than with their being more or less 'nationalistic' than their neighbours. Thus, the commonplace stereotype current among British and American journalists commenting on France, to the effect that France is a prickly nation of ultra-nationalists, has to be discarded as a half-truth.

What is more important than the degree of nationalism of the French people (or rather, the deeper cause of the symptoms that are seen as nationalism) is a more general reluctance on their part to accept wholeheartedly the full consequences of modernisation. France sees (correctly, according to many) that the way the world is going is not her way. American-English language, American (light, mass) culture, American technology, American products and American weapons are overwhelming the planet. France, which was a great global power for centuries, cannot but feel some resentment at its diminished importance in the new dispensation. It is very characteristic of French fears that, during the weeks and months that followed the attacks in New York on 11 September 2001, there was a generalised feeling in Paris, expressed among analysts and intellectuals who are not among those regarded as anti-American, that a new danger had just arisen for France and for 'Europe' (meaning, of course, for Europe as visualised from Paris). This new danger arising after the events of 11 September 2001 was what the intellectuals in question called a clearly emerging 'anglo-saxon patriotism', a feeling of solidarity and close identification between the Americans, the British and even – believe it or not, for a few otherwise credible observers – the Germans. The very fact of lumping the British (rarely called anything other than 'English' by most French commentators) and the Americans in the dubious category of 'les anglo-saxons' is indicative of living in the past, or, to put it more mildly, of the persistence of old stereotypes which are not accepted to an equal degree by the English-speaking nations in question themselves. But to add the Germans as one of the members of the group of the anglo-saxons: that was the language of Victorian and perhaps Edwardian writers! But such racially based identifications of ethnic or cultural affinities have been abandoned by those concerned for some decades now. There is no gainsaying a great degree of sympathy for the United States in the UK in the wake of the attacks on the Twin Towers, and Prime Minister Blair went out of his way to assume the role of America's best friend. But to call such manifestations expressions of a new 'anglo-saxon patriotism' betrays a degree of misperception approaching paranoia. We mention these rantings here as an indication of the profundity of the insecurities felt in France as the world is changing more rapidly than our tools for analysing it. Such changes are food for thought for all of us, certainly. But there is a distinctly French approach to these changes which tends to be more defensive and fearful than anything else. To put it simply, France has serious self-confidence problems. With its formerly predominant role in the European Community seriously diminished since German reunification, and with its global radiance fatally diminished in the beginning of this twenty-first century that inherited from the previous an unchallenged American global hegemony, France feels disorientated. All this is understandable. Yet, there is a lot to be said for the argument insinuated by Tony Judt in the text quoted in the epigraph. France will indeed have to digest the loss of its global influence and reach, the sooner the better for her. But it does have a most important role to play in Europe in the foreseeable future. President Chirac has arguably more power to shape the future of the European Union for the years and decades to come than any other leader has today or has had for a long time. The future of enlargement, the future institutional shape of Europe following the constitutional Convention, Europe's world role in foreign affairs and in defence matters – all these things will have to be decided during the five years of Chirac's second Presidency. France still has a chance to play with *grandeur*. It depends on her how she will play her cards.

In all sorts of discussions about France's international comportment and about France's attitude to globalisation/Americanisation, British and American commentators (especially in the media, but also some academics) tend to be quite critical of France. Most of them seem to think it too presumptuous of a medium-size power such as France to have the effrontery to question the uniformisation of the world under norms made in the USA. Although a great deal in such comments is understandable, as a rule, American and British commentary on France's resistance tends to be unfair on France, or unimaginative. It may or may not be out of a genuine desire to preserve cultural and linguistic diversity and diversity of modes of thought and ways of life (as they claim) that – most of – the French resist the complete Americanisation of the world and endeavour to offer France as an alternative model for universal use. But let us assume that it is sheer national egoism and pride that leads them to argue this way. So what? Does this change the fact that, by stubbornly trying to protect certain aspects of her way of life and modes of thought, France contributes to that diversity which everyone agrees is good, but very few actually do anything to preserve? In other words: some of the things the French want to preserve may be adorable, and some may be less so. It is the very fact of being determined to preserve a model that has not fully assimilated the American way that renders the French beneficial to all of us, the United States included. The more powerful a country becomes, the more in need it is of monitors, rather than of adulators. And given the extraordinary degree of power and predominance that the USA has obtained, the danger of ethnocentric *hubris* is urgent. If France (either alone or through its role in the European Union) can remain different to such an extent, as to offer its 'sister republic', America, a mirror through which to see itself better, and the rest of the world an alternative way of living and thinking than that of the *hyperpuissance*, then France will have done mankind and civilisation an inestimable service.

REFERENCES AND FURTHER READING

Aeschimann, E. and Riché, P. 1996: *La Guerre de sept ans. Histoire secrète du franc fort, 1989–1996*. Paris: Calmann-Lévy.

Agulhon, M. 1998: Qu'est-ce qu'être républicain en France? *Revue des Sciences Morales et Politiques*, 4, 117–35.

Albert, P. 1990: *La Presse française*. Paris: La Documentation Française.

Allegre, C. 1993: *L'Age des saviors. Pour une renaissance de l'université*. Paris: Gallimard.

Alphandéry, E. 2000: *La Réforme obligée sous le soleil de l'Euro*. Paris: Grasset.

Ambler, J. S., ed. 1990: *The French Welfare State: Surviving Social and Ideological Change*. New York: NYU Press.

Ambler, J. S. 1996: Conflict and consensus in French education. In J. T. S. Keeler and M. A. Schain, eds: *Chirac's Challenge: Liberalisation, Europeanisation and Malaise in France*. New York: St. Martin's Press.

Arnaud, J.-L. 2000: France and Europe. The European debate in France at the start of the French presidency. *Notre Europe Research and Policy Papers*, 10, Paris, July.

Aron, R. 1957 [1955]: *The Opium of the Intellectuals*. London: Secker & Warburg.

Arthuis, J. 1998: *Dans les coulisses de Bercy, le cinquième pouvoir*. Paris: Albin Michel.

Audac, J.-L. and Bayard-Pierlot, J. annual: *Le Système éducatif français*. Créteil: Centre Régional de Documentation Pédagogique.

Audard, C. 2001: The French Republic and the claims of diversity. In C. C. Gould and P. Pasquino, eds: *Cultural Identity and the Nation-State*. Lanham, MD: Rowman & Littlefield, 85–108.

Balleix-Banerjee, C. 1999: *La France et la Banque Centrale Européenne*. Paris: Presses Universitaires de France.

Bauchard, P. 1986: *La Guerre des deux roses*. Paris: Grasset.

Beaud, O. 1999: *Le Sang contaminé*. Paris: Presses Universitaires de France.

Benda, J. 1927: *La Trahison des clercs*. Paris: Bernard Grasset. Trans. as *The Betrayal of the Intellectuals*. Boston: Beacon Press, 1955.

Beriss, D. 1990: Scarves, schools and segregation: the foulard affair. *French Politics and Society*, 81, 1–3.

Bernstein, S., ed. 1999: *Les Cultures politiques en France*. Paris: Seuil.

Bernstein, S. and Rudelle, O. 1992: *Le Modèle républicain*. Paris: Presses Universitaires de France.

Birnbaum, P. 1998: *La France imaginée. Déclin des rêves unitaires*. Paris: Fayard.

Blatt, D. S. 1996: *Immigration Politics and Immigrant Collective Action in France, 1968–1993*. Ann Arbor, MI: UMI.

Bloch-Laine, F. 1976: *Profession: Fonctionnaire*. Paris: Éditions Français.

Boissonnat, J. 1998: *La Révolution de 1999. L'Europe avec l'Euro*. Paris: Sand.

Boudic, G. 1992: *'Le Débat'. Mutations du champ intellectuel à travers l'étude d'une revue 1968–1992*. Rennes: Mémoire.

Boyer, R. 1998: An essay on the political and institutional deficits of the euro. The unanticipated fallout of the European Monetary Union. *Couverture Orange CEPREMAP*, 9813, August.

Boyer, R. 1999: *Le Gouvernement économique de la zone euro*. Paris: Commissariat Général du Plan.

Bozo, F. 1991: *La France et l'OTAN. De la Guerre Froide au Nouvel Ordre Européen*. Paris: Masson.

Bozo, F. 1996: *Deux Stratégies pour l'Europe. De Gaulle, les Etats-Unis et l'Alliance Atlantique 1958–1969*. Paris: Plon.

Breatnach, M. and Sterenfeld, E. 2000: From Messiaen to MC Solaar: music in France in the second half of the twentieth century. In W. Kidd and S. Reynolds, eds: *Contemporary French Cultural Studies*. London: Arnold, 244–56.

Breuilly, J. 1993: *Nationalism and the State*, 2nd edn. Manchester: Manchester University Press.

Brubaker, R. 1992: *Citizenship and Nationhood in France and Germany*. Cambridge, MA: Harvard University Press.

Buron, M. 1993: *La Décentralisation. L'âge de raison*. Group 'Décentralisation: Bilans et perspectives', Commissariat Général du Plan, Paris: La Documentation Française.

Cambadélis, J.-C. 1999: *L'Avenir de la gauche plurielle*. Paris: Plon.

Cameron, D. 1995: From Barre to Balladur: economic policy in the era of EMS. In G. Flynn, ed.: *Remaking the Hexagon*. Bonlder, Co: Westview.

Cerny, P. G. 1980: *The Politics of Grandeur: Ideological Aspects of De Gaulle's Foreign Policy*. Cambridge: Cambridge University Press.

Chapman, R. and Hewitt, N., eds. 1992: *Popular Culture and Mass Communication in Twentieth Century France*. Lampeter: The Edwin Mellen Press.

Charle, C. 1990: *Naissance des 'intellectuels' 1880–1900*. Paris: Minuit.

Charlot, J. 1994: *La Politique en France*. Paris: Le Livre de Poche.

Charlot, J. 1995: *Pourquoi Jacques Chirac?* Paris: Éditions de Fallois.

Chevallier, J. 1996: La reforme de l'État et la conception française du service public. *Revue Française d'Administration Publique*, 77, 189–205.

Cheverny, J. 1966: *Ces princes que l'on gouverne. Essai sur l'anarchie autoritaire*. Paris: Juilland.

Clark, D. 1998: The modernization of the French civil service: crisis, change and continuity. *Public Administration*, 76, 97–115.

Clark, D. 2000: Public service reform: a comparative West European perspective. *West European Politics*, 23, 3, 25–44.

Closon, F. L. and Filippi, J. 1968: *L'Économie et les finances*. Paris: Presses Universitaires de France.

Cohen, E. 1996: *La Tentation hexagonale*. Paris: Fayard.

Cohen, E. 1998: A dirigiste end to dirigisme. In M. Maclean, ed.: *The Mitterand Years: Legacy and Evaluation*. London: Macmillan.

Cohen, S. 1998: *Mitterrand et la sortie de la Guerre Froide*. Paris: Presses Universitaires de France.

Cole, A. 1998: *French Politics and Society*. Hemel Hempstead: Prentice Hall.

Cole, A. 1999: The *Service Publique* under stress. *West European Politics*, 22, 4, 166–84.

Cole, A. 2001: *Franco-German Relations*. London: Longman.

Cole, A. and Drake, H. 2000: The Europeanization of the French polity: continuity, change and adaptation. *Journal of European Public Policy*, 7, 1, 26–43.

Colombani, J.-M. 2001: La France et la Corse. *Revue des sciences morales et politiques*. L'État de la France, 83–98.

Combesque, M. A. 1998: *Ça suffit. Histoire du mouvement des chômeurs*. Paris: Plon.

Commissariat Général au Plan 1994: *Pour un état stratège, garant de l'intérêt general*. Rapport de la Commission présidée par Christian Blan, Paris: La Documentation Française.

Commissariat Général au Plan 1999: *Le Gouvernement économique de la zone euro*. Paris: La Documentation Française.

Commission pour l'Avenir de la Décentralisation 2000: *Refonder l'action publique*. Paris: Premier Ministre.

Conseil d'Analyse Économique 1998: *Coordination européenne des politiques économiques*. Paris: La Documentation Française.

Corbett, A. and Moon, B. 1996: *Education in France: Continuity and Change in the Mitterrand Years, 1981–1995*. London: Routledge.

Crowley, J. 1993: Paradoxes in the politicisation of race: a comparison of the UK and France. *New Community*, 19, 4, 627–43.

Crozier, M. 1964: *La Société bloquée*. Paris: Fayard.

Crozier, M. 1988: *Comment réformer l'État*? Rapport au Ministre de la Fonction Publique et des Réformes Administratives. Paris: La Documentation Française.

Daley, A., ed. 1996: *The Mitterrand Era*. London: Macmillan.

D'Arcy, F. and Rouban, L., eds. 1996: *De la Ve République à l'Europe*. Paris: Presses de Sciences Po.

Darriulat, P. 2001: *Les Patriotes. La gauche républicaine et la nation 1830–1870*. Paris: Seuil.

Debbasch, C. and J.-M. Pontier 2001: *La Société Française* (4th edn). Paris: Armand Colin.

Debray, R. 1979: *Le Pouvoir intellectuel en France*. Paris: Ramsay.

Debray, R. 1980: *Le Scribe*. Paris: Grasset.

Della Porta, D. and Vanucci, A. 1999: *Corrupt Exchanges: Actors, Resources and Mechanisms of Political Corruption*. New York: Aldine de Gruyter.

Demossier, M. and Liner, S. 2000: Social difference: age and place. In W. Kidd and S. Reynolds, eds: *Contemporary French Cultural Studies*. London: Arnold, 69–80.

Denoix de Saint Marc, R. 1997: *Le Service Public*. Rapport au Premier Ministre. Paris: La Documentation Française.

Desportes, G. and Mauduit, L. 1999: *La Gauche imaginaire et le nouveau capitalisme*. Paris: Grasset.

Devaquet, A. 1988: *L'Amibe et l'étudiant. Université et recherche: l'état d'urgence*. Paris: Éditions Odile Jacob.

Dinan, D. and Vanhoonacker, S. 2000: *IGC 2000 Watch*, Part 2: The Opening Round. *ECSA Review*, 13, 3, Summer, 1.

Domenach, N. and Szafran, M. 2000: *Le Miraculé. Le Roman d'un président*. Paris: Plon.

Donnat, O. 1998a: *Les Pratiques culturelles des Françaises. Enquête 1997*. Paris: La Documentation Française.

Donnat, O. 1998b: Temps libre et pratiques culturelles. In *L'Etat de la France 98–99*. Paris: La Découverte.

Doublet, Y.-M. 1997: *L'argent et la politique en France*. Paris: Economica.

Downs, W. M. 1998: The Front National as kingmaker again: France's regional elections of March 1998. *Regional and Federal Studies*, 8, 3, 125–33.

Drake, H. 2001: France on trial? The challenge of change posed by the French council presidency of the European Union, July–December 2000. *Modern and Contemporary France*, 9, 4, November, 453–66.

Drake, D. 2002: *Intellectuals and Politics in Post-War France*. Basingstoke: Palgrave.

Drake, H. and Milner, S. 1999: Change and resistance to change: the political management of Europeanisation in France. *Modern and Contemporary France*, 7, 2, 165–78.

Dreyfus, F. 2000: *L'Invention de la bureaucratie*. Paris: La Découverte.

Durand-Prinborgne, C. 1994: *L'Education nationale. Une culture, un service, un système*, 2nd edn. Paris: Nathan.

Duyvendak, J. W. 1995: *The Power of Politics: New Social Movements in France*. Boulder, CO: Westview.

Dyson, K. 1994: *Elusive Union: The Process of Economic and Monetary Union in Europe*. London: Longman.

Dyson, K. 1997: La France, l'union économique et monétaire et la construction européenne. Renforcer l'exécutif, transformer l'état. *Politiques et Management Public*, 15, 3, 57–77.

Dyson, K. 1999: EMU, political discourse and the Fifth French Republic: historical institutionalism, path dependency and 'craftsmen' of discourse. *Modern and Contemporary France*, 7, 2, 179–96.

Dyson, K. and Featherstone, K. 1999: *The Road to Maastricht: Negotiating Economic and Monetary Union*. Oxford: Oxford University Press.

Dyson, K., Featherstone, K. and Michaelopoulos, G. 1994: *Reinventing the French State: Construction européenne and the Development of French Policies on EMU*, Report Number 2. University of Bradford: Department of European Studies, European Briefing Unit.

Economist Intelligence Unit 1992–2000: *Country Report, France*. London: EIU.

Ehrmann, H. W. and Schain, M. A. 1992: *Politics in France*, 5th edn. New York: HarperCollins.

Elgie, R. 1993: *The Role of the Prime Minister in France, 1981–1991*. London: Macmillan.

Elgie, R. 1996: *Electing the French President*. London: Macmillan.

Elgie, R., ed. 1999: *The Changing French Political System*. Ilford: Frank Cass.

Escoube, P. 1971: *Les Grands Corps de l'état*. Paris: Presses Universitaires de France.

L'ENA 1997: *Pouvoirs*. 80, Paris: Seuil.

État de La France annual. Paris: La Découverte.

L'État de La France 2001–2: *Un panorama unique et complet de la France*. Paris: La Découverte.

Fabre Guillemant, R. 1998: *Les Reformes administratives en France et en Grande-Bretagne*. Paris: L'Harmattan.

Faucher, F. 1999: *Les Habits verts de la politique*. Paris: Presses de Sciences Po.

Favell, A. 1998: *Philosophies of Integration: Immigration and the Idea of Citizenship in France and Britain*. Basingstoke: Macmillan.

Favier, P. and Martin-Roland, M. 1990: *La Décennie Mitterrand*. Paris: Seuil.

Feldblum, M. 1999: *Reconstructing Citizenship: The Politics of Nationality Reform and Immigration in Contemporary France*. Albany, NY: State University of New York Press.

Ferry, L. and Renaut, A. 1984: *Des droits de l'homme à l'idée républicaine. Philosophie politique*, 3. Paris: Presses Universitaires de France.

Finkielkraut, A. 1987: *La Défaite de la pensée*. Paris: Gallimard.

Fitoussi, J.-P. 1992: *La Désinflation compétitive, le mark et les politiques budgétaires en Europe*. Paris: OFCE and Éditions du Seuil.

Fitoussi, J.-P. 1995: *Le Débat interdit*. Paris: Éditions du Seuil.

Flood, C. and Bell, L. eds. 1997: *Political Ideologies in Contemporary France*. London: Pinter.

Flood, C. and Hewlett, N. 2000: *Currents in Contemporary French Intellectual Life*. Basingstoke: Macmillan.

La Fonction Publique de l'Etat 1998. Paris: La Documentation Française.

Forrester, Viviane 1999: *The Economic Horror*. Cambridge: Polity.

Freeman, G. P. 1990: Financial crisis and policy: continuity in the welfare state. In P. Hall *et al.*, eds: *Developments in French Politics*. London: Macmillan.

Fulchiron, H. 2000: *La Nationalité française. Que sais-je?* Paris: Presses Universitaires de France.

Furet, F., Julliard, J. and Rosanvallon, P. 1988: *La République du centre. La Fin de l'exception française*. Paris: Calmann-Lévy.

Gaffney, J. 2003 (forthcoming): *The French Elections of 2002*. Aldershot: Ashgate.

Galland, O. and Lemel, Y. 1998: *La Nouvelle Société française. Trente années de mutation*. Paris: Armand Colin.

Galloway, D. 2001: *The Treaty of Nice and Beyond: Realities and Illusions of Power in the EU*. Sheffield: Sheffield Academic Press.

Garbaye, R. 2000: Minorities, representation and French local politics: North African groups in Lille and Roubaix. Paper presented at the Political Studies Association 2000 Annual Conference, London School of Economics, French Politics and Public Policy: Improving Representative Democracy Panel, 10–13 April.

Gaspard, F., *et al.* 1992: *Au pouvoir, citoyennes! Liberté, egalité et parité*. Paris: Seuil.

Gaspard, F. and Khosrokhavar, F. 1995: *Le Foulard et la République*. Paris: La Découverte.

Gastaut, Y. 2000: *L'Immigration et l'opinion en France sous la Ve République*. Paris: Seuil.

Gauchet, M. 2002: *La Démocratie contre elle-même*. Paris: Gallimard.

Geisser, V. 1997: *Ethnicité Républicaine. Les Élites d'origine maghrébine dans le système politique française*. Paris: Presses de Sciences-Po.

Geledan, A., ed. 1995: *Le Bilan économique des années Mitterrand*. Paris: Éditions Le Monde.

Gerstlé, J. 1993: *La Communication politique*. Paris: Presses Universitaires de France.

Gibson, R. 1989: *A Social History of French Catholicism 1789–1914*. London: Routledge.

Gilbert, G. and Delcamp, A., eds. 1993: *La Décentralisation dix ans après*. Paris: Librairie Générale de Droit et Jurisprudence.

Gildea, R. 1994: *The Past in French History*. New Haven, CT: Yale University Press.

Gildea, R. 1997: *France since 1945*. Oxford: Oxford University Press.

Girardet, R. 1983: *Le Nationalisme Français: Anthologie, 1871–1914*. Paris: Éditions du Seuil.

Girardet, R. 1996: *Nationalismes et Nation*. Brussels: Complexe.

Goodman, J. B. 1992: *Monetary Sovereignty: The Politics of Central Banking in Western Europe*. Ithaca, NY: Cornell University Press.

Gordon, P. 1993: *A Certain Idea of France: French Security Policy and the Gaullist Legacy*. Princeton, NJ: Princeton University Press.

Goulard, S. 2000: La France 'pratiquante non croyante'? Les enjeux d'une présidence modeste. *Politique étrangère*, 2, 343–57.

Greenfeld, L. 1992: *Nationalism: Five Roads to Modernity*. Cambridge, MA: Harvard University Press.

Gregory, S. 2000: *French Defence Policy into the Twenty-First Century*. London: Macmillan.

Gremion, C. and Fraisse, R., eds. 1996: *Le Service public en recherche. Quelle modernisation?* Paris: La Documentation Française.

Groux, G. 1998: *Vers un renouveau du conflit social*. Paris: Bayard.

Guy, J.-N., ed. 1995: *Les Jeunes et les sorties culturelles*. Paris: Ministry of Culture.

Guyomarch, A., *et al*. 1998: *France in the European Union*. Basingstoke: Macmillan.

Guyomarch, A., *et al*. 2001: *Developments in French Politics*. Basingstoke: Palgrave.

Hainsworth, P. 1998: The return of the left: the 1997 French parliamentary elections. *Parliamentary Affairs*, 51, 1, 71–83.

Hainsworth, P. 1999: The right: divisions and cleavages in fin de siècle France. In R. Elgie, ed.: *The Changing French Political System*. Ilford: Frank Cass.

Halimi, G. 1997: *La Nouvelle Cause des femmes*. Paris: Seuil.

Hall, P. 1986: *Governing the Economy*. Oxford: Polity.

Hall, P., *et al*., eds. 1990: *Developments in French Politics*. London: Macmillan.

Halphen, E. 2002: *Sept ans de solitude*. Paris: Denoel.

Hamon, H. and Rotman, P. 2002: *La Deuxième Gauche. Histoire intellectuelle et politique de la CFDT*. Paris: Seuil.

Hancke, B. 2001: Revisiting the French model: coordination and restructuring in French industry in the 1980s. In P. Hall and D. Soskice, eds: *Varieties of Capitalism: The Institutional Foundations of Competitiveness*. Oxford: Oxford University Press.

Hansen, R. and Weil, P., eds. 2000: *Dual Nationality, Social Rights and Federal Citizenship in the US and Europe*. Oxford: Berghahn.

Hantrais, L. 1996: France: squaring the welfare triangle. In V. George and P. Taylor-Gooby, *European Welfare Policy*. Basingstoke: Macmillan, 51–71.

Hargreaves, A. 1995: *Immigration, 'Race' and Ethnicity in Contemporary France*. London: Routledge.

Harris, S. 2000: Cinema in a nation of filmgoers. In W. Kidd and S. Reynolds, eds: *Contemporary French Cultural Studies*. London: Arnold, 208–19.

Hassenteufel, P. 1997: *Les Médecins face à l'état. Une comparaison internationale*. Paris: Presses de la Fondation Nationale des Sciences Politiques.

Hayward, J. E. S. 1983: *Governing France: The One and Indivisible Republic*, 2nd edn. London: Weidenfeld & Nicolson.

Hayward, J. E. S. 1986: *The State and the Market Economy: Industrial Patriotism and Economic Interventionism in France*. Brighton: Wheatsheaf.

Hayward, J. E. S. 1991: *After the French Revolution: Six Critics of Democracy and Nationalism*. New York: Harvester Wheatsheaf.

Hayward, J. E. S., ed. 1993: *De Gaulle to Mitterrand: Presidential Power in France*. London: Hurst.

Hayward, J. E. S. 2001: In search of an evanescent European identity. In A. Guyomarch *et al.*: *Developments in French Politics*. Basingstoke: Palgrave, 257–85.

Hazareesingh, S. 1991: *Intellectuals and the French Communist Party: Disillusion and Decline*. Oxford: Oxford University Press.

Hazareesingh, S. 1994: *Political Traditions in Modern France*. Oxford: Oxford University Press.

Hazareesingh, S. 2001: *Intellectual Founders of the Republic: Five studies in Nineteenth-Century French Republican Political Thought*. Oxford: Oxford University Press.

Hoffmann, S., *et al.* 1963: *In Search of France*. New York: Harper & Row.

Hoffmann, S. 1974: *Decline or Renewal? France Since the 1930s*. New York: Viking.

Howarth, D. 2001a: *The French Road to European Monetary Union*. Basingstoke: Palgrave.

Howarth, D. 2001b: France. In J. Lodge, ed.: *The 1999 European Parliamentary Elections*. London: Routledge.

Howarth, D. 2002: The European policy of the Jospin government: a new twist to old French games. *Modern and Contemporary France*, 10, 3, August, 353–69.

Howorth, J. 1993: The president's special role in foreign and defence policy. In J. E. S. Hayward, ed.: *De Gaulle to Mitterand: Presidential Power in France*. London: Hurst, 83–109.

Howorth, J. 2001: European defence and the changing of the European Union: hanging together or hanging separately? *Journal of Common Market Studies*, 39, 4, November, 765–90.

Hunt, L., ed. 1996: *The French Revolution and Human Rights: A Brief Documentary History*. Boston and New York: Bedford Books/St. Martin's Press.

Hyde-pryce, A. and Jeffery, C. 2001: Germany in the European Union. *Journal of Common Market Studies*, 39, 4, November, 689–718.

Institut National de la Jeunesse et de l'Education Populaire 1999: *Les jeunes aujourd'hui*. Paris: Bayard Éditions.

Itinéraires intellectuels des années 1970. *Revue française d'histoire des idées politiques*, 2, 353–410.

Jazouli, A. 1986: *L'Action collective des jeunes maghrebins en France*. Paris: L'Harmattan.

Jaume, L. 1997: *L'Individu effacé: ou le paradoxe du libéralisme français*. Paris: Fayard.

Jennings, J. 1993: Introduction: Mandarins and Samurais: the intellectual in modern France. In J. Jennings, ed.: *Intellectuals in Twentieth-Century France*. Basingstoke: Macmillan, 1–32.

Jennings, J. 1997: Of treason, blindness and silence: dilemmas of the intellectual in modern France. In J. Jennings and T. Kemp-Welch, eds: *Intellectuals in Politics: From the Dreyfus Affair to Salman Rushdie*. London: Routledge, 65–85.

Jennings, J. 2000: Citizenship, republicanism and multiculturalism in contemporary France. *British Journal of Political Science*, 30, 575–98.

Jennings, J. and Kemp-Welch, T. 1997: The century of the intellectual: from the Dreyfus affair to Salman Rushdie. In J. Jennings and A. Kemp-Welch, eds: *Intellectuals in Politics: From the Dreyfus Affair to Salman Rushdie*. London: Routledge, 1–21.

Jospin, L. 1999: *Modern Socialism*. London: Fabian Society, 1999.

Judt, T. 1986: *Marxism and the French Left, 1830–1981*. Oxford: Oxford University Press.

Judt, T. 1992: *Past Imperfect: French Intellectuals, 1944–56*. Berkeley, CA: University of California Press.

Judt, T. 1999: *The Burden of Responsibility: Blum, Camus, Aron, and the French Twentieth Century*. Chicago: Chicago University Press.

Julliard, J. 1997: *La Faute aux élites*. Paris: Gallimard.

Julliard, J. 2000: Gauche: du progressisme social au libéralisme moral. *Le Débat*, 110, 202–16.

Julliard, J. and Winock, M., eds. 1996: *Dictionnaire des intellectuels français. Les personnes, les lieux, les moments*. Paris: Seuil.

Kaplan, S. L. 1995: *Farewell Revolution: The Historians' Feud, France, 1789/1989*. Ithaca, NY: Cornell University Press.

Keating, M. and Hainsworth, P. 1986: *Decentralisation and Change in Contemporary France*. Brookfield, VT: Gower.

Keeler, J. T. S. 1987: *The Politics of Neo-Corporatism in France: Farmers, the State and Agricultural Policy-Making in the Fifth Republic*. New York: Oxford University Press.

Keeler, J. T. S. and Schain, M. A., eds. 1996: *Chirac's Challenge: Liberalisation, Europeanisation and Malaise in France*. New York: St. Martin's Press.

Kelfaoui, S. 1996: Un vote Maghrébin en France? *Hérodote*, 1, 80.

Kessler, M.-C. 1986: *Les Grands Corps de l'état*. Paris: Presses Universitaires de France.

Kessler, M.-C. 1999: *La Politique étrangère de la France*. Paris: Presses de la Fondation Nationale des Sciences Politiques.

Khilnani, S. 1993: *Arguing Revolution: The Intellectual Left in Post-War France*. New Haven, CT: Yale University Press.

Knapp, A. and Wright, V. 1999: What's left of the French right: the RPR and UDF from conquest to humiliation, 1993–1998. *West European Politics*, 223, 109–31.

Knapp, A. and Wright, V. 2001: *The Government and Politics of France*, 5th edn. London: Routledge.

Kraits, J. and Haltzel, M. H., eds, 1991: *Liberty/Liberté: The American and French Experiences*. Washington, DC, and Baltimore: The Woodrow Wilson Center Press/The Johns Hopkins University Press.

Krulic, B., ed. 1999: *La Nation. Une idée dépassée?* Problèmes politiques et sociaux. Dossiers d'actualité mondiale, 832. Paris: La Documentation Française.

Kuhn, R. 1995: *The Media in France*. London: Routledge.

Kuhn, R. 1998: The media and the public sphere in Fifth Republic France. *Democratization*, special issue: Democratization and the Media, 5, 2, Summer, 23–41.

Labbe, D. 1994: Trade unionism in France since the Second World War. *West European Politics*, 17, 1, January, 146–68.

Laborde, C. 2000: *Pluralist Thought and the State in Britain and France, 1900–25*. Basingstoke: Macmillan.

Laborde, C. 2001: The cultures of the republic: nationalism and multiculturalism in French republican thought. *Political Theory*, 29, 5, 716–35.

Lacouture, J. 1984–6: *De Gaulle*, 3 vols. Paris: Seuil.

Lacroix, B. and Lagroye, J., eds. 1992: *Le Président de la République*. Paris: Presses de Sciences Po.

Lacroix, J. 2000: Les 'nationaux-républicains de gauche' et la construction européenne. *Le Banquet*, 15, 157–68.

Ladrech, R. 1994: Europeanization of domestic politics and institutions: the case of France. *Journal of Common Market Studies*, 32, 1, March, 69–88.

Lafargue, J. 1998: *La Protestation collective*. Paris: Nathan.

Lalumière, P. 1959: *L'Inspection des finances*. Paris: Presses Universitaires de France.

Lalumière, P. 1970: *Les Finances publiques*. Paris: A. Colin.

Lapeyronnie, D. 1993: *L'individu et les minorités. La France et la Grande-Bretagne face à leurs immigrés*. Paris: Presses Universitaires de France.

Lasoumes, P. 1999: *Corruptions*. Paris: Presses de Sciences Po.

Laurent, V. 1998: Les architectes du social-libéralisme. Enquête sur la Fondation Saint-Simon. *Le Monde Diplomatique*, 534, 26–7 September.

Lequesne, C. 1993: *Paris Bruxelles*. Paris: Presses de la Fondation Nationale des Sciences Politiques.

Leterre, T. 2000: *La Gauche et la peur libérale*. Paris: Presses de la Fondation Nationale des Sciences Politiques.

Levy, J. 2000: France: directing adjustment? In F. Scharpf and V. Schmidt, eds: *Welfare and Work in the Open Economy: Diverse Responses to Common Challenges*. Oxford: Oxford University Press, 308–50.

Lewis, H. D. 1985: *The French Education System*. New York: St. Martin's Press.

Lewis-Beck, M., ed. 2000: *How France Votes*. London: Chatham House.

Liebfried, S. and Pierson, P. 2000: Social policy: left to courts and market? In W. Wallace and H. Wallace, eds: *Policy-Making in the European Union*. Oxford: Oxford University Press, 268–92.

Lilla, M., ed. 1994: *New French Thought: Political Philosophy*. Princeton, NJ: Princeton University Press.

Lindenberg, D. 2002: *Le Rappel à l'ordre: enquête sur les nouveaux réactionnaires*. Paris: Seuil.

Long, M. 1988: *Etre Français aujourd'hui et demain. Rapport de la Commission de la Nationalité présenté par M. Marceau Long au Premier Ministre*, 2 vols. Paris: La Documentation Française.

Loriaux, M. 1991: *France After Hegemony*. Ithaca, NY: Cornell University Press.

Lovecy, J. 2000: 'Des citoyennes à Part Entière'? The constitutionalisation of gendered citizenship in France and the parity reforms of 1999–2000. Paper presented to the PSA 2000 Annual Conference, LSE, London, 10–13 April.

Ludlow, P. 2001: The Treaty of Nice: neither a triumph nor disaster. *ECSA Review*, 14, 2, Spring, 1, 3 and 4.

Mabileau, A. 1994: *Le Système local en France*, 2nd edn. Paris: Montchrestien.

Machin, H. 1990: Stages and dynamics in the French party system. In P. Mair and G. Smith: *Understanding Party Change in Western Europe*. London: Frank Cass, 59–81.

Machin, H. and Wright, V., eds. 1985: *Economic Policy and Policy-Making under the Mitterrand Presidency, 1981–84*. London: Frances Pinter.

Maclean, M., ed. 1998: *The Mitterrand Years: Legacy and Evaluation*. London: Macmillan.

Mahoney, D. J. 1992: *The Liberal Political Science of Raymond Aron*. Lanham, MD: Rowman & Littlefield.

Mamou, Y. 1987: *Une Machine de pouvoir. La direction du Trésor*. Paris: La Découverte.

Marian, M. 1999: Lionel Jospin, le socialisme et la réforme. *Esprit*, March–April, 112–21.

Marsh, I. 1999: The state and the economy: opinion formation and collaboration as facets of economic management. *Political studies*, 47, 5, 837–56.

Masson, P. 1987: *Étudiants, Police, presse, pouvoir*. Paris: Hachette.

Mathy, J.-P. 1993: *Extrême-Occident: French Intellectuals and America*. Chicago: The University of Chicago Press.

Mathy, J.-P. 2000: *French Resistance: The French-American Culture Wars*. Minneapolis: University of Minnesota Press.

Mayer, N. and Perrineau, P. 1996: *Le Front National à découvert*. Paris: Presses de Science Po.

Mazdon, L. 2000a: *Encore Hollywood: Remaking French Cinema*. London: British Film Institute.

Mazdon, L., ed. 2000b: *France on Film: Reflections on Popular French Cinema*. London: Wallflower Press.

Mazur, A. G. 1995: *Gender Bias and the State: Symbolic Reform at Work in Fifth Republic France*. Pittsburgh: University of Pittsburgh Press.

McNamara, K. 1998: *The Currency of Ideas: Monetary Politics in the European Union*. Ithaca, NY: Cornell University Press.

Menon, A. 2000: *France, NATO and the Limits of Independence, 1981–1997: The Politics of Ambivalence*. London: Macmillan.

Mény, Y. 1992: *La corruption de la République*. Paris: Fayard.

Mény, Y., ed. 1997: France: the end of republican ethic. In D. della Porta and Y. Mény, eds: *Democracy and Corruption in Europe*. New York: Pinter, 7–21.

Meyer, D. and Tarrow, S., eds. 1998: *The Social Movement Society: Contentious Politics for a New Century*. Lanham, MD: Rowman & Littlefield.

Milesi, G. 1998: *Le Roman de l'Euro*. Paris: Hachette.

Milza, P. 1999: Les cultures politiques du nationalisme français. In S. Bernstein, ed.: *Les Cultures politiques en France*. Paris: Seuil, 315–53.

Ministére de l'Économie, des Finances et du Budget 1991: *La Contribution française aux progrès de l'union économique et monétaire*. (French draft treaty.) 16 January. In English see Agence Europe, 28/29.1.91, 5419.

Ministère de l'Économie, des Finances et de l'Industrie 2000: *Politique économique 2000, rapport économique, social et financier du Gouvernement*. Paris: Economica.

Ministère de l'Education Nationale, de l'Enseignement Superieur et de la Recherche 2000: *Après le BAC: réussir ses études. Le Guide des études supérieures 2000*. Paris: Les Dossiers ONISEP.

Ministère de l'Intérieur several years: *Les Collectivités locales en chiffres*. Paris: La Documentation Française.

Mitchell, L. 2000: French education: equal or elitist? In W. Kidd and S. Reynolds eds: *Contemporary French Cultural Studies*. London: Arnold, 51–66.

Le Monde 2000: La France dans le miroir de l'Insée. *Le Monde*, 10 November, 18–20.

Le Monde 2002a: Les France de 2002. *Le Monde*, 10–11 March, 13–20.

Le Monde 2002b: Le Grand Dossier. La France des oubliés. *Le Monde*, 2–3 June, 13–20.

Mongin, O. 1998: *Face au scepticisme. Les mutations du paysage intellectuel 1976–1998*. Paris: Hachette.

Montrial, T. de, *et al*. 1996: *Agir pour l'Europe. Les Relations franco-allemandes dans l'après-guerre froide*. Paris: Masson.

Moss, B. H. and Michie, J. 1998: *The Single European Currency in National Perspective: A Community in Crisis?* Basingstoke: Macmillan.

Muller, P., ed. 1992: *L'Administration française, est-elle en crise?* Paris: L'Harmattan.

Neidleman, J. 2001: *The General Will is Citizenship: Inquiries into French Political Thought*. Lanham, MD: Rowman & Littlefield.

Nicolet, C. 1982: *L'idée républicaine en France 1789–1924: Essai d'histoire* critique. Paris: Gallimard.

Noiriel, G. 1996 [1988]: *The French Melting-Pot: Immigration, Citizenship and National Identity*. Minneapolis: University of Minnesota Press.

Notat, N. 2001: Les Relations sociales en France. Le Nouveau Contexte, le rôle des différents acteurs, les perspectives. *Revue des sciences morales et politiques*, 1 (*L'État de la France* 1), 139–56.

OECD several years: *Country Survey, France*. Paris: OECD.

Ory, P., ed. 1987: *Nouvelle Histoire des idées politiques*. Paris: Hachette.

Ory, P. and Sirinelli, J.-F. 1986: *Les Intellectuels en France, de l'Affaire Dreyfus à nos jours*. Paris: Armand Colin.

Ottenheimer, G. 1996: *Le Fiasco*. Paris: A. Michel.

Palier, B. 2000: Defrosting the French welfare state. *West European Politics*, 23, 2, 113–36.

Péan, P. 1994: *Une jeunesse française. François Mitterrand, 1934–1947*. Paris: Fayard.

Pedersen, T. 1998: *Germany, France and Integration of Europe: A Realist Interpretation*, New York: Pinter.

Perrineau, P., ed. 1994: *L'Engagement politique. Déclin ou mutation?* Paris: Presses de la Fondation Nationale des Sciences Politiques.

Perrineau, P. 1997: *Le Symptome Le Pen*. Paris: Fayard.

Perrineau, P. 1998: Le Renouveau de l'action politique. *Vingtième Siècle*, 60, 112–17.

Picq, J. 1994: *L'Etat en France. Servir une nation ouverte sur le monde, rapport de la mission sur les responsabilités et l'organisation de l'Etat*. Paris: La Documentation Française.

Pilbeam, P. M. 1995: *Republicanism in Nineteenth-Century France, 1814–1871*. Basingstoke: Macmillan.

Pochet, P. 1998: The social consequences of EMU: an overview of national debates. In P. Pochet and D. Vanhercke, eds: *Social Challenges of Economic and Monetary Union*. Brussels: European Interuniversity Press, 67–102.

Poinsot, M. 1993: Competition for political legitimacy at local and national levels among young North Africans in France. *New Community*, 20, 1, 69–82.

Pouvoirs 1999: Special issue on 'La Cohabitation' (91). Paris: Seuil.

Public Policy and Administration 2001: Special edition on 'Public administration reform in France and Britain', 16, 4, Winter.

Pujas, V. and Rhodes, M. 1999: Party finance and political scandal in Italy, Spain and France. *West European Politics*, 22, 3, 41–63.

Rapport, M. 2000: *Nationality and Citizenship in Revolutionary France: The Treatment of Foreigners 1789–1799*. Oxford: Clarendon Press.

Regional Politics and Policy 1994: Special issue on the 'The End of the French Unitary State? Ten Years of Regionalization in France, 1982–1992', 4, 3, Autumn.

Reland, J. 1998: France. In A. Menon and J. Forder eds: *The European Union and National Macro-Economic Policy*. London: Routledge, 85–104.

Rémond, R. 1982: *Les Droites en France*. Paris: Aubier.

Rémond, R. 1985: *L'Anticlericalisme en France*. Brussels: Complexe.

Rémond, R. 2001: La France d'un siècle à l'autre: continuité et ruptures. *Revue des sciences morales et politiques*, 1 (*L'État de la France* 1), 1–21.

Renan, E. 1990 [1882]: What is a nation? In H. Bhabha, ed.: *Nation and Narration*. London: Routledge, 8–22.

Renaut, A., ed. 1999: Les Philosophies politiques contemporaines depuis 1945. *Histoire de la philosophie politique*, 5.

Ridley, F. 1998: The new public management in Europe: comparative perspectives. *Public Policy and Administration*, 11, 1, 16–29.

Rieffel, R. 1993: *Les Intellectuels sous la Ve République [1958–1990]*, 3 vols. Paris: Calmann-Lévy.

Roger, P. 2002: *L'Ennemi américain: généalogie de l'antiaméricanisme français*. Paris: Seuil.

Rosa, J.-J. 1998: *L'Erreur européenne*. Paris: Grasset.

Rosanvallon, P. 1990: *L'État en France*. Paris: Seuil.

Rosanvallon, P. 1992 [1981]: *La Crise de l'État-providence*. Paris: Seuil.

Rosanvallon, P. 2000 [1995]: *The New Social Question: Rethinking the Welfare State*. Princeton, NJ: Princeton University Press.

Rosanvallon, P. 2001: Fondements et problèmes de 'l'illibéralisme français'. *Revue des Sciences Morales et Politiques*, 1 (*L'État de la France* 1), 21–40.

Rosanvallon, P. 2002: (Interview) *Le Monde*, 26–7 May, 22.

Ross, G. 1998: The euro, the 'French model of society' and French politics. *French Politics and Society*, 16, 4, 1–16.

Ross, G. 2001: France's European tour of duty, or caution – one presidency may hide another. *ECSA Review*, 14, 2, Spring.

Rouban, L. 1996: *The French Civil Service*. Paris: La Documentation Française.

Royall, F. 2000: Protestations collectives d'une minorité socio-économique en France. *French Politics and Society*, 18, 2, Summer, 69–85.

Sadoun, M., *et al.* 2000: *La Démocratie en France, 1, Idéologies, II, Limites*. Paris: Gallimard.

Safran, W. 1995: *The French Polity*, 4th edn. White Plains, NY: Longman.

Sand, S. 1993: Mirror, mirror on the wall, who is the true intellectual of them all? Self-images of the intellectual in France. In J. Jennings, ed.: *Intellectuals in Twentieth-Century France*. Basingstoke: Macmillan, 33–58.

Sartre, J.-P. 1972: *Plaidoyer pour les intellectuels*. Paris: Gallimard.

Schain, M. 1988: Immigration and change in the French party system. *European Journal of Political Research*, 16, 6, 597–621.

Schmidt, V. 1990: *Democratizing France: The Political and Administrative History of Decentralization*. Cambridge: Cambridge University Press.

Schmidt, V. 1996: *From State to Market?* Cambridge: Cambridge University Press.

Schmidt, V. 1997a: Economic policy, political discourse and democracy in France. *French Politics and Society*, 15, 2, 37–48.

Schmidt, V. 1997b: Discourse and disintegration in Europe: the cases of France, Germany and Great Britain. *Daedalus*, Summer, 167–97.

Schnapper, D. 1991: *La France de l'intégration. Sociologie de la nation en 1990*. Paris: Gallimard.

Schnapper, D. 2000: *Qu'est-ce que la citoyenneté?* Paris: Gallimard.

Schor, A.-D. 1999: *Économie politique de l'euro*. Paris: La Documentation Française.

Silverman, M. 1992: *Deconstructing the Nation: Immigration, Racism and Citizenship in Modern France*. London: Routledge.

Silverman, M. 1996: The revenge of civil society: state, nation and society in France. In D. Cesarini and M. Fulbrook, eds: *Citizenship, Nationality and Migration in Europe*. London: Routledge, 146–57.

Siméant, J. 1998: *La Cause des sans-papiers*. Paris: Presses de la Fondation Nationale des Sciences Politiques.

Sirinelli, J.-F. 1992: *Histoire des droites en France*, 3 vols. Paris: Gallimard.

Sirinelli, J.-F. 1995: *Deux intellectuels dans le siècle, Aron et Sartre*. Paris: Fayard.

SOFRES 1995–2001: *L' État de l'opinion*. Paris: Éditions du Seuil.

Stevens, A. 1996: *The Government and Politics of France*, 2nd edn. London: Macmillan.

Stora, B. 1992: *Ils venaient d'Algérie. L'Immigration Algérienne en France, 1912–1992*. Paris: L'Harmattan.

Suleiman, E. N. 1974: *Politics, Power and Bureaucracy in France: The Administrative Elite*. Princeton, NJ: Princeton University Press.

Suleiman, E. N. 1987: *Private Power and Centralization in France: The Notaires and the State*. Princeton, NJ: Princeton University Press.

Suleiman, E. N. 1991: The corruption of politics and the politics of corruption. *French Politics and Society*, 9, 1, 57–76.

Suleiman, E. N. 1995: *Les Ressorts cachés de La réussite française*. Paris: Seuil.

Suleiman, E. N. 1996: *Les Réussites cachées de l' économie française*. Paris: Seuil.

Sutton, M. 1982: *Nationalism, Positivism and Catholicism: The Politics of Charles Maurras and French Catholics 1890–1914*. Cambridge: Cambridge University Press.

Szarka, J. 1996: The winning of the 1995 French presidential election. *West European Politics*, 19, 1, 151–67.

Szarka, J. 1999: The parties of the French 'plural left': an uneasy complementarity. In R. Elgie, ed.: *The Changing French Political System*. Ilford: Frank Cass, 20–37.

Taddei, D. and Coriat, B. 1993: *Made in France*. Paris: Livre de Poche.

Tenzer, N. 1996: *Histoire des doctrines politiques en France*. Paris: Presses Universitaires de France.

Thatcher, M. 1999: *The Politics of Telecommunications: National Institutions, Convergence and Change in Britain and France*. Oxford: Oxford University Press.

Thoenig, J.-C. 1996: Les Grands Corps. *Pouvoirs*, 79, 107–20.

Tiersky, R. 1994: *France in the New Europe*. Boulder, CO: Westview Press.

Tilly, C. 1996: The emergence of citizenship in France and elsewhere. In C. Tilly, ed.: Citizenship, identity and social history, *International Review of Social History*, 40, Supplement 3, 223–36.

Tint, H. 1964: *The Decline of French Patriotism 1870–1940*. London: Weidenfeld & Nicolson.

Tocqueville, A. de 1998 [1856]: *The Old Regime and the Revolution, Volume I: The Complete Text*. Eds F. Furet and F. Melonio, trans. A. S. Kahan. Chicago: The University of Chicago Press.

Tombs, R. 1994: Was there a French Sonderweg? *European Review of History*, 1, 2, 169–77.

Tombs, R. 1996: *France 1814–1914*. Harlow, Essex: Longman.

Tombs, R. 1997: À la recherche d'une famille politique nationaliste. Les cas britannique, français et allemand de 1800 [à] 1870. In *Les familles politiques en Europe occidentale au XIXe siècle*. Rome: École Française de Rome, 315–33.

Touchard, J. 1978: *Le Gaullisme 1940–1969*. Paris: Seuil.

Touraine, A. 1999: *Comment sortir du libéralisme?* Paris: Fayard.

Tribalat, M., ed. 1991: *Cent ans d'immigration, étrangers d'hier français d'aujourd'hui*. Paris: INED/Presses Universitaires de France.

Tribalat, M. 1995: *Faire France*. Paris: La Découverte.

Trosa, S. 1995: *Moderniser l'Administration*. Paris: Éditions de l'Organisation.

Vail, M. 1999: The better part of valour: the politics of French welfare reform. *Journal of European Social Policy*, 9, 4, 311–29.

Varouxakis, G. 2001: Patriotism. In A. S. Leoussi, ed.: *Encyclopaedia of Nationalism*. New Brunswick: Transaction Publishers, 239–42.

Varouxakis, G. 2002: *Victorian Political Thought on France and the French*. Basingstoke: Palgrave.

Vasconellos, M. 1993: *Le Système éducatif*. Paris: La Découverte.

Vedrine, D. (with D. Moisi) 2001: *France in an Age of Globalization*. Washington, DC: Brookings Institution Press.

Vedrine, H. 1996: *Les Mondes de François Mitterrand. A l'Elysée, 1981–1995*. Paris: Fayard.

Vedrine, H. 2000: *Les Cartes de la France à l'heure de la mondialisation dialogue avec Dominique Moïsi*. Paris: Fayard.

Vergnerie, J. P. 1996: La Réforme de l'état, un chantier bien engagé. *Service Public*, 40.

Victor, B. 1999: *Le Matignon de Jospin*. Paris: Flammarion.

Vignes, D. 2001: Nice, une vue apaisée. *Revue du marché commun et de l'Union européenne*, 445, February.

Vital-Durand, E. 1994: *Les Collectivités territoriales en France*. Paris: Hachette.

Weber, E. 1962: *Action Française: Royalism and Reaction in Twentieth-Century France*. Stanford, CA: Stanford University Press.

Weber, E. 1979: *Peasants into Frenchmen: The Modernization of Rural France 1870–1914*. London: Chatto & Windus.

Weil, P. 1991: *La France et ses étrangers*. Paris: Calman-Levy.

Weil, P. 1995: *La France et ses étrangers. L'aventure d'une politique de l'immigration de 1938 à nos jours*. Paris: Folio/Gallimard.

Weil, P. 1996: Nationalities and citizenships: the lessons of the French experience for Germany and Europe. In D. Cesarini and M. Fulbrook, eds: *Citizenship, Nationality and Migration in Europe*. London: Routledge, 74–87.

Weil, P. 1997: *Mission d'étude des législations de la nationalité et de l'immigration*. Paris: La Documentation Française.

Weil, P. 2001: The politics of immigration. In A. Guyomarch *et al.*, eds: *Developments in French Politics 2*. Basingstoke: Palgrave, 211–26.

Weil, P. 2002: *Qu'est-ce qu'un Français? Histoire de la nationalité française depuis la Révolution*. Paris: Grasset.

Wessels, W. and Linsenmann, I. 2002: EMU's impact on national institutions. A *gouvernement économique* in the making: towards vertical and horizontal fusion? In K. Dyson, ed.: *The European State in the Euro-Zone*. Oxford: Oxford University Press.

White, E. 2001: *The Flâneur: A Stroll Through the Paradoxes of Paris*. New York: Bloomsbury.

Wieviorka, M., ed. 1997: *Une société fragmentée? Le multiculturalisme en débat*. Paris: La Découverte.

Wihtol de Wenden, C. 1998: Nationality status and foreign minorities in France. In S. O'Leary and T. Tilikainen, eds: *Citizenship and Nationality Status in the New Europe*. London: The Institute for Public Policy Research/Sweet & Maxwell, 149–55.

Wilson, F. L. 1987: *Interest-Group Politics in France*. Cambridge: Cambridge University Press.

Wilson, F. L. 1994: Political demonstration in France: protest politics or politics of ritual? *French Politics and Society*, 12, 2–3, Spring–Summer, 23–40.

Winock, M. 1990: Nationalisme ouvert et nationalisme fermé. In M. Winock, ed.: *Nationalisme, antisémitisme et fascisme en France*. Paris: Seuil.

Worms, J.-P. 2001: Old and new civic and social ties in France. In R. Putnam, ed.: *Social Capital in Comparative Perspective*. Oxford: Oxford University Press.

Wright, V. and Mazey, S. 1999: *The Government and Politics of France*, 4th edn. London: Routledge.

Zeldin, T. 1979–81: *France 1848–1945*, 4 vols. Oxford: Clarendon Press.

Zeldin, T. 1983: *The French*. London: Collins.

USEFUL ACADEMIC JOURNALS ON FRANCE IN ENGLISH

Modern and Contemporary France (UK)
French Politics and Society (US)
West European Politics (UK)

INDEX